Sojourner in Islamic Lands

Sojourner in Islamic Lands

Russell Fraser

The University of South Carolina Press

Published by the University of South Carolina Press
Columbia, South Carolina 29208

www.sc.edu/uscpress

Manufactured in the United States of America

23 22 21 20 19 18 17 16 15 14 10 9 8 7 6 5 4 3 2 1

Library of Congress Cataloging-in-Publication Data

Fraser, Russell A.
Sojourner in Islamic lands / Russell Fraser.
pages cm
ISBN 978-1-61117-316-1 (hardback)—ISBN 978-1-61117-317-8 (ebook) 1. Asia, Central—Description and travel. 2. Islamic countries—Description and travel. 3. Fraser, Russell A.—Travel—Asia, Central. I. Title.
DS327.8.F74 2013
915.804'43—dc23 2013024195

Contents

Illustrations

Maps

Figures

Preface

Sojourner in Islamic Lands, as its title suggests, tells of time spent in Islam. It is more than a travel book, however. Its primary concern is with Islamic history and culture, in particular art and architecture. I became interested in Islam a generation ago when I went to Constantinople (Istanbul) to write *The Three Romes* (1985). The First Rome, taking in all things Italian—history, culture, art, language, food and drink—had long stimulated both my heart and head. Constantinople I had known only from books as the Second Rome, the preserver of eastern Christianity after the fall of Rome. The modern city, becoming part of Islam when it fell to the Turks in 1453, now begot my ongoing interest in the Muslim world. My *Islam* is an umbrella term, comprehending a wide range of meanings. Central Asia's ancient cities, for example, Khiva, Bukhara, Samarkand, put most of them before us. They mix heart-stopping beauty with deeply shocking evil, a living oxymoron that still resonates long after I've come away.

The structure of the book is linear, an account of travels from Kazakhstan in the far north of Central Asia to Iran in the south, just below the Caspian Sea. A brief coda brings the narrative back to Italy, the conventional end point (terminus ad quem) of the Silk Road. I had thought to include, as bookends to the narrative, Mughal India to the east and Andalusian Spain to the west. But I have trimmed my sails, while remaining at least aware of the presence of these cultural and ideological outriders. In moving from place to place, I follow the line of the Silk Road wherever possible. This great network, much of it over desert sands and accessible only by camel, was the primary commercial link between Europe and Asia from the first and second centuries B.C. to the fifteenth and sixteenth centuries A.D., when the opening of maritime routes to the East made land travel obsolete.

The book centers on Islam but is much engaged with Christianity and with the secular progressive faith that aims to supplant it. Harking back to my *Three Romes*, I think of this faith as the Third Rome, initially Moscow, or in its twentieth-century version, Stalin's Third International. It aroused a young man's indiscriminate enthusiasm, sorely tried when I first went to Russia in the 1960s. What remains of that long-ago time is a skeptical state of mind, especially regarding secular progressivism, which I define as the belief that all our problems are open to contractual solutions. Skepticism on matters social and political is central to my identity, and so intense that I must make room for a quotation from Dr. Johnson, who encapsulates my point of view better than anyone else:

> How little, of all the ills that human hearts endure,
> That part which laws, or kings, can cause, or cure.

The Christian and secular panels of my "triptych" are like reflector characters in the fiction of Henry James. They set off the primary object of interest, illuminating it by comparison and contrast. Inevitably this back-and-forth suggests a point of view. Mine toward Islam mixes praise and blame. I don't have an ax to grind and have found good in people everywhere, whatever their religious persuasion. That said, there is an area over which the accepted ideology is deeply influential, sometimes in unfortunate ways. I think it important to explore that area, and I look at it closely. Perhaps some will bridle at what I see. But coming to conclusions, founded, let it be said, on the scrutiny of particulars, is the salt of what I've written.

My traveling is intentional. I seek to recover Islam and present it to the Western mind. This means describing things as they were at the height of the Islamic achievement in the High Middle Ages, and saying by contrast how they are now. The intention is complex and entails meditation on the rise and decline of a great civilization. I am out for something more than simple narration and want to say not only how and when things happened but also why. Meditation slows the pace of my narrative. There are "grace notes": some of my traveling is reminiscent, that is, I interpolate into my account journeys I made in the past, for example to Western China. Also the teller's eye is prone to wandering. I like to "expatiate and confer," a phrase of John Milton's, who interrupts *Paradise Lost* with frequent meanders, like a river in its leisurely course to the sea. The meanders are consequential, and eventually the river finds its way again.

I'd be sorry were the reader not to experience, as I have, something of the thrill of Central Asia, its vastness and endless variety. Sir Aurel Stein, to me the most impressive of the intrepid men who opened up this region a hundred years ago, wrote of standing at the summit of snowy peaks and glaciers, looking down on Bactria (Afghanistan) and the Upper Valley of the Oxus. He said "a strange and joyful sensation" overcame him. In imagination I share it, standing with him on the eastern threshold of that distant land.

I am grateful to Jane Eckelman of Manoa Mapworks, Inc., for the maps. A master of Islamic scholarship, the late Oleg Grabar of the Institute for Advanced Study, Princeton, gave me help I couldn't have dispensed with. I hope the result seems worth his pains. Part of my material appeared originally in the *Yale Review*, and I thank the editor for permission to reuse it.

Like some other books of mine, this one is for Mary, without whose intriguing presence I might have finished sooner.

RUSSELL FRASER

HONOLULU, 2012

RUSSIA
Astana
RUSSIA
Lake Baikal
Irkutsk
KAZAKHSTAN
Lake Balkhash
MONGOLIA
Aral Sea
Syr Darya
Urumqi
Turpan
TURKEY
Caspian Sea
UZBEKISTAN
Dashoguz
Urgench
Khiva
Bukhara
Tashkent
Bishkek
Almaty
KYRGYZSTAN
TIEN SHEN MTNS
Dunhuang
SYRIA
ARMENIA
AZERBAIJAN
Baku
TURKMENISTAN
Amu Darya
Samarkand
Torugart Pass
Kashgar
Dashanbe
TAJIKSTAN
TAKLAMAKAN DESERT
CHINA
Tabriz
Ashgabad
Mary
Merv
KARAKUM DESERT
Tehran
Hotan
IRAQ
AFGHANISTAN
Kabul
Lanzhou
Isfahan
IRAN
Islamabad
Yzad
Kandahar
Chengdu
HIMALAYAS
Shiraz
KUWAIT
Lhasa
NEPAL
BHUTAN
SAUDI ARABIA
Persian
PAKISTAN
Indus
New Delhi
Jaipur
INDIA
INDIA
BURMA
UAE
Gulf
Karachi
BANGLA-DESH
Cartography by Manoa Mapworks, Inc

1

Islam Past and Present

A loose and baggy monster, Asia sprawls like Tolstoy's novels, but its Islamic heartland imparts a shape to the whole. If I run my eye over the map, beginning to the east of the mountains in China, it runs west to the Caspian Sea. Along the way the eye takes in the five "Stans" on the western side of the Chinese border. Kazakhstan, Kyrgyzstan, Tajikistan, Uzbekistan, and Turkmenistan, these former Soviet client states lie like peas in a pod. They each have their separate identity, though, and I aim to say what that is. Move the eye south from the border of Uzbekistan, and it lights on Persia, now resuming its old name, Iran. This gives the periphery of the area I mean to explore. I have more than physical exploring in mind, though. I want to sort out the ideas that have governed for much of my life as I near the end of it.

Sometimes I think my branch of the family clan has a gene for wanderlust. Fighting on the losing side against the English at Culloden in 1746, many of them migrated to the New World. A nineteenth-century ancestor, Cmdr. Alexander Fraser, sailed around Cape Horn and founded the U.S. Coast Guard. His son fought at Mobile Bay with Admiral Farragut. I have Farragut saying to him, "Damn the torpedoes, Captain Fraser! Full speed ahead!" This captain's grandson, my Uncle Alex, spent his lifetime sailing the Seven Seas. I remember the haunted look in his eyes, like that of a man pursued by the insurance company that had offered him a secure berth ashore.

Modern travelers like me eschew ships of sail for jet propulsion aircraft, but whatever the transport, I'm nagged by things arcane. On my mind as I write is the English poet James Elroy Flecker (1884–1915), distinctly minor but immortal for a quatrain:

We travel not for trafficking alone;
By hotter winds our fiery hearts are fanned:
For lust of knowing what should not be known
We take the Golden Road to Samarkand.

Taking this road, I've appeased my need for the esoteric while transgressing forbidden ground. I have sought both ends when traveling the world, but the journey through Central Asia has had another and more prosaic objective. My idée fixe for a long time has been to follow every major spur of the Silk Road. I once knew an eminent papyrologist, director of the Kelsey Museum in Ann Arbor, who bored his colleagues with incessant talk of papyri. When they protested, he said, "You can never have too much papyri," and that is how I feel about the Silk Road.

The plan for this trip is to cross the entire continent, roughly from the Chinese border on, then travel back again to Italy, where I mean to lay over for a few days in Rome. Venice is the goal the Silk Road yearned for, almost mystically, but Rome is the Eternal City, "*la mia preferita,*" and every pilgrim of the heart must turn toward it. Byron said so, and definitely that includes me.

That most of this land I was traveling through is Muslim and presumably hostile qualified it, at least theoretically, as "forbidden." But the hostility I looked for was less real than fantasizing, like the spooky images of childhood. A better word for Central Asia, catching up its vast reaches that stretch to infinity, is sadness. The poet Flecker felt it, anticipating a time

When those long caravans that cross the plain
With dauntless feet and sound of silver bells
Put forth no more for glory or for gain,
Take no more solace from the palm-girt wells.

The pervasive sadness tells of the ending end, somehow in the air in this downward-tending land. Yet the welcome that often greeted me, though frequently incoherent, was friendly.

Still the question, Why travel?, remains to be answered. I'm sure that tedium vitae plays into it, also the infernal restlessness that plagues us as we are human. I am like that "insatiable peregrine" Robert Browning wondered about:

What's become of Waring
Since he gave us all the slip,
Chose land-travel or seafaring,
Boots and chest or staff and scrip,
Rather than pace up and down
Any longer London's town?

For me the road will always beckon: to Damascus, the *souk* in Cairo, Palmyra, Petra of the Nabateans, cities I remember or know only in the mind. But beyond everything else was the pull of a place I think of as veritable, without being able to locate it on the map. Call it an archetype. It has its bleak underside yet rewards me abundantly, opening to my senses all the varieties of experience. Even the questions these experiences raise, though bristling with ambiguity, hint at the chance of an answer. Somewhere in the huge expanse of rivers, mountains, and desert is a cave mouth whose archetypal features I will recognize on sight. Before it sits a cross-legged man, and when I pose him the question, "Master, what is the truth that sets us free?," he will answer.

Questions like that sound faintly embarrassing to a man grown old on the reticence of modernism, and sidling up to them seems the better part of tact. More prosaically, which comes first, the Islamic distaste for the physical world or its taste for abstraction, often met in Central Asia? Did the hard land, such as the Arabian Desert, beget a psychology on the new religion? Tillers of the soil on the Arabian plateau were creating wheel-made pots ornamented with images of flora and fauna as early as the fifth millennium before Christ. But in their art, design counted more than the representation of nature. This set a pattern for the abstract art of the future and the Islamic faith it sponsored. Or was it the faith that sponsored the art?

The religion I encountered in my sojourning is essentially unchanged from the monotheistic creed, often harsh like the desert it came from, proclaimed by Muhammad in the seventh century. Now, as then, it depends on the Koran. This foundational book is problematic in that it appeals to self-evident truth. The chain of belief it constructs, proceeding from creation through judgment, is less causal than willed, making it, as intellectual structure, at least less interesting than Christian thought. It declines to sanction the idea of original sin, opting for a happy ending to the story of our first parents' transgression. Such commentaries as I've read argue that men and women in Islam stand on the same footing. Never mind what most of us take to be the notorious superiority of men: that is only "functional," not inherent. But the day-to-day relation of the sexes belies this.

Crucially the Koran takes a more hopeful view of man's fate than the Bible—"hopeful" verging on eupeptic. Endorsing the idea of poetic justice, it acquits Jesus, the Son of Man, from his obligation to die on the cross. A revealing metaphor describes the history of civilizations, from which the bad disappears—that is, the foam on top of the torrent—while "that which is beneficial to mankind sinks down upon the earth" (13:17) to refresh it. In its psychology the good men do remains, while the evil is interred with their bones.

On the matter of style, I speak with diffidence. Those who know Arabic instruct those of us who don't that the Koran is unrivaled in the beauty of its language. If I don't always find myself in agreement, that is possibly because its special quality doesn't come through in translation. Passages such as this one seem merely comic: "So for him whose scale [of good deeds] shall be weighty, he shall lead a happy life; but he whose scale is light, his mother shall be the Ditch" (101:6–9). But let me move to a summary judgment.

Today in Islam the intellectual climate is frosty, and the auspices for the future aren't good. The birthrate is declining steeply, true across entire regions and ethnicities. Though the disproportion of young to old is huge, the average age men and women will live to is rising. At present there are far too many young people at loose ends in Islam. Eventually, however, the aging population will resemble that of the West, and the support for this increasing number of old people won't be there. Devotion to the faith is still there, though not what it was. Fanaticism is waxing, even as devotion wanes. Attendance at the Great Friday Mosque in Tehran is falling off at a rate almost as startling as churchgoing in Europe.

So it seems appropriate to conclude that Islam, having reached its apogee, has entered its long night. I think I am on solid ground in affirming that today's religion is no longer so substantial as it was a thousand years ago. The psychology that informs it today is less enlivening, the reticule that contains it no longer so capacious as in the twelfth century, the time that nourished Saladin, the sultan-general of genius, and Averroes, the renowned philosopher. That vibrant time, as great in the West as in the East, was more auspicious for Islam, not least aesthetically, than the Muslim world at present.

The religion it sustains seems verging on its end, a reason for the violence associated with it. "Dying throes" is a good apposite phrase.

THE EMERGENCE OF MUHAMMAD the holy man—out of nowhere, his contemporaries must have thought—is as spectacular as that of Joseph Smith, the founder of Mormonism. In the decade following the first "Revelation," he whose life up to then had been wholly uneventful began to see visions. Astride Buraq, a winged animal, he journeyed through the heavens all the way to Jerusalem and a meeting with the great prophets of the past, Abraham, Moses, and Jesus of Nazareth. But this privileged communion set him apart, exciting animosity, and in 622 he had to flee for his life. The flight from Mecca to Medina was the Hegira, with which the Muslim calendar begins. The hero of the Hegira was only half a man, still unmarried in middle age and apparently without a vocation. But at fifty-five he underwent a metamorphosis, taking numerous wives in succession. He created and led an army in battle, promising those of his soldiers who fell direct transit to paradise and the company of dark-eyed houris, chaste as hidden pearls (Koran 56:12–39). Transcending death, he sought to perpetuate his godlike status from beyond the grave. When he died in 632, only sixty-three, his disciples, the *ummah* or fellowship of Islam, designated a friend, Abu Bakr, as caliph (Arabic *khalifa,* supreme ruler). He and his three successors are the four "rightly guided" caliphs and presided over the first thirty years of Islamic expansion.

Violence characterizes them all. After ten years as caliph, Umar, the second of the four rightly guided ones, was assassinated, giving way to Uthman of the Umayyads. He reigned a dozen years before another assassin found him. Next in line was Ali, married to Muhammad's daughter Fatima. The fourth caliph, Ali died the same death, killed by the family of the man he succeeded. The Umayyads, back on the throne, moved the caliphate to Damascus, modern Syria. Muslims in Iraq stayed loyal to the martyred Ali. They were Shi'ites (Arabic *Shi'at*), recognizing Ali as imam but withholding recognition from the three caliphs who came after Muhammad. The rest of the *ummah* (most Muslims worldwide) were Sunni, recognizing the early caliphs but denying special status to Ali. This schism, not even doctrinal like that which describes the nature of Christ, two persons or three, seems trivial, a version of the dispute in *Alice in Wonderland* between Tweedledum and Tweedledee. But it was murderous and bred civil war.

Killing was and is its hallmark. The most important casualty was Ali's son and Muhammad's grandson Husayn, killed in 661. He died on a journey with seventy of his followers, slain by the Umayyads at Karbala in Iraq. Fellow communicants mark the anniversary of his killing with ten days of public grieving, flagellating themselves with chains. The emotional debauch says something about the nature of Shia Islam. But the victors had scotched the serpent, not killed it, and a single survivor escaped to Cordoba in southern Spain to lay the foundation of a new and magnificent culture. That was for the future. For the present the Umayyads ruled their empire from Damascus, a spectacular city. In Jerusalem they raised the Dome of the Rock. But their energy waned, and the Umayyads were overthrown by the Abbasids. Eventually they went under too.

Paradoxically, however, though Islam early on seethed with violence, its astonishing yield was the peace of high art. The Abbasids, descendants of a collateral branch of Muhammad's family, illustrate this surprising conjunction. Having deposed the sybaritic Umayyad caliphs ruling from Damascus, they moved the caliphate to Baghdad, a violent wrench. But it inaugurated a golden age, enduring for hundreds of years. John Farndon, author of *Iran* (2007), the best short book on the country, calls this period a Persian Renaissance. (Baghdad in that time was Persian.)

Unparalleled learning accompanied Islam's violent beginnings. In the tenth century, Arab scholarship, led by mathematics, deserved to be called the world's finest. The Mediterranean basin nurtured impressive cities whose Muslim culture rivaled that of classical Greece and Rome. Two centuries earlier Aristotle, translated into Arabic, came to Syria, a century later to Spain. Such was the renown of tenth-century Cordoba that the greatest Latin scholar of the Middle Ages, Gerbert of Aurillac, later Pope Sylvester II, traveled there to study mathematics and philosophy. Persia's galaxy of poets, philosophers, mathematicians, and geographers included Avicenna, a world figure in medicine; Al-Khwarizmi, the creator of algebra and our modern number system; and Al-Beruni, who compared the speeds of light and sound. The eighth-century caliph Harun al-Rashid (766–809) listened to the tales Scheherazade told in *The One Thousand and One Nights.*

The greatest work of this exuberant time is the gigantic *Shahnama* of Ferdosi (eleventh century), vindicating Persian identity in the teeth of the Arab takeover after a conclusive battle in 641. (The term *Arab* means more than an inhabitant of the Arabian Peninsula. From the eighth century on, it denotes the civilization established around the eastern and southern Mediterranean to which many contributed—Greeks, Egyptians, Syrians, Persians, Jews, and Berbers as well as Arabs.) Every literate reader of English knows or should know Edward FitzGerald's translation of the poetry of Omar Khayyám. Ferdosi's poetry, the exemplary case, met this requirement in Persia, where it was everyone's possession, literate and illiterate alike. Its enormous popularity began in the eleventh century; I wish I could say "and extends until now," but that, given what we know of the present, would need an act of faith.

The poetry is often fortified with learning, which didn't prevent Everyman from reading it. Sahib ibn Abbad, vizier of the Bayid dynasty (945–1055 A.D.), was learned on the grand scale, amassing a library of two hundred thousand books. Meanwhile Christian Europe languished in the Dark Ages. I regret the need to keep qualifying: straight-out assertion makes for smoother reading, but candor compels the admission that in an earlier book of mine, *The Dark Ages and the Age of Gold* (1973), I argue for a "dark age" that wasn't so dark after all. I wasn't less right then than now, but being younger, I enjoyed demolishing conventional points of view.

Over the centuries successive dynasties arose in Islamic Asia—Seljuks, Mongols, Ilkhanids, Timurids, Safavids—seeming to me like players in a game of squash, each new player augmenting the velocity of the ball he puts in play. The Seljuk Turks, conquering Persia in the eleventh century, raised the level of play in architecture. Their capital, Isfahan, one of the world's treasure troves of religious buildings, has for its principal treasure a Seljuk mosque, the Masjed-i-Jami. A similar upsurge, both military and artistic, signaled the coming of the Ottomans to Turkey around 1300. Where Christian churches had been, Sultan Sūleyman and his architect Sinan erected a rival creation, not inferior to the great work it displaced. In the same sixteenth century, Turkey's astronomer royal persuaded the sultan to build an observatory more sophisticated than any before it. Taq-al-Din was the astronomer, a contemporary of Denmark's illustrious Tycho Brahe. Both pursued the same objective, mapping the heavens.

"Seek ye knowledge even unto China," Muhammad told his followers back in the beginning. Doing as he bade them, they made Islam the greatest power on earth. They sailed up the Tiber, intending another sack of Rome; in France, within one hundred years of Muhammad's death, they got as far north as Tours. Muslim Tatars of the Golden Horde ruled Russia, Muslim Turks besieged Vienna. For hundreds of years, North Africa had been

Roman, ultimately Christian, but with the Arab capture of Carthage (698), all that came to an end. Until the eighth century, all the immense territory conquered by the Arabs constituted an empire ruled by a single dynasty, the Umayyads.

A thousand years ago, today's backwaters, such as Afghanistan, brimmed with intellectual energy. Asians in that remote land invented trigonometry, purified water by crystallization, arrived at a fair estimate of earth's diameter, anticipated Darwin's theory of evolution. Their art was on a par with their science, and I would mortgage the house to own a tile from Herat. One more throw was left to Islam, the pinnacle arrived at by the Safavids under Shah Abbas the Great (1587–1629). His principal achievement, Esfahan's Imam Square, seems to me among the wonders of the world.

Already, however, the writing on the wall promised decline. The Turkish astronomer who got his observatory didn't long enjoy it before it was snatched away. When Istanbul's Chief Mufti told the sultan that science endangered the faith, the observatory was razed to the ground. The power of the mullahs had a constant objective, to keep out the light, and after the early advance it insured a long withdrawal. This is at the heart of my presentation of Islam; were I writing a polemic, I would set it off in bold type.

In the thirteenth century, when intellect in the West was cresting, the light of science in Islam began to gutter. Medieval Spain is exemplary, showing how church and state, taking hands, put free inquiry to silence. Beginning in the eleventh century, fanatically puritanical Berbers from the North African desert crossed over the Strait of Gibraltar in great numbers, gaining control of Muslim Spain. Free inquiry disgusted them, and they convinced their Muslim rulers to forbid it. Averroism, Spain's greatest contribution to philosophy, was condemned, the schools were shuttered, and "the Arabic mind passed under the long tyranny of fanaticism and ignorance" (Norman Cantor, *Civilization of the Middle Ages*, 1993).

Official Islam, in the person of the mullahs, has always made a virtue of intolerance. The Koran imagines troops of unbelievers driven toward Hell "until when they reach it, its gates shall be opened" (xxxix: 70). Our modern age, which makes a virtue of tolerance, the unexamined kind, looks askance at this. But Islam is at least consistent. Sojourners in Asia's heartland took care to be circumcised; otherwise they faced instant death. Graven images were forbidden, possessing numinous power, said the imams. A trail of violence followed them, ceasing only with their destruction. Until our time a pair of massive Buddhas, the bigger 175 feet high, overlooked the Afghan town of Bamiyan. Carved from a cliff face in the third century A.D., subsequently bedecked with jewels and gold paint, they seemed a marvel to the generality of men. The imams wanted them down. Robert Byron (1905–41), a hyperesthetic traveler and writer, like and unlike the imams, looked through his monocle at "their monstrous flaccid bulk." His aversion was to bad art. But modern Islam makes nothing of criticism like his. It doesn't ask if Salman Rushdie writes well.

Mahmud, the sultan of Ghazne, not an aesthetic hair in his beard, took his hammer to Bamiyan in the eleventh century, but the Buddhas, though knocked about, remained intact. Genghis Khan had a go at them two hundred years later, leveling the town and massacring its inhabitants. Still the statues survived, and for a while longer, the Islamic world stood at the zenith. Some of its most impressive triumphs were yet to come. But by and large the great days were over. As the twentieth century ended, a new polity, characterized by violence and obscurantism, was mewing its youth. This was the Taliban. In 2001 officers of its Ministry for the Prevention of Vice and Promotion of Virtue came out to Bamiyan from Kabul with explosives. They finished the job.

My tone is perhaps more pessimistic than it need be. Even as I write, an Italian archaeologist, Luca Olivieri, is doing what he can to restore the shattered image of one of the great Buddhas. However, most of those that survived from antiquity, initially more than two hundred, are gone, defaced by Muslims centuries ago. The Taliban, contemporary iconoclasts, took aim at what is left. Climbing up ropes to reach the statues high above them, they drilled holes in the rock and filled them with dynamite. At Bamiyan the explosion blew away most of the face above the lips and cracked other parts of the carving. Partly this damage is beyond repair. The modern restorer understands that complete restoration in the absence of all the requisite data—the "blueprint"—is necessarily imperfect. But half a glass is better than empty, and if that agrees with your temperament, you will believe that there is cause for hope.

2

The Roof of the World

I am en route to Central Asia from my domicile in Hawaii, halfway round the world. I can fly east or west, pretty much a tossup. This time I take the easterly route via Frankfurt, across Russia and on to the former Soviet republics, the Stans. "Stans" is a suffix giving each of these five countries its grammatical fix, but "republics" is a joke, like that about the state where I live, ridden by bureaucrats. Cynics call it "the People's Republic of Hawaii."

As an aging traveler, I can't do without the supplementary oxygen that feeds my damaged lung. But even with its help, too many hours at thirty thousand feet leaves me feeling less than chipper, and getting off the plane in Almaty, the major port of entry for Kazakhstan, I huff and puff like a sex fiend in an old movie. I do as instructed, however, following the signs until I come to a steep flight of stairs. At the head of the stairs is customs, an obligatory stop before entering the terminal. Checkmate.

Asians must be inured to hardship, coping as they can with the hand of cards they've been dealt. Americans are more sanguine. They think all obstacles are for hurdling, and never met a problem they couldn't resolve. Hoping to deal with my problem, I look around for help. At the foot of the stairs stands a short, squat *desharnaya* whose olive drab and red epaulettes seem uncannily familiar. I'd seen her before, in cloakrooms, on street corners directing traffic, and on hotel floors, handing out room keys. Except for the florid face, there is nothing sanguine about her. I'm not as spry as I was and wouldn't have minded a hand up, but she stares at me stonily, her face devoid of expression. In the dimly lit interior, I understand that I have entered a time warp. I am back in the old Soviet Union.

Some things never change, a source of comfort or dismay depending on your point of view. My mother used to say that every glass is half full, my gloomy father that every glass is half empty. A chip off my mother's block, I thought Almaty might be like the happy valley Ronald Colman stumbles into in *Lost Horizon.* Yes and no. The city lies beneath terrifying mountains called the Roof of the World by Marco Polo. (I know I'm supposed to adulate mountains and can only say I'm sorry.) The people who live there are partners in our democracy of insufficiency and subject to entropy like everyone else. An old poet whose words I have in my phylactery, a repository of home truths, says what life offers them: "a little winter love in a dark corner." Then it's curtains and the unending night.

When Marco Polo journeyed this way, he felt his mortality, a sympathetic response to the wish for death that seems ubiquitous in a land where mutability is the one constant. Returning home to Italy, he crossed over the Pamirs, part of the stupendous chain that breaks through the earth in Kazakhstan and gives Asia its backbone. Unlike the Himalayas and other links in the chain, the Pamirs are mostly plateau, now and again climbing up high and falling away to deep valleys. Few trees and little vegetation interrupt the barren landscape, and its scorching sands are shriveled by age and the violent swings of the climate. The earth turns to water, the water leaks away and dissolves in air. Then the process begins anew.

The endless cycle that characterized the Soviet Union—mostly incompetence, partly venality—is like the landscape and the city I've come to. The Friendship Hotel, where I am staying, a relic of Brezhnev's time, has a shower with two taps, neither running hot water, and a bedsheet like a large pillowcase that engorges the blankets, leaving my feet in the cold. But the view from the window is worth a lot of tossing and turning. Lacy with snow, mountains glint in the frosty sun, their wildness civilized by the green and gold domes of the Orthodox church in the foreground. Until recently this wooden church functioned as a warehouse, but religion has staged a comeback in Kazakhstan. It downplays its recent successes, though, aware of history's penchant for doubling back on itself. Who knows, perhaps the League of the Militant Godless is biding its time in the wings.

Though Islam is elsewhere a noisy presence, in Almaty it keeps a civil tongue in its head. Praying five times a day seems like overkill to many, and I don't often hear the cry of the muezzin summoning the faithful to prayer. We aren't in Cairo or the Emirates. The world doesn't stop for Ramadan, and

I have yet to meet anyone who has made the hajj or pilgrimage to Mecca. At dinner in my hotel, I call for vodka to cut the greasy taste of mutton, and no one threatens to lop off my hands. Women don't wear the chador. The Soviet Revolution, fiercely intolerant, shuttered mosques and madrassas but set the women free. Like bra burners in the American sixties, they made a fire and threw their veils on the flames.

Fanatics such as the Taliban keep under the radar in Kazakhstan, and I feel secure walking the streets of the city. By no means a backwater, it was once the nation's capital and remains its commercial center. But the government has moved west to Astana, 1,300 kilometers away. Kazakhstan is big, though mostly empty, and when you reach Astana you still have half a country to go. Three hordes, or nomad groups, divide it among them. (*Horde,* from the Turkic, denotes the Brobdingnagian yurt where the ruling khan held court.) The Great Horde possessed the steppes, the Middle Horde the grasslands east of the Aral Sea, and the Little Horde got the leavings. For his new capital, President Nursultan Nazarbaev favored the horde in the middle. But the change he set in motion was largely cosmetic, and in Astana, under the new paint and the new plastic sidings, the buildings are the old Soviet concrete.

Within a day of deplaning, I have rented a compact from Caspian Rent-a-Car at Almaty's International Airport. With it comes a map of the road to Bishkek, the capital of Kyrgyzstan. I've got 350 kilometers ahead of me, longer than it sounds, more if I take the scenic route. I estimate a good six hours' drive. The cost of the car, computed strictly in U.S. dollars, comes to $110. My new identity is collector of potsherds. The trash of history, they turn up everywhere in the clayey soil, almost infinite in number, and it is easy to miss the rare square-holed copper coins of the T'ang dynasty (618–907 A.D.), valuable beyond price. They pair together with potsherds that are little more than detritus to make an emblem for Asia's heartland, scarred by the colliding over eons of so many disparate things. To plot the figure this unending dance describes isn't possible, unless chaos can be described as a form. As it is like atoms in flux, it disheartens. But as dance it exhilarates.

Putting myself at risk is exhilarating. In imagination I am Lt. Col. Charles Stewart of the Fifth Punjab Infantry, preparing to cross the Persian desert in the fall of 1880. The Russians, old enemies of the English in the struggle for control of Central Asia and the Indian subcontinent, are on the move in the empty lands east of the Caspian Sea. I have bet my life on finding out what they are up to. My disguise, which I have worked wonders to make believable, even including the simulacrum of a horse's hoofprint on my forehead, is that of an Armenian horse trader from Calcutta. The question is, will it get me close enough to train my spyglass on Gen. Mikhail Skobolev, the hard-as-nails commander of the Russian army assembling on the Caspian's eastern shore? "Old Bloody Eyes," the Turkomans called him, cunning, cruel, and wholly devoid of scruple. I guessed he was bound for Geok-Tepe, the great Turkoman stronghold in the Kara-Kum Desert. If that fortress were to fall, Ashkabad would follow, then Merv, and so on. My job, tricky and dangerous, was to gather enough intelligence to stop him.

I think I can do this, cast as I am in the same heroic mold as the gallant Britishers whose story I am living out in my head. To one of them especially, George Hayward, I feel an involuntary kinship. This traveler on the Pamir steppe courted risks deliberately, committing himself to a life of wandering the wilds of Central Asia until finally he might "try the effects of cold steel" across his throat. Finding what he was looking for, he died at the hands of assassins.

My romantic strain is less real than hypothetical, and leaving Hayward to his fate, I putter along the highway in my rented car. Anything out of the ordinary is grist for my mill. Outside town a Muslim graveyard decays beside the road, like an abandoned silver lode in the Old West. Slabs of stucco have come loose at the corners of the mausoleums, and the crescent and star of Islam atop their finial leans crazily into the wind. The mausoleums, row on row of them, suggest private dwellings in a housing development where the dead lie snug for eternity. Little doors open outward, as if the bony occupants were preparing to receive. But behind the graveyard rise the snowy peaks of the Tien Shan, or Heavenly Mountains, their ragged outline the color of death.

Appearances to the contrary, Islam in Central Asia is much livelier than this sad necropolis suggests. The lack of trim around the graves tells less of indifference than a laissez-faire state of mind, translated "live and let die." Muslims in this northern land are inclined to live. Also they are more laconic than elsewhere and take their faith as a matter of course. I am cheered by the absence of hysterical mullahs and the wild-eyed fellahin who do their bidding in the streets. In Kazakhstan the people, secure in their belief, don't need to parade it. But I don't want to overdo this. Perhaps they are merely skeptics, letting you know they believe by attending Friday mosque, not that different from appearing in church every Sunday.

South of Almaty the mountains turn into hills, separated by deep clefts thronging with purple shadow. Rockwell Kent's paintings are like them. Little on the land hints at life: a few cattle and sheep, a solitary vaquero slumped on his horse. Yurts in the lee of the hills are staked to the ground like air-filled balloons, their outer skin the weathered gray of old canvas. Color is for the inside, where the walls are lined with reed mats. Ceilings are lined with the felt rugs called *sherdak.* Turning away from the natural world, they favor geometric constructions, the idea of a snowflake rather than the thing itself. Color is opulent, red, green, and blue, enfiladed with yellow, but outside color leaches away.

As I drive southwest toward Bishkek, the iron land grows softer. Fruit orchards, running with the highway, are protected by a windbreak of shivery poplars. Dachas set among them look like Swiss chalets, the cut-rate version, their unpainted walls washed with lime. But some, coming up in the world, resemble the old-fashioned *izbas* Russian peasants once lived in, complete with little balconies over the front door, ornate balustrades, and blue or green paint on the windows. Before one of the *izbas* grows an apricot tree, and beneath it two old men, seated on stools, are eating salted fish, trout by the look of it. Next to them a string of fish is drying in the sun, like socks hung up on the clothesline.

This little vignette seems to mimic a scene from the other side of the world, Cezanne's pipe-smoking men playing cards around a table. But what, if anything, does the resemblance imply? You could say that one touch of nature makes the whole world kin. Sentimental Westerners believe this. Yet no two people are less alike than these codgers by the roadside and the painter's provincial Frenchmen. The former, like flies in amber, are stuck eons back in time, and their difference isn't superficial, like skin color. A census will say they are Muslim, but their abiding faith is syncretic, Islam infiltrated by Buddhism, Nestorian Christianity and its half-human god, Manichaeanism, Zoroastrianism. The last two propose a universe in which light and dark are fighting a war to the death. The prophet Mani looked forward to a happy ending when light would free itself from darkness. I think the millenarian vision, dwelling on last things, has lost its fierce clarity, worn down by tragic life. In Asia light doesn't separate out from darkness but interpenetrates it, as at dawn or the end of day.

I am aware of being a topic of conversation to the women beside the road. They stand in their doorways, big-breasted and rosy-cheeked, wearing the shapeless dresses called *parandzhas,* like old-fashioned living-room drapes. The horse carts and donkey carts that go klop-klopping by them hardly merit a look, but the secondhand car I've rented in Almaty, freshly painted as if new, gets their attention. What did it cost, and in what far-off future might it be theirs? Americans are commonly called materialistic, but they don't hold a candle to Russians.

As if dropped down from Mars, a factory sits by itself in the fields. Cyrillic characters above the entrance say it is a linoleum factory. Though handmade carpets are among the glories of Asia, many think linoleum a better way to go, and the modern world is catching up with Kazakhstan and the other Stans. Its harbinger, the railroad, marches beside the highway. A scar on the land but also a suture, it stitches together different countries and peoples. The entity called Russia is its partly fictive creation, imposed on the continent from St. Petersburg to the Pacific.

Lake Issykul is coming up, an immense presence that might be spun off from one of our Great Lakes. The map wants me to take Silk Road Street, so-called, not a street in the neighborhood but the very path the camel trains plodded over on their way from China to the West. Paved today with bitumen or some such, this spur of a once-great network of roads keeps going along the upper shore of Lake Issykul in the republic of Kyrgyzstan. The third of Central Asia's six Stans, Kyrgyzstan squeezes between Uzbekistan and Kazakhstan, all three lying side by side like the seeds in a pomegranate. Tajikistan, a fourth Stan, is smallish, like Kyrgyzstan; Turkmenistan, like Kazakhstan, mostly desert. The sixth Stan isn't on my itinerary. I have stood on the border, looking hopefully across the Oxus, but the doors and windows are closed, and today we have no Afghanistan.

Tajikistan, shut in on the north by slivers of Uzbekistan and Kyrgyzstan, lies west of China, north of Pakistan and Afghanistan. It must be an experience, living among these behemoths, and it wouldn't do to be claustrophobic. In the early nineties, within a year of gaining independence from Russia, Tajikistan lapsed into violence. Wahhabi Islam, implacably fundamentalist and an arm of Saudi religious imperialism, sought to bring the new country into its camp. Hoping to penetrate Uzbekistan as well as Tajikistan, it flooded both with zealots well stocked with cash. They cried up jihad, ostensibly to liberate Central Asia from *kufr* (unbelief). But the first round in this civil war went to an anti-Communist and moderate Islamist coalition. That was yesterday.

Today, before the new century has got well started, Islamic terrorists are out in force again, sowing confusion. Making good use of the long border with Afghanistan, they have learned from their neighbor how to ambush military convoys, ram police installations with dynamite-packed vehicles, explode bombs in nightclubs where pleasure-seekers congregate for an innocent evening. I have two addenda to this tale of rising atrocities, both reported in the American press. One is a throwback to the nineteenth century, the other as current as now. The attack on a convoy of soldiers in a mountainous valley east of the capital, Dushanbe, is uncannily reminiscent of the First Afghan War, when a British army battalion, shepherding its women and children home to India, was set upon by tribesmen on the heights and annihilated to the last person, soldier or civilian, but one.

And the second addendum: the organizer of a jailbreak from the detention center in Dushanbe, a terrorist eager to find work for his hands, had been extradited to Tajikistan from the American prison at Guantánamo Bay. I think of Lenin in 1917, released by the Germans into Russia to foment revolution. That was with malice aforethought, and of course the Germans were complicit in freeing this poisonous bacillus from its bottle. But the Americans were naive and only doing what the courts said they had to.

Issykul, "hot lake" in Kyrgyz, never freezes but doesn't tempt me to put my toe in the water. Twice as big as the Aral Sea, it is ringed by white-capped mountains, the Kungey Ala-Tau, whose peaks disappear in the heavens. Some go nine thousand feet. In Central Asia the key is often minor, inclining to gloom, but the scale is inevitably major. My hotel, in its palmy days a Soviet sanatorium where Stakhanovites got their health back or died trying, is hideously grand, like a set for *The Ring*. A few leaves the color of malaria still cling to the skinny birch trees outside the window. The trees stand up like the masts of old schooners bound for the edge of the world. On the wide front lawn topiary evergreens are cut in the likeness of outlandish beasts. "Here be dragons."

The savage-looking country reminds me of my ancestral Scottish Highlands, but taller, wilder, claiming remote kinship to the Peruvian Andes. Crows flap across the leaden sky, and big shouldering hills piled on top with snow "beetle over their base." Below them men scratch out a low-level existence. All day long cold tightens its grip, and in the night an electric storm slashes the pitchy darkness with lightning. I hear it and partly see it as I lie snug abed, and in the morning I get a good look at the road I am driving. Statues of animals stand beside it, the environmentally friendly kind you see on postage stamps promoting the natural world. I note an eagle, a snow leopard, possibly an elk. A heavily muscled man, naked to the waist and shaking his fist at the universe, must be a version of Soviet man. Behind his statue the bluff flattens out suddenly, smooth as a dish of custard. The glacier has been through here, cuffing aside whatever pretended to stop it, but the naked man seems not to have noticed.

On high ground above the lake, a brick orphanage for boys is losing its bricks to the weather. Its facade is pitted like the face of a man with old acne scars, and the field it sits on is littered with boulders painted over with a pale wash. The boulders have the look of an ordnance map, crosshatched with lines N, S, E, and W. As I get closer, the lines resolve themselves to signs of the solar system and sketches of ibex, antelope, and deer. Long ago sun worshipers lived on this plain and had for company only the lake and the mountains. They seem incredibly far off in time but not alien, and I feel more akin to them than to Socialist man, here and gone only yesterday. Surely little communities must have settled themselves on the plain, but I see no evidence of them. Vacancy is the rule. Breaking the silence, ricky-ticky music falls on my ear from an open window. The Soviets were both murderous and prissy, the people who have replaced them following suit, and the music, diluted rock 'n' roll, is filtered of anything distinctive.

Beautiful little Kyrgyz boys appear at my car window, wanting a stick of gum or a throwaway ballpoint. They wear leather caps like workingmen's caps, and their elegant sweaters and vests are colored with vegetable dye. Chain-stitch embroidery, either on felt or fabric and featuring geometric designs, ranks high among this country's crafts. You can buy it by the yard (fabric only) in the big Phillips department store in Bishkek. The store sells pillow covers, made by clever seamstresses from pieces of sliced-up antique fabric. More expensive are the felt *sherdaks,* bright with large and high-colored rectangles. I covet one for my bed.

But gloom is growing on me, perhaps a function of the cold wind and no human habitation to fend against it, and I see this handmade art being superseded any day now by machine-made, cheap, and shoddy. The boys' faces, though shy, are bright with candor. I wish them well, while supposing that the place they live in has them in its gun sights.

Man is free, not fated, Henley's famous poem assures us, "the master of his fate, the captain of his soul." That isn't altogether false, despite the tub-thumping, but needs qualification. Character, a maze of contradictions, is fate and includes a man's physical makeup, also the environment that nurtures or thwarts him. Survival depends on coming to terms with this governing constellation. Disability plays into it, whether given at birth or, as with me, arriving in medias res. I used to kick against it and still see it as the cross I must carry. But going with its limitations, I exercise a kind of control. The control is doubtless circumscribed, emphasis falling on what a man can't do more than what he can. Something salutary in that, however: we are all fastened to a dying animal.

Behind the hills in the far distance rises a wall of mountains, on the other side of it China. An arrow on a signboard directs me to the Torugart Pass, leading up and through. The road, like a barren cleft in the hillside, is empty of traffic. I would give much to follow it, up and up, until I reached the border and looked down like "stout Cortez" from his high place. My dinged-up lung said no to all that years ago, however, matter for regret. But for better or worse, you have to play the hand that's been dealt you. This is true for the beautiful Kyrgyz boys I've left behind me, but no homily I can think of would offer them more than cold comfort.

SILK ROAD STREET, going south and west, keeps going until it lands me up in Bishkek, the capital of Kyrgyzstan. This city of a million has the feel of a small town but looks a little ramshackle, not *la douce France.* In Kyrgyzstan what's up front seems unimportant. Next to my upscale hotel, patronized by international businessmen carrying briefcases, the vacant lot is sprouting weeds, and the houses beyond it and extending to the corner are settling in on themselves as if embarrassed. For want of something better, I take in the historical museum, which turns out to be worth the visit. Roses are blooming outside the university, grandly sentineled by Corinthian columns. In the park red salvia the size of philodendrons surrounds the statue of the national hero. Amir Timur, known in the West as Tamburlaine, sits astride a general issue charger, pointing the way to his people. Though his record is a bloody one, he looks avuncular, another instance of appearances deceiving.

I don't find a lot to comment on in Bishkek, perhaps validating Tolstoy on the way only bad marriages have a story. Bishkek bespeaks sobriety, and if I lived there I would be grateful, at the same time looking over the fence at the greener grass on the other side. It used to be Frunze, remembering the Red general who won it for Russia in the aftermath of the October Revolution. Born in the city, he was popular with its inhabitants, and Stalin, taking thought, had him shot in the back of the head.

Reflecting on the up and down of things, how the first shall be last though not necessarily the other way round, I have my own head in the clouds and don't notice the traffic cop until his face is six inches from mine. Frantically I riffle through the papers in the glove compartment, looking for my international driver's license. Suddenly I realize that the cop doesn't want my license; he wants a bribe. Awareness dawning, I extract a wad of their national currency, the som, and hand it over discreetly as if dropping a Kleenex out the window. A moment later I am back on the road.

Kyrgyz cops, as everybody in Bishkek will tell you, are like that. In the joke one of them comes home unexpectedly at lunch, hoping to catch his wife with her lover. *Where is he?* and so forth. Tearing through the house, he flings open closet doors, checks out the shower, even the pantry. In the bedroom at last, he pulls off the bedspread and looks under the bed. A hand appears, waving a bill, and a voice says, "There's nobody here."

A Mongol with a ropey mustache and a large brown head as bald as a cue ball sits beside me on the flight from Bishkek to Tashkent. It is seven in the morning, but Uzbeki Air aims to please, and no sooner are we off than the drink cart appears in the aisle. Reaching across me, my seatmate drags a bottle from the tray. Wearily the stewardess takes it back again, wagging a reproving finger. He laughs, a weird cachinnation, like one of his ancestors about to put a defenseless city to the sword. "Way to go, Genghis!" I tell him.

Amir Timur was a native son, and in Tashkent, the capital of Uzbekistan, his likeness is everywhere, like Lenin's before the taste in Lenin staled. Buildings are named after him, and the history museum is modeled on his crown, topped with a tugh or yak's tail, the emblem of the Mongols. No Mongol himself but a Scythian shepherd, he redid his lineage to create a more glamorous past. The official biography does this too, sponsoring a lifeless figure like Lenin under glass in Red Square. But the flesh-and-blood Tamburlaine, a living oxymoron, blended glamorous and monstrous, and the age he gave his name to did the same. This is why we remember it, an amalgam like life itself. In both violence that isn't thinkable and beauty without peer exist together, a hand in a tight-fitting glove.

Everywhere I go in Central Asia, I meet this comprehensive coupling. Vice supports virtue, and the present is a new moon cradling the old in its arms. Tashkent is the exception. In this ancient-modern city, they have spirited the old out of sight. That is only partly owing to the earthquake of 1966. The truth is that the Soviets, filled with a superstitious dread of things past, liked starting out from scratch. Tashkent, ignoring history, seems created by parthenogenesis.

There is a lot about it to like, beginning with its green space. Both the parks and the concrete towers that rise around them have been lowered in place from the flies, though, and what appears to survive from the past is confected. On Amir Timur Street, the National Bank, an architect's fantasy in steel and black glass, is shaped like an Uzbeki peasant's hat. The handsome rose-colored building on Pushkin Ploshad is English Regency; the pale yellow low-rises on the main thoroughfare are baroque. Mama's Fun Pub near the station recalls an American sitcom. Streetlamps, their amber glass bulbs enclosed in metal filigree like the petals of a tulip, are left over from Third Empire France.

But beneath the froufrou is a no-nonsense integrity. Essential Tashkent, faithful to the Soviet planners who rebuilt it, defines modernity in their brutal yet finicky sense of the word. The subway system, unique in Central Asia, takes its cue from Moscow's. Each bright with decorative art, preachy but otherwise independent of function, lets us know where its priorities are. The city's public art is Red Fascist. Its tone is minatory, exemplified by the three huge statues that stand before the offices of the National Security Service. Grotesque in their muscularity, impossibly resolute, they represent the end of the road Michelangelo started us out on. Communism liked walking that road.

With a start I recognize the layout of the city, dreamed by the inventors of the modern age when rationalism was flexing its muscles. Edmund Wilson tells about them in his memorable account of mythmakers on the left, *To the Finland Station.* French, German, Italian, and Russian, they used to be my heroes. Sharing a morbid passion for hospital corners, they saw to it that the city's avenues ran straight as a saw cut, no whimsical twistings or turnings. Against the grid, spokes move out from the center, the same spiderweb effect you get in Moscow inside the Ring Road. Order and control define the rebuilt city, a spiritual descendant of Jeremy Bentham's imaginary Panopticon. In this ideal prison, the warden, from his station up top, could look into every cell. No hole-and-corner activity escaped him.

Paris, after Baron Haussmann got through with it, is a little like that, but Paris has the *je ne sais quoi* that words fumble at. It is itself, and we take it on its own terms. Washington, D.C., beneath its white marble overlay approximates the ideal modern city, not a good thing. But no sooner is the pejorative out than admiration, even awe, turns it into a positive. In Washington patriotism is of its essence. In Tashkent the impulse to rein in stands naked, and no amount of tarting up can suppress it.

But the Argus-eyed social scientist meets his match in Tashkent's people. The same as people everywhere, they have a way of wriggling out from under. In the sprawling Chorsu, an open-air market, everything is lowercase, defeating the synoptic view. "Pigeonhole me if you can!" say these wily Asiatics. They bring to mind a modern poet I like going back to. "A great disorder is an order," says Wallace Stevens. He sees how this coincidence of opposites runs the rationalizing idea off the rails.

Each of the hundreds of stalls in the market is sui generis. You can't lump them together under a single head but have to take them one at a time. Framed by arches swirling with arabesques, perfect apples, tomatoes, and bananas are piled up at random. Hangers of pale green grapes called Ladies Fingers descend from the arches, each grape long and pendulous, the size of a large thumb. Calves' legs, half a hundred, look sinister, as if about to walk off under their own steam. But fresh eggs, filling an ancient truck bed, look wholesome. Figs, glowing darkly in their woven baskets, look sexy. A vendor, reaching down for a pomegranate, splits it open for me. Inside the rough-red skin, the dark seeds, six of them, make a tiny cluster. Persephone, who couldn't say no to the seeds of the pomegranate, pays for her greediness with six months a year under ground.

On the arches that bend over all this profusion, the painted figures are purged of mortality. Appealing to a bloodless world where abstraction governs, they challenge the rough-and-tumble of the market and its hydra-headed self. Inscriptions are in Arabic and are all Greek to me. But that seems not to matter, the beauty of the calligraphy being in its form. Presiding over chaos, this elegant form functions as a magnet, drawing the myriad of willful filings to its center. In the Chorsu struggle between the one and the many is a condition of life. Were particulars to inundate us or be absorbed in general statement, we would know that the last days are at hand.

Across from the market, the long, colonnaded street is reserved to pedestrians. "Broadway" is their name for it, "just like NYC." Shops offer bunches of wildflowers, single cigarettes, besoms, shashlik, ice cream, and BARF, a popular detergent. Recorded folk music, nothing of the folk about it, can't be evaded. A tout, catching my eye, indicates his Strong Man machine and the bearded face of Amir Timur stenciled on the glass. With the wooden mallet he hands me, I drive the ball up the shaft, not far enough, however, and onlookers, shrugging, melt back in the crowd. Some in the crowd are old men, their beards "sable silvered," their faces worn like old coins. Hand-me-down clothes from the Salvation Army seem the rule, and even the young men wear rusty black suits and black and white prayer hats like Hebrew yarmulkes. But pretty girls are themselves. Vivid and daring, they balance like ballerinas on their stiletto heels. Afloat on this sea of life and not doing anything with it, I'm happy.

On impulse I buy a hat from one of the men and perch it on the back of my head. He has his face in a bowl of plov, a glutinous rice dish dotted with bits of meat and bits of yellow, possibly saffron. Putting down his spoon and fork, he considers my hat and me and gives me a thumbs-up sign. The girls teetering along the sidewalk smile their approval. They wear dresses that look like leopard skin, the spots glowing like fluorescent lightbulbs. Curling up at the tip, their shoes resemble courtiers' shoes in old Venetian paintings. I could hang out in Tashkent for a long time.

But I want to look in on the Telashayakh Mosque, home to one of the world's oldest books. This eighth-century Koran, bigger than a Shakespeare folio, was once on display in Samarkand's Bibi Khanum Mosque. Imams far up in the balcony could read the letters without straining to see them. Osman, founder of the Ottomans, owned the book early on, and Tamburlaine carried it off when he captured Damascus. Later the czars took it for St. Petersburg, but Asia got it back after the 1917 revolution. Uzbekistan's dictator, Islam Karimov, made much of this transfer, saluting a win for democracy and the indigenous peoples.

Karimov, an ex–Communist Party boss, understands how ideas are often virulent and throws a sanitary cordon around them. Solicitous on his people's behalf, he gathers all thought in the country, including religious thought, and presses it under his thumb. If Uzbekis want to examine the Osmani Koran, they have to have the dictator's approval. But censorship, far from infringing on their rights, guarantees them. The government newspaper, a latter-day *Pravda,* quotes him with approval. "I keep tabs on what my people can read," he says. "That way, they won't get the wrong ideas."

The forecourt around the Telashayakh Mosque, laid out in rose beds enclosed by clipped boxwood, resembles a medieval cloister. Brick walkways mark off the beds, and at their edges the persimmon trees, hung with bright orange globes, flare like candles. Inside the fabulous book is in the keeping of an ignorant mullah to whom all visitors, fish, flesh, or other, are heathen. He reminds me of a rare-book librarian I knew at Harvard who divided the world into people and books. With people, even fellow cognoscenti, he tended to brusqueness, but books he treated lovingly, like pressed duck under glass. I still see his plump, manicured fingers as he hefted one in both hands. The mullah, loving neither books nor people, pockets up the coins I give him and watches sullenly as I pay my respects. Though the crinkly pages are yellowing, the ink is still legible after more than a thousand years. For a while longer, young mullahs in the madrassa can scrutinize it for home truths. I wouldn't bet on another thousand years, however.

Would the book be better off in a vault in St. Petersburg? The czar thought so, my rare-book librarian concurring. Books are for safekeeping. On the other hand, books are everyone's possession, a repository of the truth that sets us free. This holds for the sister arts of painting and sculpture. Give the people custody of what the people have made, liberal friends of mine tell me, a sentiment I want to fall in with. Two cheers.

But if Lord Elgin hadn't carried off the Parthenon marbles for the British Museum, would the Greeks have preserved them? Would the Chinese have preserved Dunhuang's antiquities, including the world's oldest book? Sir Aurel Stein, having his doubts, shipped them to London where they are still on view. Had Muslims, getting to Dunhuang first, broken into the hidden cache in the desert, would they have spared all that glory of learning? Would the lion lie down with the lamb? These are questions worth entertaining, and I do my best to sort them out. Meanwhile I am grateful to the British Museum for preserving the past to the future.

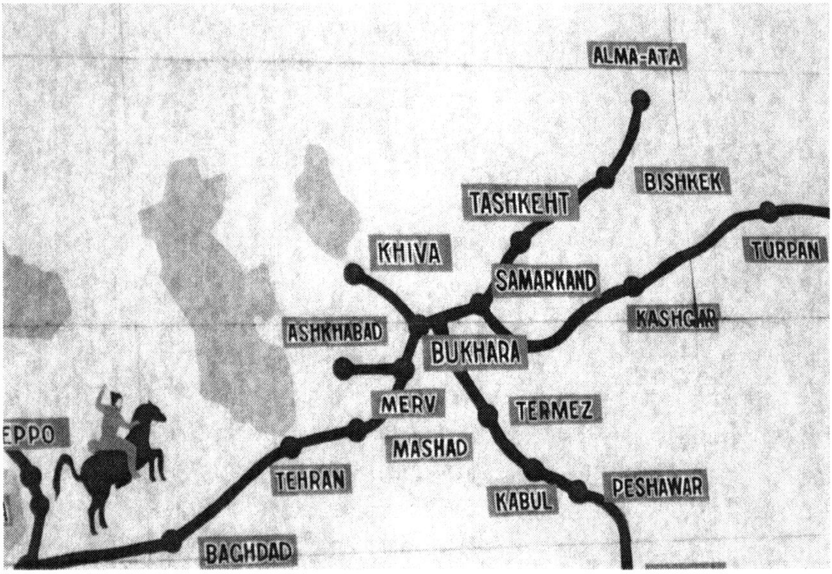

Wall map of the Silk Road. Photograph by the author from Museum in Bishkek.

Statue of Tamburlaine in Tashkent, Uzbekistan. Photograph by the author.

Pamir Mountains between China and the "Stans." Photograph by the author.

Shir-dor Medressah, seventeenth century, Registan, Samarkand, Uzbekistan. Photograph by the author.

Registan, Samarkand. Photograph by the author.

Flying Angels, from Dunhuang Caves, China.

KAZAKHSTAN
Almaty
Bishkek
Lake Issykul
Karakol
KYRGYZSTAN
Naryn River
UZBEKISTAN
Valley
Fergana
Syr Darya
Osh
TIEN SHEN MTNS
Torugart Pass
CHINA
Kashgar
TAKLAMAKAN DESERT
TAJIKSTAN
Cartography by Manoa Mapworks, Inc.

Aral Sea
Syr Darya
Lake Balkhash
KAZAKHSTAN
KAZAKHSTAN
UZBEKISTAN
Bishkek
Tashkent
KYRGYZSTAN
Fergana Valley
Dashoguz
Urgench
Khiva
Bukhara
Caspian Sea
TURKMENISTAN
Samarkand
Shakhrisabz
Amu Darya
Torugart Pass
Kashgar
TAJIKSTAN
CHINA
Ashgabad
Mary
Merv
IRAN
KARAKUM DESERT
Tehran
AFGHANISTAN
PAKISTAN
Cartography by Manoa Mapworks, Inc.

3

Looking for Tamburlaine

A four-lane highway takes me southwest to Samarkand, from ancient times the heart of the Silk Road. Not bothering with a rental car, I go by bus. I am looking for Tamburlaine, Central Asia's greatest hero. Staring out the window at the endless fields of cotton, I try to imagine what he looked like. I have a clue in the plaster cast made of his face by a Soviet anthropologist. In 1941 he unsealed the crypt in Samarkand, ignoring the warning inscribed on the coffin: "Whoever opens this will be defeated by an enemy more fearsome than I." The next day, June 22, Hitler invaded the Soviet Union. But Hitler got his comeuppance, and the anthropologist, M. M. Gerasimov, found what he was looking for, confirmation that Tamburlaine was tall beyond average and deformed in his right arm and leg. Contemporary accounts piece out his portrait. Lean and muscular, he had eyes like burning candles and could ride for days on end. Whether or not he descended from Mongols, his country was the back of a horse.

His provenance is mysterious, like that of many great men. Emerging from nowhere in the late Middle Ages, he invented a past and fulfilled it in his future. Barred from holding higher rank in his clan than emir or commander, he married a rival Mongol's widow, creating a direct link to the great khan. On another side he claimed descent from a maiden, Ahngoa, ravished by a moonbeam. This is like Greek Danae, impregnated by a shower of gold, or the Virgin Mary, by the beating wings of a dove. How else should self-made men find a parent?

In the century after his death, Christopher Marlowe, Shakespeare's contemporary, wrote a famous tragedy about him. London's Old Vic staged it memorably half a lifetime ago, and I was there in the audience, thrilling to Donald Wolfit in the lead role. "Is it not brave to be a king?" he asked us, a version of Marlowe's "mighty line," both trademark and limitation. His play is all one-liners, but only an ingrate would complain. He wrote it in his twenties, full of youth's exuberance, and also its crudity of feeling. The ills our flesh is heir to didn't vex him, not yet, and like his superb hero, he held his fate in iron chains. "I am the captain of my soul," he might have written, had the banal meter not been beneath him. Shakespeare, the same age but colder, paid him the tribute of parody.

Marlowe died at twenty-nine, stabbed through the eye in a barroom brawl. In his art and temperament, he is certainly perverse, and a whiff of inhumanity about him repels us. He longed to express the inexpressible, though: "One thought, one grace, one wonder, at the least,/Which into words no virtue can digest." The longing, coupled with the awareness that it won't ever be satisfied, puts him among the immortals.

His robustious hero is one of history's heavyweights, only in his thirties when he bestrode Asia's heartland like a colossus. Six hundred years later, his fame hasn't dimmed. For much of the vast region between the Caspian Sea and the mountains of China, he is their George Washington, and few cities lack his statue in the park. Tashkent, the biggest city in that part of the world, has him seated on a charger in Amir Temur Square, his out-flung arm pointing at the acacia trees. This statue replaces one of Karl Marx, for whom the city's main street was named before the demise of the USSR. In Asia street names change often and statues get a new head depending on who's in, who's out.

The historical Tamburlaine called himself "a poor, lame, decrepit mortal," emphasizing his frailty even as he sought to transcend it. He smiled when the Turkish sultan Bayazid was brought before him, not to mock a defeated rival but because God should have given the dominion of the world to a lame man. Evidently he was cut from a different cloth than the uncouth Scythian of legend. Contemporaries knew him as Timur, but "foreign words are turned in a circle like a ball by the sporting cudgel of the Arabic tongue," said the chronicler Ibn Arabshah, "so they say sometimes Tamar, sometimes Tamarlang . . . and Tamar in Turkic means iron, but lang means lame." The lameness was just deserts for early misdemeanors, in particular cattle rustling. The historian Ibn Khaldun reports that he was crippled during an unlucky raid. But he revenged himself on the world for what it did to him, and his subsequent bloodletting "imitates" the decadent art of Antonin Artaud.

He liked to shock and liked being cruel for its own sake. Sacking a Turkish city, he buried some of its defenders alive and threw others in the moat with their heads tied between their thighs. Children he trampled under the hooves of his horses. Virgins, nine thousand of them, he handed over to his troops. Poe, perhaps sensing affinities, called him "a diademed outlaw!" His career is so awful—in the primary sense of the word, also in its sense of filling us with awe—that we are almost inclined to salute him. He shortened enemies by a head, a million in Baghdad alone. His sinister artist's eye for effect reminds us of Browning's icy connoisseur in "My Last Duchess," and consulting it, he built a pyramid of skulls. Hungering for more the more he gorged himself, he was bent on the conquest of China when he died. But he had another side. Overstepping the limits of humanity, he created a heavenly city on earth, and some of it survives to delight us.

Samarkand is built beside a river west of the mountains that form Asia's spine. On the north are the endless steppes, on the south and further west the deserts, red sand or black sand, a distinction without a difference. But Samarkand in its essence isn't bounded by space and time. The word itself is magic and, like Keats's magic casements, opens on a world of romance. For at least ten thousand years men have lived here, but until recent times few have found their way in—about one every hundred years since the death of Tamburlaine. This changed in the 1860s with the prizing open of Central Asia by Russian bayonets. Samarkand's history begins with its ancient predecessor, Afrosiab, named, some say, for the first Sogdian king. His writ ran between Central Asia's two great rivers, the Amu Darya (Oxus) and the Syr Darya (Jaxartes), a land famous for the work of its looms. Felt, silk, and the crimson cloth called cramoisie are code words evoking the magical city, whose carpets, lustrous with vegetable dyes, might have covered the floor of heaven. Transoxiana, another uncanny word, means the land across the river. Between the two world wars, the travel writer Robert Byron reported what he found there. Art criticism better than the Blue Guide's distinguishes his account, *The Road to Oxiana* (1937), but its chief merit is as a *plein de rêves* kind of book, and the city it summons lives in the unconscious mind.

This city stopped Alexander in his tracks as he marched across Asia. "Everything I have heard about the beauty of . . . [Samarkand] is indeed true," he said, "except that it is much more beautiful than I imagined." Like a famous courtesan, it passed from one hand to another, belonging to Greeks, then Samanids and Persians, Seljuk Turks and Arabs. Early in the thirteenth century, however, Genghis Khan torched the city, and its desolation became a byword for centuries to come. Mehmet II, the conqueror of Constantinople, thought of it as he contemplated the ruined palace of Justinian, home to so many successors of Constantine. Reflecting on the vicissitudes of human greatness, says Gibbon (aloft, it seems, on a howdah and writing to suit), "he repeated an elegant distich of Persian poetry: 'The spider has woven his web in the imperial palace, and the owl hath sung his watch-song on the towers of Afrosiab.'" This was the storied place where Tamburlaine pitched his tent.

He did that literally. Though he had his Blue Palace, he preferred the al fresco life, camping out with his entourage in pleasure gardens adjacent to the city. In the middle of his journey, about 1370, he began the work of glorification. Rebuilding Samarkand, he laid the world under tribute, from its four corners scooping up material wealth, also monuments of the intellect and spirit. The Indian elephants that transported much of his plunder covered his front line in battle, their turrets filled with archers and Greek fire. In peace they became beasts of burden. I have seen an elephant lumbering down a busy street in Asia, not part of a circus act but minding its own elephantine business. A sight not easily forgotten, it would have been commonplace in Tamburlaine's city.

The city of the Timurids, continuers of his line, is also a modern city, and its "monuments of unaging intellect" share the limelight with attention getters such as the Spartak Stadium, the GUM department store, and the Club Sharq, a popular disco. But cream rises to the top, and above the swales and tacky vistas of modern times rise the major peaks of the city we remember. I pick them out of memory as if palpably present, first the Registan, then, dominating a second group, the mosque of Tamburlaine's consort, the Bibi Khanum, and last the Gur-i-Emir, his burial place, and two lesser tombs in its orbit.

Of these focal points, one is visible from the balcony of my hotel. The past merges with the present in the city I have returned to, and the hotel I am staying in is called the Afrosiab. Leaning over the balustrade, I make out the greenish-blue dome of the Gur-i-Emir (Tomb of the Ruler). Glazing or enameling redeems the homeliness of its brick understructure, and the glitter of majolica gives it the look of suavity that even Italy in its great days didn't surpass. Painting on plaster or papier-mâché, made of the special-quality silk paper of Samarkand, adds another dimension. Tamburlaine's artisans employed a technique called *kundal.* They used a gypsum-like material native to the surrounding country, carving it while still soft and often spreading it over their painting. The eyes dazzle at these bas-reliefs, painted with gold in solution.

Sometimes their attention to detail is so meticulous as to seem extrahuman. Even so they divided their attention, keeping one eye on heaven, the other on their craft. The mausoleum makes an octagon, girt round on its interior with indentations called *mihrabs,* niches hollowed out in that wall of the mosque facing Mecca. Rome's Pantheon resembles it except that the Pantheon, by comparison, looks plain. Green alabaster tiles create an oversize dado encircling the wall at its base. Above this an inscription from the Koran, thirty feet high, proclaims the faith: "There is no God but Allah, and Muhammad is his prophet." Neither Virgin nor Child nor Holy Spirit nor panoply of saints participates in the faith, only the one impalpable presence. Mixed in with the calligraphy are floral designs called *girikh,* intimating flowers but reducing them to their form. In some such way, late Cézanne sees through nature to the cubic structures behind it. Gilded stalactites, honeycombs of them, descend from the inner ceiling. They look like themselves but are finer than stalactites in nature.

A skin of glazed tiles stretched across the dome conceals the bones that give it its structure. It doesn't conceal them entirely, and the bones look through the skin, creating the famous ribbed cantaloupe dome, a version of our ghostly paradigm and its fleshly integument. I am paraphrasing Yeats, whose Plato thought nature but a spume that plays upon an underlying paradigm of forms. Much Islamic art advances the claims of the paradigm or naked word against the word made flesh. But not here.

I would stoop to italics if they didn't shirk a writer's job, so tempted am I to hammer home the point: how talent picks a momentous quarrel with convention in the late fifteenth-century in Asia. For the Gur-i-Emir revolutionizes the conventions it inherits, bringing to birth something new beneath the sun. This is the special achievement of the Timurids and the ambiguous man, "darkly wise and rudely great," they descend from. Look again at the tiles that roof the Gur-i-Emir and you see how they shatter convention only to reinvent it. The old imperative wants us to come as close to the naked truth as may be, but this architect wants a nakedness with her clothes on. Whatever his motive, esteeming our physical world or contemning the void, he traces patterns on nothingness. A pattern of lozenges covers the dome, mingling greens, yellows, and turquoise. To my astonishment I realize that these must be the colors of death and transfiguration.

All this the architect of the Ruhabad (literally "Abode of the Spirit") denies. This domed mausoleum, below and west of the Registan, is above and east of the Gur-i-Emir. It sticks to convention, and grace notes are banned. Its aesthetic, the same as that of our poet Milton's, bets on pure form against the welter of lowercase exemplifications. Christianity, though a house of many mansions, doesn't favor this aesthetic. Islam, born of the desert, makes it central to the faith. But in some great historical moments it lapses from the faith, in Moorish Granada, in Ottoman Constantinople, in India under the Mughals, and this is a version of the fortunate fall.

South of the Gur-i-Emir is the Ak-Saray (White Palace), where the last Timurid is buried. In the foreground the Ruhabad honors a fourteenth-century mystic. Its sober dome, bare of tiling, gives off waves of feeling like heat waves. Bordering the door frame are a few majolica tiles, otherwise nothing until the nineteenth century and its tarting-up impulse came on the scene. So lacking is it in self-importance that I confer importance on it, reminded as I am of sober Christian churches of the older time, for example San Lorenzo in Florence.

But how should Christian and Muslim, those types of antipathy, make a nexus? This question is before me as I inspect the tomb of Tamburlaine. He finished his first version of it in 1404, as he neared the end of his life. It is as if he knew this and meant to build a mausoleum that would put all others in the shade. Five years earlier he had broken ground for the Bibi Khanum, a mosque so colossal as to redefine its kind, the way Beethoven's late quartets demolish the kind, hoping to create a new one on its ruins. He didn't build from scratch but completed and reconstituted the madrassa and *khanaga* complex begun by his favorite grandson, killed fighting in Turkey. (A *khanaga* is a hostel for wandering dervishes.) He himself meant to be buried in his native place, Shakhrisabz, the Green City, but death overtook him at the outset of his China campaign, and his body, bathed in rose water and adorned with pearls like a work of art, was brought back to Samarkand, his most artistic achievement.

NO MAN-MADE PLACE is visually more stunning than the Registan. The Spanish ambassador described it on the day its artisans painted the last glowing lozenge, their brushes charged with gold in solution. He was favored with a place beside the sovereign in his plane tree gardens, the walls hung with rose-colored silk "ornamented with spangles of silver plate gilt, each spangle set with an emerald or pearl." Ermine and squirrel fur lined the tents in the garden; the gold tables were set with gold flasks studded with gems. Trespassers in this *hortus inclusus* were shot on sight, their bodies left where they lay. Robert Byron, whose thin skin became him, felt the colors like a blow: the turquoise of Tamburlaine's domed mausoleum, its ribs scattered with black and white diamonds. Byron was an aesthete, and the dead bodies didn't concern him.

But they are important for our sense of Tamburlaine's great square, whose beauty has something to do with its name, literally the place of sand. Strewn across the square, the sand soaked up the blood from public executions, a horror that still resonates under the chatter of vendors and tour guides. Romantic poetry makes much of the connection of horror and beauty, supposing that one is contingent on the other. Shelley wrote of the leprous corpse exhaling itself in flowers, and Oscar Wilde posed the naked Salome against the gory head of Jokanaan. Whether these conjunctions are contingent or only bizarre is a question, however. Dr. Johnson said that he who thinks causally must think morally, a saying I used to keep in my phylactery. But confronted by the Registan, I wonder. Perhaps the sequence it presents is more a matter of energy than morals.

Tamburlaine's was demonic. In high summer 1401, a time of heat so ferocious that birds fell dead from the air, he sacked Baghdad. Each of his soldiers was ordered to bring in a pair of heads. He had them piled up in towers, 120 towers, says Ibn Arabshah. After he was done, only owls and crows built in the ruined city. But the treasure he brought back to Samarkand needed all the army's elephants to convey it. A tree of pure gold was part of the loot and went to beautify the pavilion of the empress.

Samarkand is a coat of many colors, none so arresting as those on display in the Registan's three principal structures. That suits propriety, for the square is the city's hub of commerce and learning and was its major market until restless Tamburlaine swept it clean in 1404. (He was always knocking down and rebuilding.) If you lay a string across the map from southwest to northeast, the Registan lies in the middle, below it the Gur-i-Emir and its satellite tombs, above it the Bibi Khanum Mosque and the royal necropolis called Shah-i-Zinda. A new addition to an old city, the Registan waited for its development on Tamburlaine's grandson Ulug Beg and his Timurid successors. They raised the dome that crowned the whole, but his energy fueled their fires. It did this the way a grain of sand provokes the oyster into making a pearl.

But energy alone doesn't rationalize Tamburlaine's achievement. Children and wild animals have it abundantly, and we are glad when it flags. Largeness of spirit seems key to the achievement. The state of his soul, damned or saved as we once put it, has to play into this—not only because use and wont says so, but also because a reading of history with eyes close to the page argues for such a conclusion. The trouble is in the calibrating: how to do it so exquisitely as to see just how cause relates to effect.

Early in the fifteenth century, Ulug Beg erected the first of the Registan's buildings, a functioning madrassa on the west side of the square. This house of learning accommodated more than a hundred students taught by the best scholars Islam could muster, including the ruler himself. His passion for astronomy is reflected in a mosaic of blue stars on the huge *pishtak* (portal) that opens on the interior courtyard. Around the courtyard four vaulted arches called *iwans* give access to the student rooms (*hujira*). The lecture halls (*darskhana*) lie under the corner domes, and four slender minarets stand at the corners. It seems right to use the old Islamic terms, for like the technical vocabulary of Romanesque and Gothic, they tell of things worth recalling.

Time, an ill wind that blows no good, has winnowed the student rooms, turning those that remain into gift shops. *Molti anni fa* (long time passing), when I climbed Giotto's bell tower in Florence, I found a Coca-Cola machine at the top. No muezzins call to prayer, but the minarets have another function, holding up the heavens. The northern minaret is famous for its lean that can't be corrected. Even the Soviets tried and failed, and perhaps it is appropriate that perfection should always elude us.

Ulug Beg's madrassa is like a handsome old face seamed with wrinkles. It isn't old, or wasn't when finished, but the proliferation of detail is fantastic, even over the top, not an inch of the surface remaining unadorned. Some will call this art decadent, a word to use warily in speaking of the Registan, but I put it on the table. Floral patterns are painted or sculpted on tiles around the doorways, spirals climb up the pillars, stripes of Kufic calligraphy come alive on the inside of the *iwans*. *Girikhs*, those reminiscences of flowers in nature, embrace the minarets as if they were ivy hugging old trees. Do we say that Ulug Beg so loved the world, or was his true passion elsewhere, the surface serving him as a jeu d'esprit?

Whatever he meant, his concern with superficial things—astronomy, theology, history, mathematics, poetry, and music: all of them superficial under the aspect of eternity—sealed his death warrant. Had not his teacher, the astronomer Qazizadeh Rumi, said, "Where knowledge starts, religion ends"? Enlisting the help of his son, the mullahs had him beheaded in 1449. Soon after his observatory, the best equipped in the medieval world, was demolished. In 1908 an amateur Russian archaeologist, Vladimir Vyatkin, excavated the astrolabe's huge semicircular track. This Vyatkin slept through the Bolshevik Revolution, remaining in Samarkand as director of its antiquities. He wasn't political, an innocent rather, but had the powers that be estimated his priorities, he would have gone the same way as his master.

Work on the Registan began again under the Shaybamid Emir Yalangtush. In the early decades of the seventeenth century, he raised the second of its buildings, the Shir Dor, or lion-bearing madrassa. Facing its predecessor on the other side of the square, it approximates its dimensions, not more than that, and the distaste for perfect symmetry that makes Islam a more credible faith makes it a more persuasive aesthetic. In its psychology particulars are out but idiosyncrasy is insisted on, and oddly no two beings are the same.

The lion-bearing imagery above the *pishtak* arch comes as a wrench, violating the Islamic taboo on representational art. Striped lions that look like tigers pursue a pair of white does across a tapestry of stylized flowers. The lions are grotesque, and human faces fringed with sunbeams rise out of their backs. No one knows what prompted this break with tradition, surely not an impulse to naturalistic art. The Shir Dor Madrassa, like each of the others, loads every rift of the surface with ore, but nature never knew the figures on the facade. Some say they remember the solar symbolism of the ancient Zoroastrians, a cult driven underground long before but still quick. I think the resort to physicality, cartoonish at that, suggests that Islam was losing its nerve.

In the last of the Registan's major buildings, the impulse to pure form is back in the saddle. Fitting a third madrassa into the square, Emir Yalangtush placed it at right angles to the others. Nature abhors a vacuum, and so does his Tilly-Kari, literally "gilded" like a baroque fantasy. Daylight was too coarse, and he filtered it into the student rooms through *panjera*, carved plaster windows. He and his collaborators, Soviet restorers of the 1970s, so bathed the interior walls in gold leaf that they smite us like a sunset. Appeasing our senses, even overwhelming them, he went back to the old kundal style, hardening mortar over the image, then turning it incandescent with gold in solution.

By 1660 the work was done and the huge square boxed in on three of its four sides. Huge it is but not gargantuan, not Red Square or the Zócalo in Mexico City or even overbearing St. Peter's. Space is on the human scale, and we feel ourselves in an enclosure where men congregate to worship, study, or chaffer, as in the old bazaar that occupied the middle ground. The first time I saw the Registan, looking idly from the window of a passing bus, my head snapped back. Something outside my control took hold of me and hasn't yet relinquished its hold.

This apparition is engraved in memory as on a photographic plate. I see shimmering towers that lean from the perpendicular. Their bright facing goes on sans intermission, a weave of terra-cotta tiles whose turquoise coloring seems to come from within. A wick has been turned up inside a lamp chimney. The glittering majolica reverses this effect, and its white surfaces, painted over with gold, are like Danae's golden shower. I am looking at a theophany, as when the god descends from above. The facades, brushed with sun in the declining light of late afternoon, evoke Keats's rosy stubble fields in his "Ode to Autumn." Is the color real or imposed? Here and there on the surface, the modern restorer has left a few rectangular spaces untouched by restoration to show us how art improves nature.

Tamburlaine was primarily a fighter, conquest absorbing most of his life. He spent the last thirty-five years of it outside Transoxiana. But he wasn't monomaniacal, and as one hand busied itself with the coming campaign against China, the other built the Bibi Khanum. A favorite consort began this gigantic mosque that bears her name while he was off at the wars. She wanted the job done in a hurry, meaning to surprise him, and the architect demanded a kiss in return. When she complied, he bit her. He was a passionate architect. Tamburlaine, aware what the telltale blemish must mean, had him hurled from his own tower, but instead of falling to earth he flew off to Mecca. Bibi Khanum, though permitted to live, had to hide her face ever after, and this was how women first took the veil.

A great pity if the story isn't true, for the mosque in its heyday was fit for a queen. This one, attended by three hundred ladies-in-waiting, came there when she wanted to pray. The portals she passed through rose a hundred feet, the dome even higher. Tamburlaine thought it too low. A stage set surrounded her, plunder from the sack of Delhi in December 1398. Ninety-five elephants hauled the marble for the pavement she knelt on. Stonemasons from Fars, Azerbaijan, and Hindustan dressed the walls, and crystal workers from Damascus worked their magic on the ceilings. Running round the base of the dome, inscriptions from the Koran loomed so large (my sources say) she could read them a mile off.

In the seventeenth century, an earthquake tumbled half the mosque; in the nineteenth its mammoth walls were quarried for brick and its great gates melted down by an avaricious emir of Bukhara. The czar's officers, when they seized the city, used the Bibi Khanum as a stable. What goes around comes around, they said to each other, remembering how Tamburlaine had come close to sacking Moscow. Though Soviet restorers sought to put the huge mosque back together, the money ran out before they were done. Today a giant crane stands beside the site, imposing but idle. History, not only melancholy, bores us with its recurrences, and the fate of the Bibi Khanum is step by step the fate of Cluny, once the light of the world, now a bucolic spot where Maçonnais picnic on Sundays.

I needn't take off my shoes when I enter the mosque. Its floor has gone back to dirt, its walls are stripped down to the bare brick, and I must work on my imaginary forces to picture the building that was. But the sense of grandeur, different from grandiosity, isn't a casualty of time. Even in its enfeebled state, the Bibi Khanum seems to soar. Though rising to a dome, its spirit is gothic, like Michelangelo's ruined Church of the Angels and Martyrs next to the Piazza della Repubblica in Rome.

The gray marble lectern in the center of the courtyard is still there. A gift from Ulug Beg, it held the world's biggest book, the Osmani Koran. What did Tamburlaine think when he carried it off as a trophy from Damascus? Did he think its talismanic verses would stand to him in the final exigent? Was he captivated by its size, like all of us on our vulgar side? Did it have any intrinsic value, or was it only hocus-pocus? Nine legs support the lectern, and beneath them a youngish woman is crawling in and out on her knees. I assume she is barren, but if she can make the circuit three times, her infertility will leave her, and she will bear the children she craves.

Miracles are the stuff of every day in Islam, and not far from the hopeful goings-on in the mosque, a man picked up his severed head, walked with it through the wall, and was gone. This happened in 676 A.D., and the man was Qsim ibn-Abbas, a cousin of Muhammad the Prophet. The Shah-i-Zinda or Tomb of the Living King commemorates his dramatic exit, though some have him jumping down a cistern or walking through a cliff face. I prefer the wall, recalling as it does the fall of Constantinople, among the most touching of all the great stories. When Mehmet II began his last furious assault, the priests in Sancta Sophia raised their voices to heaven, chanting before the high altar until the very end. Then they collected the sacred vessels and stepped through the sanctuary wall. Like ibn-Abbas in his tomb, they are still hidden behind it, waiting for time to come round.

The Prophet's cousin meant to convert the local Sogdians from their Zoroastrian faith, but a group of fire-worshippers stole on him while he was praying and chopped off his head. St. Denis, patron saint of France, suffered a similar fate with the same composure. Putting his head under his arm, he kept walking until he came to the right place to stop. Blood marks the spot outside Paris, the site of France's first Gothic cathedral. Both Christianity and Islam seem drawn to the conjunction of blood and beauty, finding it fruitful. The Shah-i-Zinda bears this out.

In the second half of the fourteenth century it became a popular burial place for princes of the realm, and a modern graveyard on the bluff above it still accommodates dead Soviets and their Uzbeki successors. Displayed on gravestones, framed photographs show men in business suits with rolled lapels, white shirts and ties, and full heads of hair. As I watch, a funeral is beginning and the procession winds its way toward me. The pallbearers, all men, wear black and white caps, and the casket they are carrying is slung between poles. The bizarre photos notwithstanding, everything tells of the boneyard. Against it the Shah-i-Zinda sings a jaunty song of protest. "O Death, where is thy sting?" it cries. "O grave, where is thy victory?"

Ulug Beg built its *pishtak* or entrance portal, a gateway to heaven. But his portal opens also on an ambiguous country, neither heaven nor earth, in which our normal progress from life to death is rejected. Through it the once and future king will return to his kingdom. Domed transit halls called *chortaks* conduct the visitor through the tombs and mosques, a pair of the latter, a madrassa, and a prayer room, the *ziarakhona,* which goes back a thousand years. Most of the mausoleums are small, and most house a dead Timurid. They swing out in a line like human vertebrae, the line curving slightly as it reaches its term. A steep staircase links them, the Stairway to Heaven, suggesting another parallel to the Christian story. As with Rome's Scala Santa, good things happen to those who climb the holy stairs. Thirty-six stairs lead to heaven, but if you err in your count you won't get there.

As I walk the cobbled street, a brick wall rises on my right hand, on my left a row of brick mausoleums. The facades are much worn but show enough of their original facing to rivet the eye, caught as it might be by a woman still beautiful, though past her prime. Contrast is of the essence of the Shadi Mulk Aka Mausoleum, about a third of the way down the line: plain brick work on the melon-shaped dome, beneath it carved and glazed panels of terra-cotta and majolica. An artificial stalactite hangs in the space above the entrance, the windows are trellised (*panjera*), and the lacelike portal seems made of wool. Once more I see how art betters nature.

Inside the mausoleum the tile is more nearly intact, most of it blue in endless permutations. The tombs on the floor are cenotaphs, and out of sight in the crypt are the bones. The dome, a gleaming blue, is painted with frescoes on a white ground. Not crowning the whole, it seems to float in air above it. I am looking at an artist's reordering of heaven and earth from which all trace of grossness has been purged.

A final *chortak* connects the tomb of the martyred saint with that of Tuman Aka, a favorite wife of Tamburlaine's. Admonishing the visitor, her inscription reads: "The tomb is a door and everybody enters it." This sounds gloomy-Hebraic, but the Shah-i-Zinda is less a necropolis than a celebration of life. Nowhere else in Central Asia has ceramic art so flowered. Its high point is a grave, the holy of holies (*gurkhona*) where Ibn Abbas lies buried. To reach the grave chamber, I pass through the Door of Paradise, six hundred years old. Like everyone else I press my nose against the wooden trellis enclosing the tombstone. It isn't cemetery gray but majolica and strikes on the eye like a sunburst.

TAMBURLAINE, anticipating Peter the Great, was hands on, involving himself with the work up to his elbows. There is an anecdote that has him cheering on the laborers constructing the Bibi Khanum Mosque, tossing down coins and slabs of meat while they raised the foundation. He craved the company of artists and men of science, bidding them all come in. He didn't ask them to check here if they were Christian or Muslim. Craftsmanship trumped ethnicity, and the best craftsmen from India, Persia, and Azerbaijan collaborated in his grand instauration. One, Muhammad ibn Mahmud Isfahani, left his name on the portal of the Gur-i-Emir mausoleum. Glory enough, he thought, to let them know he had been there.

The man who butchered impartially was a syncretist, and there seems a grisly propriety in that. He took strength from different faiths and intellectual persuasions, and perhaps the greatest men, artists included, have his accommodating instinct. It wasn't tolerant, our modern shibboleth, but provident. In 1402 he stormed the city of Smyrna, the last Christian stronghold in Anatolia. His soldiers decapitated everyone inside the walls, sacking up their heads as pious tokens of a job well done. But in the same years he dug up the bones of the Old Testament prophet Daniel, reinterring them in Samarkand. He meant them for a prophylactic against moral or physical disaster, also as an inducement to travel. Tour guides point out the lion's den, not far from the tomb. It needs enlarging each year, they say, to make room for the prophet, whose body keeps growing in death.

In the gorgeous mausoleum prepared by Tamburlaine for his own death, seven coffins sit on the floor in the octagonal hall, six of white marble, one of jade. But the coffins are empty, and the bodies are interred below in the crypt. That the jade tomb is his goes without saying. It doesn't have an epitaph, and he didn't need one. As he lay dying, he said, "Only a stone, and my name upon it," the ultimate arrogance. "Not to know me argues yourself unknown," Milton has his Satan say. The man whose mere name was enough planned to conquer Egypt and Africa, march from the Nile to the Atlantic, enter Europe by the Strait of Gibraltar, impose his will on the Christian world, then return home by the deserts of Russia and Tartary. He came close.

Pious when it suited him, he checked out the stars in the summer of 1402 as he prepared to settle accounts with Bayazid. The astrologers looked grim and didn't dare speak their minds. So much for them, and he brought in new astrologers. "Neither fortune nor affliction depends on the stars," he told them. The new man of the Renaissance, "himself alone," speaks in this pronouncement. For example, Cassius in *Julius Caesar:* "Men at some times are masters of their fates . . . (the fault) is not in our stars but in ourselves that we are underlings." Moderns are inclined to take this for sound doctrine, but Shakespeare means us to look askance. It isn't true, his play discovers, that men are masters of their fate, not sometimes, not ever.

But Tamburlaine's story says there is much a man can do of himself, and doesn't argue for passive behavior. He had an agenda, pursuing it deliberately. This was the control of trade along the Silk Road from Merv and northern Persia through Samarkand. One by one he picked off his competitors, until it came the turn of Kunya Urgench. This powerful city state didn't cave easily. Once home to two million people, it lay between the Caspian Sea and the northern border of Iran. It was famous for music, and enthusiastic chroniclers said its children cried in harmony in their cradles. Five times between 1372 and 1388, Tamburlaine came back. The last time he leveled the city, first smashing the wooden dam that kept out the Amu Darya. When the men were all dead and the women and children sold into slavery, he sowed the land with barley. If you approach it as I did across the waste of the Kara-Kum Desert, you see rising from the sterile soil the tallest minaret in Central Asia. But that is all you see, and Kunya Urgench is gone.

Next in Tamburlaine's sights was Isfahan in Persia. Stacking seventy thousand decapitated bodies in the shape of minarets outside the city walls, he meant to teach the Persians a lesson. That done, he turned north, crossing the Caucasus into Georgia and coming close to Moscow. South of the Oxus in present-day Afghanistan, he cut a swath from Balkh to Herat, famous for tiles. I would give much to see Herat, knowing that isn't likely to be. At dawn its terrified citizens heard the sound of Tamburlaine's seven-foot trumpets.

Before he died, having defeated the Ottoman Turks and secured the submission of the Mamluks of Egypt, he brought his empire to the shores of the Aegean. All that remained for him to conquer was China, the richest country on earth. Methodically he set out to do this. But Nature, a greater power than he could contradict, frustrated his purpose. He had always worn his body lightly, like a cloak to be shrugged on and off, and now it began to betray him. As he prepared to set out on his last adventure, the Castilian ambassador Ruy Gonzáles de Clavijo was startled to observe his decline. Suddenly he had become so old and infirm "that his eyelids were falling over his eyes."

But dreams of Cathay led him on, and he struck his tents in midwinter. For the four-thousand-mile journey, his personal baggage train numbered five hundred wagons. He carried grain for food en route and to be sown when he got there, and each of his soldiers brought two milch cows, both for milk and meat. But snow covered the land to the depth of two spears. In the bitter cold, men's spittle froze and their ears and noses fell off. Tamburlaine, though borne in his litter, could never get warm. His health worsened; he drank heavily, first wine, then spirits; and his doctors shook their heads. In the night of February 18, 1405, he died on the plains of Otrar beyond the Syr-Darya, the second of Central Asia's great rivers.

Gibbon, who noticed Tamburlaine often in his *Decline and Fall,* concludes that he "was rather the scourge than the benefactor of mankind." But Gibbon's moral judgment is perhaps off the point, for Nature's darlings are not the children of the Lord, nor do they come out of Sunday school, nor weigh their food, "nor punctually keep the commandments." This conclusion is Emerson's in his essay "Experience," a logical throwing-forward from the stand-on-your-own-two-feet position he makes memorable in his famous "Self-Reliance." Emerson himself hoped to inaugurate the rule of morality, but the Emersonian hero deserves the name not because he is moral but because he is great, beautiful, and strong. He is like Tamburlaine, or like Shakespeare's villainous Richard III, "himself alone."

Tamburlaine, one of nature's darlings, is also a surrogate: he stands for something as well as himself, and to ask about the meaning of his spectacular career is to ask about the meaning of history. Is it all sound and fury? Another of history's captains and kings, Charles XII of Sweden, hints at an answer. In the seventeenth century, he blazed across his times like a comet, the metaphor implying that at the end he petered out. Before that happened, however, he decimated his country, killing off huge numbers of its young men, and few in his time could have had reason to praise him. But nearly three centuries after Poltava, the strong pull of his glamorous spirit is the only reason I think about Sweden.

His empire, like Tamburlaine's, fell to pieces after his death. In itself that isn't remarkable. Nothing human lasts, true of the Registan not less than Nineveh and Tyre. But to say that nothing matters is to say more than I know. Though I am chary of pronouncing, leaving that to priests and mullahs, I will say at a minimum that what matters most is superficial. A word for this is style. Tamburlaine, a killer more thoroughgoing than most, was dowered with it, and it saves him for the future. Unlike many who are morally his superior, he had an eye for beauty, the will to embody it, and the wit that let him know how to do this. A contemporary, Sharaf-al-Din, remembers him saying, "As the only creator of the world is God, so there should be only the one king in the world." He was that king, and living up to his perfect sense of himself, he became a work of art.

Merged in his creation, he took pride in what he was and what he had made. "Truly our works represent us!" he said, words that seem to echo from high minarets in Samarkand. The domes and towers of his capital city are so many emblems of his capacious spirit, and yearn for a harmony beyond human achievement, the perfect thing "no virtue can digest." (Virtue, as Marlowe meant it, is power.) The Castilian ambassador saw him, toward the end of his life, feasting at a golden table in his silken tent. In front of the table stood "a gold tree made to resemble an oak," on its branches "many birds made of enameled gold of various colors." These birds, though the product of dreams, were substantial.

Yeats has birds like them, "of hammered gold and gold enameling," on his golden bough in Byzantium. Tamburlaine's outdid them. A type of the Romantic poet, he gave imagination free rein. But he had a soldier's arm, and it conferred reality on the things he imagined. Unexpectedly Marlowe's reading, though he could only have dreamed it, comes closer than any other to stabbing the heart of his greatness. "Still climbing after knowledge infinite, / And always moving as the restless spheres," he reached for the heavens, not resting until he achieved them.

4

Shakhrisabz and the Once and Future King

The Khudjum Embroidery Factory in Shakhrisabz, the birthplace of Tamburlaine, is having its annual gala. So reads the colored brochure handed to me by the clerk at the checkout counter in Samarkand's Hotel Afrosiab. The colors in the brochure are garish, too bad, for it is promoting Oriental carpets. Better stick to black and white, avoiding odious comparisons. But I would walk a mile for an elephant-foot carpet, unique to this part of the world, and you never know where you will find one. It's only a morning's drive to Shakhrisabz, and according to the map, the carpet factory is a mile or two south of town. The stars are aligned, and I decide to go prospecting for carpets.

I have the road to myself, nothing to distract me from the unvarying sameness of the landscape. Mile on mile of stunted tamarisk trees, pulsing against my eyeballs like highway markers, flash by in the other direction. A callow poem of Keats's I like for its callowness tells about the eyeballs, and I begin to recite it. "O ye who have your eyeballs vexed and tired."

Despite a good night's sleep, it's a struggle to keep my eyes from closing. I am like the old hajji in the watercolor that hangs on my study wall at home. This pilgrim to Mecca has had his fill of life on the road, and his body language says he wants to turn in at the next caravansary. He leans on his staff, one arm supporting the other at the crook of the elbow. His heavy-lidded eyes are drawn down at the corners, but his arched eyebrows ask a question. *What am I doing here?* The same question has occurred to me. But like the decrepit pilgrim, I am sojourning for truth, and turning back isn't an option.

Suddenly the scene changes, and in front of my windshield are the foothills of the Zerafshan Mountains. Fearsome rocks, the playthings of heavenly bowlers, lie nearly athwart the road. To either side of it, the ground, denuded of vegetation, sends up heat waves as it bakes in the sun. I could wish my life balanced on a more nearly even keel. Soon, however, the arid land turns a filmy green. Trees in leaf, crowning the hills, overlook a lush valley, beyond it high mountains. I am in a parenthesis, like life between birth and death. Fittingly, I make out below me an old graveyard, some of the stones tilted at angles like traffic cones brushed by the traffic. In the midst of death sits a still-lively brick *khanaga,* imposing order on its surroundings. These hostels for Sufi dervishes are often so uncompromisingly plain they might be taken for ostentatious. A broad dome, faced with steel and reflecting back the sun, rises from this one's brick walls, and nearby a famous holy man is buried. Over his grave flies a telltale, the white flag of sainthood.

Meeting up with the Sufis in this remote corner of Asia seems more than chance. On my night table at home is an abridged volume of one of them, the Persian poet Rūmī, who lived eight hundred years ago. His translator, A. J. Arberry, says he is the supreme genius of Islamic mysticism. I ask myself how a mystic's perception of the world, by convention nonrational, can possibly close with the truth. As I travel south through Central Asia, I am in its pursuit, and finding out how things cohere is the end of my sojourning. Like the old Hungarian traveler Ármin Vámbéry, "a wanderer through the world for many a day," I look for a pattern in flux. This end was present to my mind in the story of Tamburlaine, blood-boltered but magnificent, yet again (to compare great and small) in the art of carpet making. A superior carpet on the floor of the house imposes coherence on everything around it. But replace it with cheap-and-shoddy, and unity fractures." "All coherence gone." So wrote John Donne in the backwash of the Copernican revolution, when the earth was displaced from the center and man became a wanderer on its face.

In Central Asia man has always led a wanderer's life, but not because science has cut him loose from his moorings. The rootlessness that besets him is intrinsic to his being. In this respect men in the West are his brothers, and comparing the two helps us to apprehend both. Rūmī's poetry, like Sufi poetry as a kind, means to lead men back home. His poems celebrate a cosmos both brilliant and familiar. When we look at the heavens on a starry night, the same panoply is always spread before us, and Rūmī, step by step, offers few surprises. A highly structured poet, he returns to the same verbal patterns over and over. Connecting the bizarre to the matter of everyday, he gives first place to the emotions:

Have you heard that basil and carnation in the garden are laughing surreptitiously because affairs have become easy?
Have you heard that the nightingale has returned from his travels, joined in the concert and become the master of all the birds? . . . .
Have you heard that the anemone's cheeks are suffused with blood?. . . . (and) that the rose has become the head chamberlain of the divan? (poem 98)

Obviously this poet doesn't rack his brains for knowledge. But where does he get it? The scholars say by revelation or through ecstasy, induced by singing and dancing. But his parallel constructions aren't revealed or ecstatic: they come from craft. So the Sufi, supposedly a type of everybody's Romantic poet, his eye rolling in a fine frenzy, is actually a cold-blooded artificer, even counting on his fingers. In that respect, Rūmī is like all credentialed writers. He anticipates a well-known poet of Shakespeare's day, whose famous precept, "Look in thy heart and write," turns out to be borrowed from books.

But Rūmī isn't self-conscious, though he uses his wits. Some of what I read of him transcends intelligence, like Runic language "felt in the heart and felt along the blood." "In the desert," he says, "a great silence overcomes me, and I wonder why I ever thought to use language." He sought God like a traveler advancing slowly down a path to the goal of union with the one reality. But his conclusions were enunciated rather than worked out. No peeping and botanizing along the way. He had to travel all the stages, though, plant life, the lower animals, man, to reach the highest planes of consciousness, and there is something of Buddhism in this offshoot of Islam. Ultimately the Sufi and the Buddhist are pantheists whose one god is everywhere, but more in the heart than the heavens. Sufis especially have a foot in either camp, emotional and rational. This ambiguous posture makes them appealing, if you believe as I do that awareness of ambiguity is the condition of knowing.

I park in front of the *khanaga*, its portal facing the saint's tombstone, conspicuous on a raised platform. Next to it on this *dakhma* is the tombstone of his son, identified by an inscription. An old man, his bonnet at his feet, is kneeling on the *dakhma* dressed in the Sufi uniform, coarse woolen cloth (*suf* = wool). Muslim ascetics wore it in imitation of early Christian anchorites in the desert, and not for the first time Islam and Christianity announce their connection.

Only minutes away, according to my Blue Guide, is a cistern of supernatural power. I get down from the car to pay it a visit. The cistern sprang into being at a touch of a saint's walking stick, and drinking from it is said to open your eyes to the truth. The poems of Rūmī originate in some such mysterious way, welling up like the miraculous water. Though deeply learned, a theologian, a student of the Koran and its exegeses, he was clearly no intellectual, and it is by miracles that he comes to the truth. In one of his ghazals, number 190, an intoxicated man, drunk with the blood of enemies, is likened to a ring on the door. What can this mean? Can he be telling us that wisdom is entered through the gates of excess?

Rational-minded moderns are apt to shy from his incoherent-seeming art, wanting their art true to life. The same bias dictates their choice of Oriental carpets, not abstract in design, my choice, but realistic, the increasingly popular choice. But realism, as with all interesting matters, is open to different meanings. The same description holds for Rūmī's poetry. As a thinker he is 1) acute or 2) wooly-headed. For example how should drainers of pure wine be located on "the path of poverty"? Can poverty-stricken and intoxicated make a sequence? Are we to say that the poor (or meek) shall inherit the earth, and that their poverty, far from diminishing them, sets them free? Does it blinker their eyes or let them see things as they are?

Born in what is now Afghanistan, Rūmī is buried in Konya, Anatolian Turkey, homeland of the dervishes down to modern times. He wandered far. To symbolize his search for the lost oneness before the fall into life, an almost Wordsworthian idea, he invented the whirling and circling dance that so offended Ataturk, Turkey's modernizing ruler and through-and-through rational, like most modern men. But the dervishes are more than irrational, and the Sufis who tutored them more than know-nothings: they are "the elect of the Muslim community," quoting R. A. Nicholson, *The Mystics of Islam* (1989). Coming together in formal fraternities—think Franciscan or

Carthusian—they constitute a school for saints. These schools are like *fasces,* the unbreakable bundle of twigs carried by the Roman lictors. They constitute the hierarchy on which coherence in the visible world depends, and though they are invisible, you can't break them.

From their knowledge of our concupiscent heart and fallible mind comes their skeptical reading of the human condition. But in the teeth of what they knew, they believed that men, though imperfect, could be saved. Salvation isn't achieved by fiat, however, a mere sprinkling of holy water. It needs a total redoing. Let me invoke etymology to suggest what this means.

Dervish is from Persian, its first syllable the same as the English word *door. Vish* is Persian *vihtan,* begging, and the dervishes were mendicants who begged from door to door. But *dar* also means "in," and *vish* can mean "thought," so the dancer, despite his outlandish activity, is a meditative man who seeks to dance his way out of life's fury into the stasis of art. Conventional Islam has little patience with any of this, spurning the body and its claims. At the center of its intellectual structure is Allah, an impalpable God without affections or emotions. The Sufis wanted more, just as, you might say, St. Francis and his followers wanted more than the cold rigor of St. Thomas, the rational philosopher par excellence. But though Sufis attempt to escape the prison house of phenomena, they make the body a bridge to the real.

Sufism manhandles the Koran, to put it crudely but justly, using it the way Alexandrian allegorists used the Pentateuch, the first five books of the Bible. They took it as a halfway house en route to a more plenary truth. This truth is the oneness of body and soul, an interpenetrating as opposed to a Cartesian duality. Down with dichotomizing; inclusiveness is all. "I am God," cried a Sufi mystic, wanting no doubt to get his hearers' attention and, more crucially, to let them know that the body is the equal of the soul. Another of his brethren asserted that the *ah* in Allah forms the very sound we make with our breath. The orthodox crucified the first for blasphemy, the second, forestalling his coreligionists, died in a jihad fighting the Mongols. I doubt we have seen the last of them. The return from the dead is a theme sounded often in Central Asian folklore, and perhaps these martyred Sufis will come back to enlighten their people.

The old man, still kneeling beside the tombstone, is looking at me intently. On closer inspection, however, I see that his upraised eyes are blind. He is a poor man (*faqir*) and beggar (*dervish*) who has thrown away everything that might divert him from God. Gandhi, said Winston Churchill bitterly, was a "cheap Middle Temple fakir," doubtless this word, as he meant it, comprehending "faker." Some may think that London's Middle Temple, where lawyers learn their trade, has made more mischief than either fakir or dervish. I am considering this question as I approach the old man, bow silently, and drop a handful of coins in his bonnet.

THE ROAD WINDS through cultivated fields as I near Shakhrisabz, and I see why Tamburlaine renamed his birthplace Green City. The beauty of its gardens in spring are said to have entranced him, and I want to locate him in this original habitat. First, however, I must pay tribute to Mammon. Ignoring the highway signs to the ruins, I keep on resolutely to the Khudjum Embroidery Factory, a little south of town on the same road I have been traveling.

The owner, a portly man in a weskit, stands in the doorway as I pull up. He smiles at me affably, greeting an old friend. "English?" he says. "German?" I shake my head. On the third try, he has it. "Vous êtes français, n'est-ce pas?"

"Might we speak English?" I ask him.

"As Monsieur pleases," he says. "Our distinguished clientele includes many of your nation. Earlier this year, President Sarkozy and his charming wife favored us with a visit. You find that surprising?"

My head shaking doesn't deflect him. "In this emporium," he continues, "synthetic dyes are a no-no. Only natural dyes color our carpets. You see those deep blues in the far corner? Indigo." A hand on my elbow, he urges me toward the rear of the building. "We import it from India. The red root of the madder vine gives us that bright red, crushed walnut the darker browns. Over there."

Rainbows of color cascade from the walls, carpets heaped against them almost as high as the ceiling. There are gobs of color on the parquet floor, like new-fallen snow with a few lanes cutting through it. But the indiscriminate profusion leaves me dazed, even slightly repelled. Orders to come are stockpiled in the warehouse like cabs in a queue at the airport. Consumer goods, they are the product of the loom, with an assist from electric-powered machines. How do they relate to the village craftsmen who conspired with their mother earth to create them?

If you think me a primitive, think again. Half the beauty in my life is owing to the machine, and I'm grateful. But I don't demand that it work wonders, like updating my take on things, nor do I blame it that I don't cope that well with its mysteries. Unlike my children, I'm not part of the "on-line" generation. My model, I tell them, is the lilies of the field. Though they neither toil nor spin, they do all right being themselves.

The emporium's product aspires to something more. It wants to be useful, as by offering an index of value. Not the value of the rugs, my value. That sounds paradoxical, so let me explain. Surfaces to walk on are useful, and even those carpets we hang on the wall. In a well-ordered economy, objets d'art have their use. But the Oriental rugs in the emporium are like calculators, computing my worth in dollars and cents. The seller, if I encourage him, will whisper it in my ear. "You are a thousand-dollar man, then. Five thousand, perhaps?" Not wishing to insult me, he rejects as unworthy his less expensive carpets and proffers the top of the line.

The workroom behind his shop opens out at either end, approximating the size of an airplane hangar. It has to be that big to accommodate the workforce, he explains. "Twelve hundred women. They work in shifts, three per day." A glance along the rows confirms that all of them are young. Standing in front of their looms, they caress them like mechanical harps.

"We have a firm rule in our company," says the owner, showing me around. "The girls must be no younger than eighteen. We don't want them frivolous, you see. One thing more," he continues. "All our girls must have acquired a good education."

That seems a lot to ask for a job like this one. I'd think education would breed sullen workers who know more than they need to. But they look like happy campers, and when I smile at them they smile back. Some are pretty, some lumpish. It doesn't matter, and they ply the loom eight hours a day. Backbreaking labor, it isn't work for an educated man. Possibly in Islam women are different.

"Our specialty is fine carpets," says the owner, "but this factory produces a wide range of goods." Like a doyen in an art museum, he indicates a bundle of mats that feature the face of Tamburlaine (it manages to be both baleful and benevolent), wall hangings, elegant gowns, skullcaps embroidered with *iroki* cross-stitch. The owner follows my eyes. "Some, as you see, are decorated with rosettes, others with geometric figures." Wanting to be agreeable,

I buy an embroidered skullcap. "You choose for me," I tell him. But the owner is after bigger game. He wants to sell me an Oriental carpet.

The big room makes my flesh creep, like a hostel for geishas. Thrown in on themselves, the girls bicker, cherish favorites, cast eyes at the owner. Sexuality, overheated, hisses like steam from a radiator valve. The owner ignores his charges, his mind toting up profit and loss. "I could give you a very good price," he says, eyes probing my face.

But I have had enough of carpets. All are good to look at, it goes without saying, but their beauty-in-a-vacuum overwhelms me like the ice cream sundaes of youth. What's the matter with these carpets and those sundaes? Casting about for an explanation, I think of the relation between the end and the means. "What are you worth, sir?" the carpets are asking me, pursuing their function. Such a trivial end!

The owner is tenacious. "What kind would please you?" he wants to know, his eyes darting about the room. In terms of carpet design, I am a conservative, and I want the design to be nonrepresentational. No palm trees, mosques, or camels, no idealized portraits of Lenin. Surprising me, many of the carpets are representational, featuring human or animal figures. "Isn't that sort of thing taboo in Islam?" I ask the owner.

"It used to be," he says. "But Islam is changing. Besides, my best customers, especially in Europe and America, like their art true to life. They're the ones who pay the bill, and who's to argue?"

But what does it mean, true to life? Must it mean naturalistic? I like the kind of art that trains an eye on the least little detail, for example the cigarette butt on the dance floor in Renoir's *Bal à Bougival.* But the life of the design depends on more than observant reporting. If it is going to speak to me, it has to declare a personal reading of things rather than a photographic likeness. Looking beyond the real-life image, perhaps looking through it, I want a reality more persuasive than verisimilitude. In this room overflowing with carpets, craft is meticulous and the labor intensive, but the end seems less than the means.

The owner's handshake is a limp one as we say goodbye. Sighing at my obtuseness, he gives me his card. Perhaps I will come back to the Khudjum Embroidery Factory?

"The world is full of winding streets," I tell him, putting on my best hajji persona.

DOUBLING BACK on my tracks, I reenter the Green City, coming at it from the south. It is oddly reminiscent of the New York World's Fair of my boyhood, pylons and perispheres looming through the grainy air. The conqueror's grandson Ulug Beg left his mark here. For six hundred years, the great blue dome and two smaller domes of his Blue Mosque (Kok Gumbaz) have tilted at heaven. They remember his father, Shah Rukh, Tamburlaine's most accomplished son, and though the blue tiles that once brightened the dome are gone, I use my binoculars to focus on a cluster of radiating stars on the tiling of the rectangular arch. Slim pickings, perhaps, and the closer I get the more the city, hacked about by time, shows its age.

Decay is everywhere, suggestive of Islam's faded glory. Below the Blue Mosque, the immense dynastic tomb known as the Seat of Power and Might (Dorus Siadat) has shriveled to a single mausoleum. Jehanjir, Tamburlaine's eldest son and the apple of his eye, is buried under the conical dome. He died at twenty-three, an inconsolable loss, and every day in this place, said Clavijo, the Castilian ambassador, the meat of twenty sheep was cooked and given to the poor by order of a grieving father. After his son's death, he never smiled again.

Leaving the crumbling tomb, I walk north up Ipak Yuli Kuchasi, Silk Road Street. Like other streets in Uzbekistan, it used to be named after Lenin. I am heading for the Ak-Sarai or White Palace, Tamburlaine's most extravagant creation. As spoils from his conquest of Kunya Urgench in 1379, he carried off its craftsmen to Shakhrisabz and put them to work on this latest testimony to his inability to sit still for long. He meant it to surpass the Bibi Khanum Mosque in Samarkand. Clavijo gives the dimensions, the twin towers, each 125 feet high, flanking the portal arch, 70 feet wide and almost twice as tall. Beyond another gateway, the huge room that did duty as a reception hall goes back to the origins of Persian art, for example the immense vaulted arch of the palace at Ctesiphon. The walls of this chamber, said the ambassador, were "panelled with gold and blue tiles, and the ceiling . . . [was] entirely of gold." Not anymore.

In the banqueting hall, like most of the palace a casualty of time, Tamburlaine's wives dined on horseflesh and mutton. They drank wine with their men, who weren't satisfied till they had "drunk themselves silly." Clavijo noted the fruit trees that leaned over pools of water outside in the garden, hallmark of summer days. In the sixteenth century, a barbaric khan of

Bukhara, indifferent to history and misliking anything greater than himself, destroyed this work of great price. The gigantic portal and the two flanking towers are all that remain. Agreeably melancholy, I sit on the fallen stones like Hubert Robert, painter of moldering antiquities. *Sic transit gloria mundi,* true for Tamburlaine, like Lenin to come.

The master builder began building his royal residence to end them all late in the fourteenth century, leaving the work unfinished when he died. Clavijo, who inspected it in 1404, saw a work in progress, astounding, however, never before anything like it. Over the entrance a lion or leonine creature postured against the background of the sun, both figures repeated on the summit of the arches around the courtyard. How this imagery relates to the lion and sun emblazoned on the mammoth portal of the Shir Dor Madrassa in the Registan is a question worth pondering. It surfaces again in Persian art of the eighteenth century on a wing of the Gulistan Palace in Tehran, its timing agreeing with Islam's turn to realism. Clearly realism was in the ascendant when, in the next century, Vámbéry was honored by the Shah of Iran with the Order of the Lion and Sun.

But the bizarre imagery appears in Asian art long before, and realistic it isn't. China's Emperor Wu glances at it in his poem of 101 B.C., written in praise of the Heavenly Horses of Ferghana. When they rose from the water, he saw their tiger's backs that looked like striped lions. The T'ang poet Li Po (701–62) saw them too, complete with dragon wings. In the very beginning, sun and lion represented the two tribes, Pars and Medes, encamped on the ground that was to be Persia. As symbols they stood for the prevalence of warmth over cold, spring over winter, life over death. The sun was the absolute lord of creation, the lion was power, and together they connected men to the gods. The mythical kings of Ferdosi's *Shahnama* chose the image of a lion holding a sword in its hand for their national flag, and Shah Abbas the Great the sunlike face rising from the lion's back for his flag of Esfahan. Clavijo called this "the emblem of the sovereign of Samarkand." It seems apt for Persia as well, triumphant but ambiguous in the sum of its parts.

The triumphant days of the White Palace are past, but even in the wreckage there is much to feast the eye. Pieces of the sumptuous wall decoration at the base of the big arch are still visible, together with fragments of the tiled floor. Bits of the mosaic faience cling to the rear wall of the reception hall (*iwan*). The faience, glazed earthenware, is colored in vivid hues of turquoise and lapis, milk white, black, green, and aubergine, embellished with gold. Blending by design with the changing lights and shadows of day, the colors seem alive.

After centuries they are still fast and as brilliant as the day the painter applied them. While you are putting a name to the color before you, it changes, however, like the god Proteus, who changed his body as the color does in texture and hue. The warm ochre of the terra-cotta portal deepens, as your eye travels down, to dark blue and violet, studded with geometric tangles of glazed brick. The portal is like the carpets in the Khudjum Embroidery Factory, but the latter, if still faithful to the old abstract imperative, are altogether themselves, not suggesting some other thing. That is what metaphors do. "I chew the cud of grief" is a metaphor, implying more than itself. Rūmī (in poem 192) goes on to say that this is "like a raging camel (bringing) up foam." The classical carpet won't allow of equivalences, no likening to the cud of a camel, etc., and that is its distinction. High praise to the work that is itself alone. Tamburlaine is like it, hence his mysterious nature.

The design in the carpet is circumscribed, though. This isn't a fault but a limitation, a purview. Think about it and you will see that the same is true of the design on the portal. It appears to be a perfect representation of our mother earth, pairing the blue of ocean with the gold of sunrise and the white of an unflecked sky. But though it may yearn after unalloyed truth, its truth is qualified by particulars that by their nature diminish. It remains a figure of speech (like metaphor, like simile), suggesting the truth, not closing with it. The figure of speech wants to get above itself, nailing the truth as it is. But our human insufficiency, unable to bear the weight, puts limits to understanding.

Perhaps, as Hamlet thinks, we are kin to the angels. But in us, as in the artifact, gain and loss mingle their spurs, and he tells us that too. That we cast our net wide doesn't make any difference for value. I used to believe that a great work of art demands a great thought, but I'm afraid that is mere piety. A work of miniature painting, Persian or Indian, may tell of a sensibility more capacious than that of the creator of "half-acre tombs." (The derisive phrase is John Donne's.) Much painstaking went to the Churrigueresque churches of eighteenth-century Spain and the mock-Gothic churches of nineteenth-century England, but the end doesn't justify the means. So how does it happen that the end crowns the work rather than simply ends it?

The answer, it seems to me, lies with intensity. Bridled by form in the service of nature, it is the truest index of value.

Involving nature in the highest art, as I do, doesn't exclude art that moves toward abstraction; otherwise how should we deal with the art of Islam? Its abstract designs appeal to the "ghostly paradigm" of nature, increasingly true of the late art of Monet. I think we admire the daring of his departure from nature and are grateful that he never quits it altogether. Putting it that way seems to imply a negative judgment of art that has no apparent point of reference. But Bauhaus students, though they didn't draw from life, even from plaster casts of Greek and Roman originals, were hardly working in a vacuum. What did they have before them, then? Inevitably this aesthetic I am intimating must suppose an appeal to a "substrate." In Islam the substrate, underlying the myriad forms of life, is synonymous with abstract truth.

The Ak-Sarai is faithful to nature and hopeful of more than a partial version of it. I imagine the crescent moon hanging in the portal's white sky, absolute in its disdain for qualification. The sky is an image for Islam in its great days when, lusting after absolutes, it turned away from lowercase things. It did this triumphantly. But the sun has begun to set, and there's a chill on the air in Shakhrisabz this evening. In the waning light, the domes and towers of the Green City appear to dwindle, as Islam, bit by bit, dwindles from its apogee. What is left is passionate, give it that, unlike the Christian denominations of modern Europe, sick to death, all of them. But modern Islam's is the passion of mindlessness, the "passionate intensity" that characterizes the worst.

THE "SCRAPS AND ORTS" of delicate artifice that survive in the Ak-Sarai are almost shocking after the bleached-bones look of the Zerafshan Mountains I have come over to get here. It is as if the people of the dry land were responding to their deprivation in art. History is a palimpsest, the gravity of the past showing through the near-hysterical present. One overlays the other, as my life overlays that of my forebears. Ages ago Alexander the Great, bent on conquering the world, followed this branch of the Silk Road I am traveling now. Tamburlaine, his successor, took the same road, on his way to India and the sack of Delhi. Czarist General Abramov followed him when he stormed the city in 1870, annexing it to Russia. In recent memory Soviet tanks came this way, bound for Afghanistan and disaster.

Central Asia is a petri dish awash with ideologies, some dying, others resurgent: Buddhism and Christianity, both the Latin and Nestorian kinds, Islam, once riotous with color, now a dim monochrome bidding its faithful turn away from the world. Let it be remembered that Islam used to throb with a passion for sensuous things. My wife's pashmina shawl, among the glories of Northern India, is the work of the Mughals, Muslim emperors. They built on the grand scale but had an instinct for the miniature as well. The Mughals left their signature on Shakhrisabz a century after Tamburlaine created the outsize palace I am doing my best to imagine. Babur, his great grandson and the first of the imperial line, remembered it in his autobiography. Over the portal he recorded the inscription: "If you are not sure of the power of our miraculous deeds, look at our construction." He was thinking of the Registan in Samarkand, the tomb of Ismael Samani in Bukhara, and the White Palace itself. The achievement justifies the unstinted praise, which isn't less credible than Christopher Wren's: "If you want a monument, look around you." Around was the city of London.

Babur's monument, like Wren's, honors an intensely physical presence. His early-sixteenth-century autobiography, the *Babur Nama,* declares it often. He feels the events he describes on his pulses, for example the death of his father, who "flew with the pigeons and became a falcon," soaring, after assassins killed him, away from the earth. The tendency in his prose to pictorialize informs his distaste for slovenly Hindustan (that is, India and Pakistan), conquered by him in the 1520s. He has none of the Islamic yearning for abstract thought. Mundane matters preoccupy him. He complains of the Hindustanis' lack of running water. "It came to my mind that water should be made to flow by means of wheels . . . and also that grounds should be laid out in an orderly and symmetrical way."

In Agra after he took it, he surveyed the land, looking for a patch of it that might support a garden. But the whole was "so ugly and displeasing . . . that the idea of making a Char-Bagh"—a formal garden in a cruciform shape—"passed from my mind." He was himself, though, and persevered, to the end that "in disorderly Hindustan, plots of gardens were laid out with order and symmetry, with suitable borders and parterres in every corner, and in every border there rose a narcissus." In the future was the Taj Mahal.

But the Ak-Sarai has yet another inscription, suggesting that Babur is dead and won't come again. On the east tower of the portal we read that "the Sultan is the Shadow of Allah on Earth." So far, nothing surprising. The west tower's version abbreviates this, however. Its inscription reads: "The Sultan is a Shadow." What can these words intend? Is the once and future king we are waiting on a fiction? The coherence Babur established, the Mughal dynasty, fell to pieces at last, and perhaps only death is permanent. Or perhaps the worker on his scaffolding ran out of space. Tamburlaine, not inclined to conjecture, is said to have punished his delinquency by pushing him from the top of the tower. Local boys in Shakhrisabz still climb its perilous height, looking for eggs in the swallows' nests at its apex.

Weary of the past and its muted melodies, I retreat to a park bench in Victory Park, a few paces south of the Ak-Sarai. Little boys with close-cropped hair stroll past me, arm in arm. They are wearing what I take to be school uniforms, black pants and a white shirt, and their innocent earnest faces turn in my direction. Curiosity satisfied, they turn back to the wedding party coming up the path. I see that it isn't a uniform they're dressed in but their Sunday best, and they are kin to the groom or the bride in her white bodice and billowing white skirt that looks like an old-fashioned hoop skirt. An unbidden guest at the wedding, I watch the procession go by.

Heading it up, photographers snap pictures and professional musicians blow on the long horns, fully six feet long, called *dzharchis*. Their deep throbbing, horrifying to my ear, basses the action in John Huston's movie *The Man Who Would Be King*. In the older time, repeated blasts on these gigantic copper tubes let the enemy know that Tamburlaine had arrived before their gates. Immense on a pedestal, he overlooks the park, a hand resting on his sword, the tugh coming out of his helmet. He seems impossibly substantial, "the greatest man who ever lived in the tide of times," but he is also a figment of the imagination, a hero created by the folk in their hoped-for image and likeness. They wanted assurance of the continuity of things, also coherence in their own lives, more than merely linear. The great man embodied both. His legacy of violence is certainly enduring, but what of the impulse to artistic achievement? Will there be another Registan?

The bride, eyes downcast, seems not to notice him or anyone around her, including the groom who has her by the elbow. She is his goods, his chattel, and he has borne her from home, her father assenting cheerfully, her mother indifferent. Unless barren, she will bear a child inside the year, best if a man-child. She knows she will be beaten and knows her husband's family will welcome a slavey. Many of her sisters in Muslim Asia will die by their own hand. Back home in American University, my feminist colleagues are aware of her plight. All are multiculturalists, however, and one piety trumping another, they keep silent.

I AM ABOUT TO HEAD BACK to my hotel when a small boy sits down beside me. He is decently dressed and, except for the absence of knickers, looks the way people of my generation looked at his age. "May I have a moment of your time, sir?" he says formally, his voice not timid but respectful. "I am Ulugbek Mukhammad and I want to speak English. You can call me Ulug."

Small-boned like a sparrow, he has keen, serious eyes in a handsome face. I am looking at John Keats, born in Uzbekistan and still in his early teens. Ulug speaks better English than some of my countrymen and has two passions, English language, his major subject in school, and computers. He recognizes the make of my computer when I name it, and I am sure he can work its levers better than I can. "I would do anything to study in your country," he tells me, earnest eyes searching my face.

I don't see how, and his face falls.

"Perhaps I could get a scholarship to one of your colleges?"

"All things are possible," I say, sounding like an oldster and avoiding his eyes. "But what you're asking is very unlikely."

We take each other's measure on a dusty street in Shakhrisabz, he whose life is all before him, mine like a ship's wake off to stern. I've taught thousands of students, most an unleavened lump whose angle of repose is at the bottom or near it. But I would walk on hot coals for a student who cared about learning. In this remote corner of Central Asia, I confront what I've been looking for all my life. Now that I no longer teach, I go out on the roads, like the man in the Book of Judges who is looking for a place that can use him.

Ulug is persistent. "I know your government has programs," he says. "You could show me how to apply, sir."

"I suppose I might," I say, the beginnings of involvement making me look for the exit.

"We could exchange e-mail addresses," he says. He scribbles on a slip of paper, whisked out of his satchel. I don't have a pencil, but he hands one over. He's a magician. "You will hear from me, sir!" he says.

"I should warn you," I say. "The chances are slight—"

"I shall hope, sir!" he says.

I am incorrigibly a skeptic, and in my view of the world shapes and colors may change, not the thing itself. Perhaps Ulug might challenge that. Perhaps, grown to manhood in a less insular society, he might challenge the Muslim hatred of any order not its own.

"I am going to surprise you," he says. "You will see!"

My smile as we part company is of the cut-rate variety, meant to put a damper on all the conviction. Tone it down, young man! But I wonder. Looking after him as he passes the statue of Tamburlaine, I imagine a younger version of the hero, not wholly made up yet. His glowing face-of-a-poet says he is of a finer grain than the killer of multitudes. But the question is how he will dispose of his portion. Does he have it in him to leave the world better than he found it? Tamburlaine did that. He could have sunk his restless spirit in sensual torpor but chose to beautify his capital city. The choice he made is open to every man. Which shall it be, young Ulug?

TAMBURLAINE, the man of blood, wasn't wholly that, and the House of Meditation (Dorut Tilyovat) he built in Shakhrisabz included the mausoleum of a Sufi sage who tutored both his father and him. That is an unexpected conjunction. He wanted to be buried in his birthplace, and inevitably the tomb he commissioned is near the tomb of his firstborn son. It seems a matter of some urgency to find it. Off an alley behind Jehanjir's mausoleum, a green door leads to an underground chamber faced with sandstone and limestone. In the courtyard is a large marble block carved in arabesques, perhaps Tamburlaine's throne, or after his time a coronation stone like the Stone of Scone. The chamber is empty, except for a few Koranic inscriptions over the arch and a single stone casket, meant for the emir. But the casket holds the bodies of two unidentified persons, and his body lies in Samarkand, fifty miles to the north. Like a cenotaph, his tomb still waits to be filled.

For centuries no one knew of its existence. But our time has recovered it, and I get the details from an old vendor in the Chorsu, the big market. He remembers the very day in 1943 when a boy, playing football, blundered into the crypt. Or perhaps this happened just before the war, and the boy was a girl who followed an earthen tunnel to a room filled with light. What she saw made all the pieces in her little world of disconnects come together. In the center, upright in his casket, was the once and future king. He was holding the orb and scepter, the crown on his head, and his eyes, focused on hers, burned with compassion. But when she looked again he was gone.

5

Medea's Magic Bath

Shakhrisabz is behind me, but before getting under way again, I want to rethink the ground I've covered. What strikes me most about it is the recurring of the past in the present. But though it keeps confronting me, I don't find it inevitable, like the Marxist reading of history. On the contrary: it depends on human agency. I follow that with another important distinction. More than once in these pages I encounter truth, the way I put it, and I had better say at the outset that I don't intend a once-and-for-all truth. Mine is lowercase or provincial. Everything I care about partakes of this truth. Given its limitation, it is anathema to secular progressives. On the lookout for a comprehensive truth, they suppress particulars in favor of general statement.

Muslims, who worship an abstract deity, evince the same preference for the general over the particular. They denigrate the past (history before Muhammad), calling it lies or half-truths. Looking to salvation, they suppose it can be compassed within historical time. But like Christians before them and secular progressives after them, they can't get rid of the past. All, in my trinity of reigning ideologies, want to repeal it, a tangle of particulars wrapped around us (they think) like Laocoōn's snakes. None of them can do it, though, and the past hangs on.

Muslims and Christians have an expedient, however. Assimilating what they can't get rid of, they take it into the house. In Anatolia, where I've been before and will be again, Christian churches once summoned the faithful to mass. Now mosques and minarets rise on the same ground. In Rome old Perseus is reincarnate in the character of St. George the Dragon Slayer; or a Mithraic temple, buried below ground but still quick, lends its aura to St.

Clement's Basilica. I like the opportunism, friendly to such activity as poetry that grapples with truth. Being a comparativist, I like the assimilating too. I note, however, that the survival of the past in the present puts the future at risk. Another way to put this is to say that "the cask still smells of the wine that steeped it first," remembering rueful St. Jerome, who wanted to reject his classical legacy but couldn't.

The killing of Muslims by Christians in modern-day Kosovo recapitulates the killing of Christians by Muslims more than six hundred years ago on the same site. Even the name, Kosovo, the Field of Crows, is the same. Christian Serbs don't forget what happened to them on that field. Modern heads of state who led their people into the Balkan cockpit are ignorant of it: a reason history keeps folding back on itself. (This isn't the same as coming round again involuntarily.)

With ignorance of the past goes its well-known tendency to repeat itself, but not for fate or willed reasons à la Marx; let us say rather it reflects some inner imperative. The land the Silk Road traverses from Jiayuguan south and west along the Tibetan border looks to have been moribund from the beginning of time. As Peter Fleming and Ella Maillart rode into the Cherchen oasis along the Southern Silk Road, "the country-women fled, hiding their faces with a fold of their white veils" (Maillart, *Forbidden Journey: Peking to Kashgar,* 1937). They might never have seen a Caucasian! Who could suppose that civilization in our Western sense ever took root there? But it did and perhaps it will again.

Beautifully carved furniture, preserved by the arid climate, has been unearthed in the desert. Charged with the feeling of the man who made it, dead many years, it says he took pains. The Swedish explorer Sven Hedin, when he came this way a hundred years earlier, traveled by boat. He shared the marshes with grebe, heron, and osprey, also a feral pig, swimming for its lair on an island in the reeds. But sixty years later, the water had gone. Coins and arrowheads lay on the dry land like pirate treasure brought to light. The wheel that keeps turning hasn't come full circle, though, and inexorably the oasis settlements are going back to the desert. Central Asia is a lime kiln, and in a few decades even these remnants of the past will have mutated or returned to their elements.

In Central Asia the land, decaying in every particle, renews itself forever, as if dipped in the magic bath Medea prepared for old Aeson. The father of Jason, hero of the Golden Fleece, Aeson despaired when the Argonauts sailed away and took his own life. But Ovid says that Medea restored him. He furnishes the model for the endless metamorphoses that characterize this part of the world. But in Central Asia the transition from death to life is less like a wheel than a version of musical chairs.

If you cross into the Stans from China, you go back in mind eleven hundred years to a time when the T'ang dynasty was dying. But history abhors a vacuum, and a Mongol tribe called the Tangut saw its chance to claim a place in the sun. Taking power in Gansu, the great corridor running west from Lanzhou to Dunhuang, it built a genuine civilization, distinguished by sculpture and painting. An impressive clay statuette of a double-headed Buddha survives from what is left of its capital, Kharakhoto. But after three centuries, Genghis Khan gave the Tangut its quietus, and it disappeared from history, leaving a few relics in a solitary stupa.

The Great Khan, a butcher without a peer until our own time, conquered Central Asia from the Caspian Sea to the mountains, then struck southeast across them and extended his domain to Peking. His ferocity was appalling, his energy boundless. He attacked Russia and Eastern Europe, his army reaching the gates of Vienna in 1242. By then he was dead, but he had a savage successor in Tamburlaine (1336–1405), who led his armies to Baghdad and Damascus, after that to Delhi (1399). A century later his descendant Babur, like a runner carrying the baton, founded the Mughal empire in India. Sylvia Plath has an apposite line, remembering a Polish town scraped flat by the roller of wars. "But the name of the town is common."

Lord Curzon, one of the great Victorians, moralizes this tale of the present reenacting the past in his *Russia in Central Asia* (1889). "The imagination of the Europeans," traveling eastward and arrested at every step by some relic of the past, "cannot but be impressed by the thought that he is mounting the stream of ages" back to the beginning. "History lies outspread before him like the page of a Chinese manuscript, to decipher which he must begin at the bottom and work his way up to the top." This is moving, not least as we feel that "reading in an inverse direction the long route of humanity," we are coming nearer its source. All of us are sojourners in a difficult country, an older poet tells us, but the "mighty maze" we are laboring through is "not without a plan."

I am willing to go with the first clause, but jib at the second. The incessant rise and fall of men and nations seems less moral than physiological, like the systole-diastole of the human heart. First the expanding, then the contracting. After the Sogdians came the Tangut, then the Mongols, the Timurids, descendants of Tamburlaine, then the Uzbeki Turks. This chain of events resembles a necklace of multicolored beads whose connectives are linear, the unity of that which comes next.

How poignant to find Christianity, so insistent on cause and effect, arguing its claim among all these diverse people. But Nestorian Christians, a heretical sect, had been at home for a long time in Central Asia. Nestorians emphasized Christ's dual nature, divine but also human. A stele locating them in the China of the T'ang as early as the eighth century is syncretic in its imagery, that is, it mingles disparate traditions without assigning priority to any. Normally we live by priorities, giving hegemony to one of many possibles, but in Central Asia, as in our Middle Ages, everything seems foreground. The Maltese cross that crowns the stele rises from a Taoist cloud with a Buddhist lotus flower underneath it. This congeries of belief is like an emulsion from which nothing precipitates out. Endlessly accommodating, it has no meaning but itself. If we think of today's multiculturalism, we will note the critical difference. In my image of the mingling of different traditions, all of them have varying degrees of value. But in the multicultural world, one thing has no more value than others, meaning that nothing has value.

Whatever meaning the heap of images declares to us is written in a minor key, Wordsworth's "still, sad music of humanity." To the point is a snippet of poetry from the Han dynasty (206 B.C.–219 A.D.), the song of an imperial princess sold by her father for a thousand Ferghana horses. She went to an old man "on the other side of heaven" and unburdened her grief in verse. "My family sent me off to be married. . . . They sent me a long way to a strange lord. . . . I live with constant thoughts of my home, my heart is full of sorrow." That was woman's lot, no doubt, but in last things a man's lot was the same, both subject to mutability, the only constant in a turning world.

MY TRIP SOUTH by car from Kazakhstan has led me through its fellow Stans, Kyrgyzstan and Uzbekistan, each showing us how the past infiltrates and even determines the present. No river or desert or mountain chain separates one place on the map from another. Boundaries are prescribed by politicians and the wars they set in motion. Kyrgyzstan lies north and east of Tajikistan, but the lay of the land won't tell you when you cross from one to the other. Uzbekistan, west of Tajikistan, is a cut-and-paste job and appears to be devouring its neighbor. Afghanistan pokes an intrusive finger into its southern flank. Tiny Tajikistan abides what it can't change. In all these countries, the abiding constant is power.

Kipling made it central to *The Man Who Would Be King*. He set his story in Kafiristan, not a genuine Stan but like a sept to a clan. In this corner of eastern Afghanistan, two strong men can still "Sar-a-whack," and Daniel Carnehan, the hero, wants to be one of them. Modeling himself on Sir James Brooke, the famous White Raj who made himself master of Sarawak in Borneo, he determines to take over the country. But Carnehan, though his will is all for whacking, lacks the power, and the "utter brutes" he meant to subdue gauge his weakness and destroy him.

Kipling doesn't point a moral to adorn the tale, but I wonder if his fictitious past isn't prologue. In the locale in Afghanistan where his story unfolds, Muslim terrorists and American and allied soldiers face off in a war that seems not to end. The enemy shows no signs of backing away. But Americans have a plan to pacify this unsubduable land. Optimism is strong in the national character, and I have my share of it. "Tomorrow" I am determined to throw away the oxygen I carry and climb to the top of the Torugart Pass. From its crest I shall look across to China, like Moses glimpsing the Pisgah sight. Central Asia is a powerful narcotic.

I think about Afghanistan, germane to my narrative though I must be satisfied to know it only in imagination. The British, when they ruled the country in the nineteenth century, might have been puffing on a hookah, the "hubble-bubble" water pipe that takes the reason prisoner. They thought themselves invincible and thought the backward land they had occupied would slip easily into their orbit. We must "take it in hand and make it a British dependency," said Lord Palmerston, the foreign secretary. Acting on this imperative, a British army invaded in the spring of 1839. By summer Kabul was theirs. "Our glorious success," said Palmerston, "will cow all Asia."

In the capital its occupiers settled into the good life. The families of officers came up from India to the glamorous new hill station. They organized race meetings, including a steeplechase, skating, and fancy-dress balls. Trains of camels brought them tinned foods, vintage wines, cigars for the men. They played cricket, attended concerts, drank, and womanized, taking the Afghan women. Later Kipling admonished them:

If drunk with sight of power, we loose
Wild tongues that have not Thee in awe,
Such boastings as the Gentiles use,
Or lesser breeds without the Law—
Lord God of Hosts, be with us yet.
Lest we forget—lest we forget!

It turned out that the army wasn't invincible. The conquest of Afghanistan had come with a price, and the men, worn down by fighting, wanted a time "for frighted peace to pant." In January 1842 the army left Kabul bound for India, via the Khyber Pass. Sixteen thousand civilians, mostly woman and children, accompanied the four thousand soldiers on their march. The mountain roads were clogged with heavy snow, and behind them the land was in flames. They had put off leaving too long.

Back in Kabul chaos reigned. Already Alexander Burnes, famous as "Bukhara Burnes," who had got into that notorious city alone disguised as a Muslim, was dead at the hands of a mob. Still young when he died, of great native wit, charming to both sexes, accomplished in languages, courageous, sometimes foolhardy, he was "first among equals" in the roll of those Britishers who built an empire in Asia. Attached, on joining the service, to the First Bombay Light Infantry, he was transferred from his regiment to do a solitary's job in intelligence. When he went to Kabul for the first time, in 1832, it agreed with his hedonist self. Singing birds, including doves, delighted his waking hours. He marveled at the fruit trees, apricots, plums, quince, cherries, and pomegranates. Kabul, he said, was paradise on earth. But beneath its idyllic surface was a powder keg.

The natives, though beaten into submission, were neither crushed nor intimidated. Each of them was a soldier, if need be. They were practiced in shooting, swordplay, and stabbing with their long knives. They lived on the land, loved fighting, and believed that death in jihad guaranteed them an afterlife in Jannah, the Muslim paradise. They hated their English masters. Above all the rest, they singled out Burnes.

He was quartered then in the old city, isolated from his fellows, who were billeted in military cantonments a half hour's march away. Best to join them promptly, said his trusty aide-de-camp, an Afghan. Brave but rash, he ignored this counsel and, on the night of November 1, 1841, emerged from his compound to face a raging mob. The Afghans who attacked him thought he had stolen their sovereignty, also their women, and among them were men he had cuckolded. He knew the game was up and tied a black cloth over his eyes so he wouldn't see where the blows were coming from. In short time the long knives of the Afghans hacked him to death.

Responding to the violence, the British in Kabul tried appeasement, surrendering most of their artillery in exchange for free passage out. Sir William Macnaghten, representing the imperial Raj, led the appeasers. He went in person to treat with the rebel leader, who bowed and salaamed like a respectful native. That he "spoke sooth," Macnaghten was sure, unaware that he had already been measured for death. A day later he hung from a pole in the bazaar, minus head, arms, and legs.

The British, on their march to India, were ignorant of what was happening in their rear. They focused solely on home and getting there. They sent out no flankers. In the mountains, however, the Afghans were waiting. From the heights, taking aim with their long rifles, *jezails,* they fired down at the redcoats, a bull's-eye. Many survivors, men of the Forty-Fourth Regiment of Foot, fought their way to the village of Gandamark, thirty miles from Jalalabad and safety. When their ammunition was gone, they fought on with bayonet and sword. More than a hundred years later, their bones still poke up through the soil. Of more than twenty thousand British, only a medical doctor survived, wounded but outracing his pursuers. None of the women and children made it back.

In the new year, the British retaliated with overwhelming force and fury, fighting their way north over the skeletons of their slaughtered comrades. "They lay in heaps of fifties and hundreds, our gun-wheels passing over and crushing the skulls," said one of the participants. The Scottish Highlanders were in the van as the army marched through Jalalabad, the pipes playing "Oh, but ye've bin lang a' coming." That was predicable of Scotties, but for once they struck the wrong note. In one village in their path, British soldiers killed every male over the age of puberty, raping the women and killing some of them too. When they reached Kabul in September, they gave it over to plunder. At last on October 11, having slaked their lust for revenge, they ran down the Union Jack and marched for home.

Forty years later they hungered for a rematch. Reducing the emir in Kabul to their puppet, they installed Sir Louis Cavagnari, whose father had been a general of Napoleon's, as British resident. But the Afghans, true to their nature, threw off his yoke and killed him. The mayor of Kabul paraded his severed head through the city. As before reprisals followed. Some hundred Afghans were hanged on the site of Cavagnari's murder. Bloodied but unbowed, the Afghans mustered an army of sixty thousand *ghazis*, Muslim fanatics, and stormed the much smaller British force in Kabul. But the British had the big guns. Three thousand Afghans died to five British.

Back in England politics went on as usual. The Whigs had made a "bloody balls-up" of it, as the British like to say, and even before the debacle in the mountains, a Tory government under Sir Robert Peel replaced them. Economizing radically, it wanted to scuttle the war in Afghanistan. Today's present harks back to the past, with "Peelites" in the American Congress willing an end to our Afghan war. But the Tories bungled things in turn, and Gladstone's Liberals, old Whigs in sheep's clothing, came in. Pledged to abandon the aggressive foreign policy of the Tory leader Benjamin Disraeli, they closed the book on a half century of warfare without any issue even a politician could point to. The story of the Afghan wars reads like a version of Medea's magic bath, except that its central figure, the man who was to be made whole again, is no different after than before.

But the story isn't finished. In the next century, the Russians, learning nothing from history, had their own Afghan experience. Over a period of ten years, they sent in 620,000 soldiers, sustaining casualties in the range of nearly eighty percent. Then, having taken a licking, they stood aside to watch others go at it. In life as in art, the past is often prologue but hardly ever in a straight line. Art is, however, more intelligent than messy life, and the narrator, if competent, lets us see, from the shape of his material, how today follows from yesterday. His business is to delineate the cause of the effect.

Let his protagonist be an American of the early twenty-first century, not a fictitious character but flesh and blood. He is, as we say, lifelike. But the artist who brings him forward makes him self-conscious, endowing him with the intelligence that life rarely supplies. Equipped with it, he asks why he is there in the first place. If from self-interest, to destroy his enemies and deny them a base across the porous border, he may find it appropriate to gird up his loins. Marxists argue that history is ineluctable, the outcome of a conflict between capital-letter abstractions, that is, the moneyed class and the proletariat, but I see history as the lengthened shadow of a man. The nature of his intervention, crude or subtle, brave or pusillanimous, will be decisive for the future, and it has yet to unfold.

IN THE HISTORY of Britain's Afghan wars, Henry Rawlinson (1811–95), a disinterested protagonist, typifies the artist. Sir Henry, as he became, served in the punitive expedition that followed the massacre of 1842. But his soldiering is secondary to his skill in threading the maze of Anglo-Russian politics in the days of the Great Game. J. A. MacGahan, the *New York Herald*'s war correspondent, said he was the man to consult if you wanted to understand the machinations of Russia in Central Asia. Distrustful of Russian imperialism, he favored a forward policy in Afghanistan, promoting it as a Conservative MP and a member of the India Council. He did without university training, perhaps finding it gratuitous, electing instead to join the East India Company as a cadet officer. He went on to reorganize the Iranian army of the Qajar dynasty (1795–1925) and to act as military adviser to the Shah's brother at his palace in Kermanshah. Already the British in Iran had their hands on all the ropes.

But Rawlinson is memorable primarily as the possessor of "useless knowledge." He had a taste for esoteric learning and a mind-boggling talent for pursuing it. Like more than a few Britishers in his time, he lit up every quarter of the spectrum. The energy that drove these extraordinary men seems to have dissipated in their descendants, another comment on entropy in men as in nation-states and religions. Rawlinson's distinguishing achievement was the deciphering of Darius the Great's *res gestae* (account of "things done"), carved on a high rock near the palace in Kermanshah. The site, Behistun, was known to the Achaemenids as "the place of the gods." Darius chose it deliberately to proclaim his achievements: the Silk Road, so-called later, led past it, connecting Babylon and Baghdad with the Iranian upland.

A cuneiform text records the king's triumphs. "I am Darius," he said of himself, "the great king, king of kings, king of the peoples of every origin, an Achaemenid." The proclamation, repeated in three languages, Elamite, Old Babylonian, and Old Persian, tells how Ahura Mazda, the supreme deity of the Achaemenids, chose the king to dethrone a usurper, put down rebellion, and defeat his enemies abroad. A large relief shows him, his bow carrier and lance carrier, and ten representatives of conquered peoples, above them all the winged deity. When the carving was finished, the ledge below the inscription was knocked away so that no one could ever stand there again and read what Darius had written. I think he meant the words to be between him and the gods.

Ancient authors wondered at the illegible writing high above their heads. Ctesias (c. 400 B.C.) imagined a monument dedicated by Queen Semiramis to the supreme being. This Greek physician, roughly contemporary with Plato, is memorable to my younger days for his version of what I took to be the artistic process, a fabulous beast that ate its own paws without knowing it. Alexander the Great stood below the inscription, guessing at a different meaning. In the time of Shah Abbas I (late sixteenth century), a French traveler saw as in a vision the twelve apostles under the cross of Jesus. It was left to Rawlinson to determine what was actually there.

Earlier he had come on a word whose letters appeared again in the Behistun inscription, and he had discovered that the meaning of a phrase of Darius's was the same in Sanskrit. This confirmed a relationship between Sanskrit and Old Persian. Building on these connections, and the notes of a fellow scholar on the cuneiform alphabet, he established the meaning of all forty-two signs in Old Persian. In a letter to his sister in 1835, he described the way he reached the inscription. Ladders were indispensable, but even with their help the risk was great, "for the foot-ledge is so narrow, about 18 inches, or at most 2 feet in breadth, that with a ladder long enough . . . sufficient slope cannot be given to enable a person to ascend, and if the ladder be shortened to increase the slope, the upper inscriptions can only be copied by standing on the topmost step of the ladder." Upright on the top step with no one to support him, he pressed his left arm against the rock, while the right arm busily scribbled in his notebook. "In this position I copied all the upper inscriptions and the interest of the occupation entirely did away with any sense of danger."

His ambition was high, not less, he said, than "to do for the cuneiform alphabet what Champillion has done for the hieroglyphics." He wasn't out to fix the truth in aspic: our temporal world, running away every hour, makes that impossible. He wanted to resolve the riddle of the Achaemenid tongue, up to his time a babel of mysterious sounds. Leaving changeless truth to others, he sought a particular manifestation. Such conclusions as this narrative engenders are like that.

THE FABLE OF MEDEA is in the nature of a parable, true of the legendary tale of the Heavenly Horses. They lived in the uplands of the Ferghana Valley on the Tajiki side of the Torugart Pass. I can't climb up and over the pass, but I can ponder the stories nourished in its thin air. I needn't exert myself to do this, and the reader will be aware that my narrative mixes traveling and reflecting. Having left Shakhrisabz, I am traveling to Bukhara. But my head is in the clouds, and I am busy reflecting. The Heavenly Horses, a story of great antiquity, depends on both: travel first, then the "reflection in tranquility."

In 101 B.C. the horses came to China as spoils of a military campaign. China's Emperor Wu, having heard they could fly, made up his mind to possess them. Like many in this narrative, he yearned to get beyond the body's limitations. The old artificer Dedalus, who made wings for himself and his son, is their prototype. Moralists find his story grist for their mill. But though Icarus the son falls to his death, his fate is more than a caution against overreaching. It is the yearning that redeems the story and gives it its poignancy.

The emperor, believing that his trophy horses would draw him up to the Holy Mountain of Kunlun, wrote a poem in their honor. On their backs, he said, "I shall reach the Gates of Heaven/I shall see the Palace of God." The liberal-secular psychology scoffs at the emperor's land of heart's desire, but the Kunlun Mountains that march with the Southern Silk Road provoke speculation. Who can say what beings beyond our ken dwell in their higher reaches? On the plain far below, dreary prose, the coarse grass called *kumash* holds down the thin soil, its desolation broken only by the occasional tamarisk tree. This unenlivened surface doesn't lend itself to speculation.

Secrets are at the core of Central Asia's wilderness: in the high mountains and under the desert floor. In the museum at Urumqi, the capital of Sinjiang Province, the visitor stands before a pane of glass, separating him from mummified bodies four thousand years old. Sir Aurel Stein recovered them at Loulan, on the edge of the salt water lake of Lop Nor. Except for the parched skin, they might have been sleeping. He noted their "peaked felt caps decorated with big feathers and other trophies of the chase, the arrow shafts by their side . . . the neatly woven small baskets holding food for the dead." The land they hunted over wasn't desert, not then. When Han Chinese first ventured in this remote area, Loulan was still a major caravan stop on the middle Silk Road. It had food and was plentifully endowed with water. Then the lake disappeared, leaving salt flats.

The water stood for continuity. Sustaining life, it guaranteed a viable future. Loulan's mummies suggest what was lost. Astonishingly they are Caucasian, tall of stature, their hair fairish or red, their noses high-bridged. They wore leather and felt, furs and wool, often in a plaid pattern. Cherchen Man (buried south of Loulan about 1000 B.C.) died in his fifties, looks European, and wears a deep red robe and white deerskin leggings. Inside them his felt socks are striped horizontally in blue, red, and yellow. Documents found nearby and dating from the third century A.D. are in Tocharian, a lost language with affinities to Latin. What faraway place did these people come from, to lay their bodies in the anonymity of the sands?

The frozen earth at Cherchen yields a more painful secret, the body of a male infant, three months old. Lifted from its shallow grave, it is dressed in a brown wool romper, wrapped around the body and meant to keep it warm on its journey. On its head is a bright blue felt bonnet; blue glass stones close its eyes. With the baby is his drinking cup, made of cow horn, and his nursing bottle, a sheep's udder.

Urumqi is in the country of the Uighurs, non-Chinese and Muslim, a people I am grateful for knowing. Progress seeks to destroy them, and the other minorities, Buddhist Tibetans and Muslim Hui, that share the country with them. They are the past, inimical on a progressive view to the future. China's war on all three is ongoing. Living on the periphery of this huge and still expanding nation, they arouse its cupidity. The Hui wear white pillbox hats. Uighur hats are festooned with rickrack, while Tibetans are recognized by the saffron robes of their monks. The identities of these people run deeper than costume, however, and none of them welcomes China's attempt to drown it in a flood of Han Chinese. China's Leviathan has enough gross tonnage to flatten protest without a word said. But physical might doesn't always trump do-or-die, and sometimes David is a match for Goliath. Perhaps that is merely wishing and willing. Stay tuned.

Uighurs live in one sixth of China's land mass, a huge sickle shape sweeping west, south, and back east from Inner Mongolia to the Burmese border. They have spoken their Turkic language for eleven centuries, not the same as the speech of the Han. By edict of the government, Mandarin Chinese is supplanting the old Uighur tongue. "Out of step with the twenty-first century," Kashgar's Chinese mayor calls it. Real men don't talk that way, except in bad novels. Uighurs have their own culture, sometimes startling. The men, splendid to look at, are volatile in temper and as quick to embrace you as to take offense. I can't imagine a more attractive people. They wear thick, curling mustaches and scimitar-like knives in their belts at the small of the back. Lord Byron might have invented them.

Living in the borderlands between China and the Stans, they move across the borders at will. Modern states such as China, following the practice of all big organizations, public and private, make a fetish of order and would prefer that they stay in one place. The Uighurs fail to see why they should. Because they won't accept Beijing's dictate, China calls them terrorists. Americans, angling for China's support in other areas of the world, such as Iraq, have been willing to go along. Uighur men, fallen into American hands in Afghanistan and Pakistan early in the decade, have spent years in Guantánamo prison. China wants them back.

It undertakes not to mistreat them. Following the ethnic rioting of July 2009 in Sinjiang Province, China executed an indeterminate number of Uighurs, sentencing others to life in prison. Still others, including children, have fled to Cambodia, seeking political asylum, but have been forced to return. Coincidentally China has agreed to business deals with the Cambodian government worth a billion dollars. You need a long spoon if you sup with the devil, and Cambodians might want to notice what is happening in Kashgar. Site of Western Asia's great Sunday bazaar, it has long been the Uighurs' special preserve, but China is literally knocking it down, another instance of the war of the present on the past. The city's berm, an earthen wall twenty-five feet thick and thirty-five feet high, has nearly disappeared, and the ancient two-story houses that lean over alleyways and open on secret courtyards are being replaced by Soviet-style apartment buildings, concrete tumors on the city's outskirts.

The wooden houses, added on to over the years to accommodate bigger families or burgeoning wealth, are like old clapboard houses in America, accordions that stretch wider as the music demands more range. I suspect that in the winter of 2000, the date of my last visit, I saw them for the last time. The alleyways they front on are like Italian *rioni,* complete neighborhoods in themselves. Tinkers, bakers, shoe repairmen, wood-carvers, makers of cutlery live above their shops, a self-sufficient web where the work place and the home place are the same. Generations of the same family have lived in these houses. I have broken bread with one of them, sitting cross-legged on the Oriental carpet that served as their dinner table. The house I visited, like its neighbors, keeps intact the relationships that hold up society, the way piles, driven deep in the water, hold up the bridge that fords it. Progress wants to demolish the houses and make a fresh start. It will supersede the past, all right, but the future will die of inanition. The instant slums Kashgar's families are being moved to are sure to meet the wrecker's ball before their children are old.

This is a dismal view of the future, and I try not to pull a long face. Sometimes doing that can't be helped. Stein, in the Taklamakan Desert, felt overwhelmed by sadness when he found himself in the midst of death where life had been. But as he traveled on to Tashtaurgan, the Stone Tower, his spirits rose. Ptolemy, the Alexandrian astronomer and mathematician, had been there before him, and he was aware of that. Continuity was the thing that sustained him. Sharp-eyed traders from the West had stood on the very spot where he stood and where Parthians, Romans, and Indians had met the Chinese bringing silk. The embodied past, still present, buoyed him up, a life preserver thrown on the waters.

To the east rose the giant mass of Muztagh-Ata, and he determined to climb it. He was a man prone to gratuities, relevant to me as I consider how to cope. At a height of twenty thousand feet, he looked down on "a seemingly endless succession of valleys and ranges . . . the 'Roof of the World.'" Up there he spoke the language of the gods, not indifferent but aloof from vexation. A little before he ascended the mountain, he got news of the Boxer Rebellion in Peking (1900). Terror stalked the foreign concessions but hardly ruffled his composure. From the Roof of the World, he could see the branching of the old caravan roads that connected China to Central Asia and on to the West. One road ran back to Kabul, another east to Kashgar, another to Khotan, the oasis town on the southern rim of the Taklamakan. From such a perspective, war and the rumors of war could mean little.

Detachment such as his on the mountain is rare. The two Chinese in Yeats's poem "Lapis Lazuli" possess it.

> On all the tragic scene they stare.
> One calls for mournful melodies;
> Accomplished fingers begin to play.
> Their eyes mid many wrinkles, their eyes,
> Their ancient, glittering eyes, are gay.

Like Stein they have learned to acquiesce in the vagaries of things, and who's in or who's out no longer matters. This doesn't say they are free of the circular course of the Wheel. All of us must ride it as we are human, the imposition of the Fall.

MILLENARIANS, both Christian and Muslim, deny that. Weary of life's repetitive round, they look forward to the last thousand years of time, the millennium, when the meaningless course of life will end. My vocabulary is archaic, and readers may feel that the people I am dealing with and the ideas they embrace are no longer relevant. Not so. I have acquaintances who are millenarian, though they wouldn't use the word, root-and-branch leftists who look forward to the kingdom of heaven on earth. Emotionally Icarus, spurning earth for the heavens, is of this mind-set. Fundamentalist Christians share it, except that the better time they anticipate waits on death. All of them want to escape the vagaries of life in the present in favor of life over yonder. Like Aeson they have only a mortal's narrow scope and must count on extrahuman agency to enlarge it. (Details and citations follow two earlier books of mine, *The Dark Ages and the Age of Gold*, 1973, and *The Language of Adam*, 1977).

First of all Christ must return to his kingdom. A great battle, Armageddon, will precede this event (Rev. 16:16), ratifying the triumph of virtue. Its earthly manifestation will last a thousand years, a millennium precisely, after which temporal life will be replaced by life in heaven. Rejecting the ebb and flow of time, the Nicene and Ante-Nicene fathers of the church are millenarian. Tertullian in the second century speaks for them, St. Cyprian in the third. St. Augustine (d. 430), the greatest of the early fathers and the subtlest thinker among them, stands apart.

I have been reading him all my life, first as a young man in Paris, turning pages in *The City of God* while I smoked Gauloises and sipped Marc de Bourgogne. I have his intellectual profile in my phylactery. He wasn't a millenarian, and the church, mostly faithful to the identity he prescribed for it, follows his lead. Like his predecessors Augustine affirmed that the more the soul approaches God's immutable essence, the less likely it is to lust after the lowercase world. But he parted company with the millenarians in his skeptical view of our nature and portion, and skepticism like his is at the heart of this discourse. Millenarians expect the earthly paradise in the present or immediate future, in any case in historical time. Muhammad is of their company. Augustine perceived, however, that our concupiscent nature won't let us enter paradise, not a punishment exactly, an inborn limitation. We can never achieve perfection on earth, and a stunning line from *The City of God* all but says this. Echoing down the centuries, it sums up his psychology and sets him apart from more hopeful psychologists, for example, Descartes. "If I err, I am."

The millenarian fervor, dying down when the church's temporal power increased, boiled up again as the Middle Ages neared its conclusion. On the periphery are wistful ideas like that of the once and future king and the enduring legend of Prester John, whose fabulous kingdom bordered on the earthly paradise. Islam has similar traditions, among them the Lord of Time, sponsored by the murderous cult of the Assassins. These Persian fanatics were "antinomian" in their psychology, released from the obligation to follow the law. The Lord of Time, abducted as a child like the Mahdi of the orthodox, will reappear to save them at the end of days.

Hassan-i Sabbh, the twelfth-century Shi'ite who created the Assassins, pledged to free them from worldly tribulation. The key that turned in the wards was emotional fervor, kin to magic. It needed in addition a messianic figure, identified by Jews and Christians with a scion of the House of David, by Zoroastrians with a savior who would emerge from the seed of the prophet. All of these criers-up of good hope appeal against the temporal world, forfeit to death. I invoke them in this context to suggest how millenarianism puts its stamp on the faith of Islam.

On Islam, not Christianity. Christians after St. Augustine locate the better time to come beyond history. Muslims move this time forward to the present. They do so affectively, in language that glorifies our everyday life. Paradise is in prospect when the Mahdi or Hidden Imam returns from concealment, his so-called Occultation, and peace and justice signalize the universal rule of Islam. This event, occurring in historical time, is the result of jihad or struggle. The violence that goes with the struggle seems intrinsic to the faith. A new caliph or supreme ruler can only ascend the throne by killing his rivals. That isn't written, only what history tells us. The guttering of old candles (before the days of the self-consuming wick) offers a reading of the *khalifa*. "There lives within the very flame of love," says the King in *Hamlet*, "a kind of wick or snuff" that quenches the light.

The struggle for ascendancy needed foot soldiers, and none have fought more fiercely than the Islamic mujahideen. Some say the jihad they wage is directed against the carnal side of our being, but most Western scholars take it to denote a holy war on behalf of Islam. The Koran seems to support them: "Those believers who sit at home free from trouble, and those who do valiantly in the cause of God . . . shall not be treated alike. . . . God hath assigned to the strenuous a rich recompense, above those who sit still at home" (Sura 4:95). This better recompense is paradise to come. Bernard Lewis, whom I follow, asserts that the overwhelming majority of interpreters equate jihad with doing valiantly in the cause, that is, going to war.

Jihadists are rewarded with eternity in the Muslim paradise, where rubies and pearls beautify the valleys and gardens are laid out in exquisite geometric patterns (*chahar bagh*). Fountains scent the air with camphor or ginger; rivers are fed with milk, honey, and wine. Succulent fruits, but no thorns, hang from the branches of the trees. The mountains are made of musk, the palaces of gold and silver. Men and women in paradise recline on couches inlaid with precious metals. They need not earn their bread in the sweat of their brow. Perfume is sprayed over them, they wear gorgeous costumes, like ours only more splendid. Drinks, including wine, forbidden on earth are poured by good-looking youths from priceless goblets; meals are served on platters fit for a king.

Sexual pleasure is part of the scene, famously the seventy virgins reserved for the brave. Commentators stipulate the number seventy, the Koran promising only "perfected spouses and counterparts." But it holds out a vision of endlessly obliging women. "And by flowing waters, / And with abundant fruits, / Unfailing, unforbidden, / And on lofty couches, / Of a rare creation have We created the Houris, / And We have made them ever virgins" (Sura 56:30–36). The commentators, like Christian glossarians filling the margins of their texts with footnotes that raise eyebrows, go on to say that those who have had multiple partners on earth are permitted to choose among the most agreeable in paradise. An additional plus, Allah will reinvigorate the elderly, both men and women, making them virgins once more. In its insistent sensuality, this scenario verges on comic.

AS I DRIVE SOUTH from Kazakhstan, always bending west, the land is a kaleidoscope, its shape and colors ever varying. The cities I pass, especially gorgeous Samarkand, give me the sense that a wonder-working deity has created a miracle on earth. Allah, who has a plenitude of power, could do that if he cared to. Having built the Tower of Babel, says the poet Hāfez, he shot Abraham into a great fire, changing it by miracle to a field of flowers. The Christian God, though a miracle worker, favors less spectacular turns. Step by step the Christian doctrine of the afterlife, compared to the Islamic version, passes through a fine sieve. Before the Coming of the Kingdom, the church must undergo a final trial in the form of a religious deception. This is the pseudo-messiah, or Antichrist, who glorifies man in place of God and his son. We are in the time of the Antichrist: secular progressivism precisely.

Its sign and flag are deception, except that where the Antichrist fools others, secular progressives fool themselves. Basically they claim that our ultimate salvation can be realized in historical time. This is what millenarianism means, and the church condemns it out of hand (Catechism of the Catholic Church, Vatican Archive, p1s2c2a7; the mysterious numbers come from the Internet). The church's victory over evil, pronounced in the Last Judgment, will occur not before but after the death of the ephemeral world.

Christianity is intellectually rigorous where Islam is kindlier to our concupiscent selves. Only give allegiance to the faith and expect to be stroked beyond satiety. If the fasting, many-times-repeated praying, and sundry inhibitions aren't thought excessively onerous, Islam is a popular choice for the millions. That explains the relative facility with which it gathered up North Africa, much of Asia, and the huge populations to the south, like Indonesia. It is an easy faith to adhere to, not asking its followers to swallow head-knuckling doctrines such as the Trinity and the Immaculate Conception. On one side, however, it remains as hard as the desert it came from.

For example Saladin, who ruled in Egypt when the last caliph lay dying. A great man and many-sided, he is utterly without ruth in his determination to wage unending war against the infidel. The Latin states were marked for annihilation. "Or I die," as he put it. Having recaptured Jerusalem after his victory at the Horns of Hattin (1187), he promised to "cross this sea to their islands," Venice and beyond, and "pursue them until there remains no one on the face of the earth who does not acknowledge Allah." The one alternative to death was conversion. From its beginnings in seventh-century Arabia, Islam has endorsed this division into chaff or wheat. The world is bipartite, on the one hand *ahl al-kitab*, the People of the Book, whose book-learning is frivolous, on the other *ahl al-bait*, the People of the House of the Prophet. Terrorists accept the dichotomy, making it easy to kill.

Islam, though aggressive in its posturing, seems a curiously negative faith, appearing to define itself by what it is against. It forbids more memorably than it affirms: wine or other alcoholic drinks, the representing of nature, the separation of church and state. The face it shows the world, at least in our time, is a gloomy one. When I pull over to stretch my legs, a bird perches on my side mirror. It is a *bulbul,* a nightingale, and it looks at me steadily without making a peep. I decide it must be a tame *bulbul,* trained to silence by the mullah who owned it.

The mullahs brook no appeal against the dictates of the church, embodied in sharia, the law of the faith. If Muslims are given the vote, as they are in Southeast Asia, the majority is likely to disenfranchise the minority, at least to tyrannize over it, as when, in Indonesia, Christians and Buddhists are persecuted by the state. A death cult seems to live at the heart of the religion, manifest in the immolation of its suicide bombers. They have no program and present no concrete political demands. What drives them is their hectic constancy to the archaic age that produced them, rife with Old Testament hatreds. This is another instance of the cask smelling of the wine that steeped it first. St. Jerome, who used the metaphor first, was only deploring the unshakeable claim of his classical legacy. Modern Islam has no regrets.

6

Thieves of Mercy

When I first traveled to Central Asia, I took the westerly route, over the Pacific to Beijing. An ongoing flight brings you to Lanzhou in the center of China—a huge city, but I remember coming in when darkness had fallen and nary a light was visible below the wings of the plane. You can continue on by propeller plane to Jiayuguan, an old fortress town on the Silk Road where the Great Wall ends and the desert begins. It sounded to me like the end of the world. But the Chang Chen Hotel has A/C, in-house movies, even a beauty parlor. Women in curlers sit in the chairs. If you want to get on the road to China's Wild West, they will rent you a car at Reception. A word of warning is in order, though. Civilization is behind you, before you the endless sands.

Peering through the crenels of Jiayuguan's west-facing portal, you stand at the gateway to Sinjiang Province, backed by its immense mountains. "The most important door on the farther side of the fortress might be called Traveler's Gate, though some spoke of it as the Gate of Sighs. Every traveler to the northwest passed through the gate, and it opened on a great and always mysterious waste." So wrote two dauntless ladies, Mildred Cable and Francesca French, in their book *The Gobi Desert* (1942). The road from Jiayuguan, bypassing Dunhuang and the Mugao Caves, picks up the old Silk Road at the oasis of Hami. At that point it turns west, crossing through Turfan, among the lowest places on earth, arriving at Urumqi, my choice for the grittiest. The last time through, in dead winter, I scuffed the snow on a filthy street with my boot and uncovered a human ear.

The end of the line in Sinjiang is Kashgar, home to the biggest bazaar in Central Asia. Bearded men from the Old Testament make their way there on

Sundays from the mountains and desert to barter, buy, and sell. They will sell you a camel, a hawk trained for hunting, a purebred horse, a cornucopia's worth of spices. Not far out of town rise the Pamirs, on the other side of them the Stans of what used to be Soviet Russia. They looked like a problem my battered lung didn't want to confront, and I beat an inglorious retreat, returning to the coast of China by plane and riverboat. This time is different.

Flying east from Europe, I took care to land in Almaty this side of the mountains, and didn't have to worry about getting across them. As I get back on subject, moving southwest from Kazakhstan, Shakhrisabz is already behind me. I am heading for Bukhara via the land of the Sogdians. Dushanbe in Tajikistan was the eastern extremity of Sogdian country, inhabited a thousand years ago by a people long lost to history but still quick in my imagination. The Sogdians controlled the trade between China and the string of oases that nourished the Silk Road all the way to Samarkand. Controlling the desert was the key to survival. It meant deep-dug wells, date palms, leafy arbors, and fruit trees, all laboriously tended, the work of man. Before the desert could bloom, it had to be broken. That was borne home to me when I traveled to Israel, today a cultivated land, before the Jews came an oven where nothing grew. In Central Asia oases, imposed on the desert, made cultivation possible and at the same time facilitated trade. A thousand years ago, oasis towns such as Khotan functioned as major entrepôts on the China-to-Samarkand leg of the Silk Road. Their existence depended on keeping the desert at bay.

My time in the desert plays into my life as a writer, instructing me to keep my hands on the reins. Otherwise the horse, or the id, or whatever name you give to letting it all hang out, will take over. The camel, known to the Arabs as the ship of the desert, is prone to taking over. This refractory creature is controlled by a rope tied to a pin in its nostril. Tugging on the rope brings the camel to heel. Some call that cruel, but it works. Sogdians understood this. Their hand was heavy on the great swatch of the land to either side of the Pamirs. I have made these people my particular study, admiring their artistic side, also because their story makes a cautionary tale.

Hard weather didn't faze them, and they often journeyed west in winter, driving their yaks through the snows of the Kunjerab Pass. Trade was survival and had to go forward, whatever the weather. In defense of their trade, Sogdians were redoubtable warriors. But in the fourth century B.C., Alexander the Great smote them with a calculated ferocity—first a general massacre, followed by enslavement and forced transportation—and their military power never recovered. But human beings are wonderfully resilient, dowered by nature with the strength and coarseness survival requires. Both terms apply, and the energies of Sogdiana shifted without ado to commerce. Henceforward they were the factors, go-betweens who did the buying and selling for others.

They cast their net wide, taking in the Stans on the other side of the mountains. The way they raked and combed the land, uncovering every penny, earned them the title, Venetians of the East. A Han Chinese said of them: "At birth honey is put in their mouths and gum on their hands." The people of Khotan knew all merchants as *suli,* the word for a Sogdian, whether they were Sogdian or not. They traded in spices, an all-purpose term including pharmaceutical drugs, dyes, exotic fruits, and culinary plants such as cumin, cinnamon bark, and ginger, five different types of it. The alfalfa they transported to China fed the "Heavenly Horses," famous in Chinese folklore. Chinese wanted "mare's teat" grapes, and Sogdians found them near Turfan, packed them in ice, and sent them on in lead containers. They supplied the West with Persian silverware, the East with coral from the Mediterranean coast near Naples, amber from the Baltic, purple woolen cloth from Rome. Civilization owes them the chair. Chinese of old sat cross-legged on the floor, but from Sogdians they learned creature comfort.

Samarkand, anciently Marakanda, was the Sogdians' capital. I remember them, however, for a city that used to exist, over the Uzbeki border in modern Tajikistan. Built on a hill above the Zerafshan River, still flowing through the land, Pendjikent was the city. It looked east from its walled ramparts to the snowcapped Pamirs. Inside the wall people lived at close quarters, and their houses rose vertically, leaning toward each other over dark, narrow streets. The "lands" or tenements of Edinburgh, the old town, are like them. Outside the wall, on less confining ground, were the markets and caravanserai, hostels for travelers.

Pendjikent was a welcoming city, also a transit point on the road going east to China and west to Samarkand and beyond. A potpourri of races traveled along it from every part of the Far East. Many years later a trio of valiant women, Mildred Cable and her two friends, Francesca and Evangeline French, took this road on their way to Jiayuguan, writing about it affectionately in *A Desert Journal* (1934). They discriminated among the people traveling with them, an act of generosity not often conceded by the cursory eye, which doesn't see particular men and women but man in the mass. Their different kind of eye surveyed the "stream of living men and women who moved up and down the great road," not amorphous but "acquainted with life and full of knowledge about distant places."

I impute this generous sensibility, perhaps fancifully, to the inhabitants of Pendjikent. Its wall surrounded something like an atelier of the arts, a reason for keeping these people before us. Houses of the well-to-do stood cheek by jowl with the meaner dwellings of the hoi polloi. The former featured large reception rooms hung with paintings from floor to ceiling and adorned with elegant carving. The paintings, some forty-five feet long, showed soldiers in combat, knights at a banquet, religious observances, scenes from myth, handsome ladies. The sculptures, like those of Hindu Bali, favored ferocious demons. Arabs destroyed all of this, or all that was visible, but in 1933 a shepherd found a trove of manuscripts, ninety in all, on Mount Mug east of Pendjikent. They furnish the basis for describing the city as it was.

Its physical remains—though not remotely comparable to the ruins of Rome—preserve a sketchy sense of what the people were like. They looked at the world out of deep-set eyes in long, thin faces, their big noses almost Italian, their beards curly and luxuriant. Priests of their Zoroastrian cult wore felt hats, knee-length tunics of silk belted at the waist, close-fitting trousers, and high leather boots. They would have been prosperous. Today Pendjikent survives as scattered mounds of yellowish-brown loess heaped up on the riverbank.

Central Asia is sown with memorials like it, memento mori rather. Konya Urgench, capital of the once-mighty Khorezm-Shah state farther to the west, lasted fifteen centuries. The tall minaret is still there, visible far across the plain, and the big palace of the granddaughter of Genghis Khan, in their desolation like those scattered leaves that hang upon the boughs when all the rest have fallen. But Pendjikent is one of a kind. It gave birth to a prodigy sixteen hundred years ago, creating a tolerant society, not Laodicean, where everything goes because nothing matters, but one that looked at a world it cared for through different windows. It did this equably. Zoroastrians, Manichaeans, Buddhists, and Christians, each believed themselves in the right but didn't send their dissenting neighbor to the stake. The leaves were many but the root was one, and they lived on easy terms in Sogdiana.

But Pendjikent neglected to keep a wary eye on its borders, where Arabs were mustering. Perhaps the men of Sogdiana discounted the danger. Or perhaps they were magnanimous or had moral qualms, characteristic of cultivated people, and declined to confront the enemy in his true character. Their long history inclined them to philosophize, and they chose a quiet conscience over honing their swords. Perhaps they thought wistfully that right makes might or that truth crushed to earth will rise again. A pleurisy of goodness was their death, the fate of a society that can't or won't believe in evil. Arabs would have been glad to meet an enemy for whom the truth was its own best defense.

In the eighth century, an Arab army broke through the walls of the city. At first the prince of Pendjikent, last of his line, eluded them. But they hunted him down, crucified him, and reduced the ancient city to rubble. With the destruction of Pendjikent, its truth disappeared. The indestructible nature of truth seemed axiomatic when I was young, almost like a law of physics, but history gives it the lie.

Only a hundred years before, Arabs boiled up out of the desert, swept across the Near East, Africa, and the Mediterranean littoral, and scalded to death whatever lay in their path. Few eruptions in history have burst through earth's mold with such terrifying force. Attila and his Huns and Genghis Khan and his Mongols, breaking the chains that bound them in the underworld, drove everything before them until death took their leaders. Arabs were different. Fuelled by the ideology of Islam, they lost the Prophet but threw up a myriad of savage and brilliant successors. Not until the Christian West balked them at Tours in 732 A.D. did the tide of conquest begin to recede. This happened too late to make a difference in Central Asia, costing me my chance to wander the streets of Pendjikent as they were in life. But the vanished city, though a dream, still haunts about the buried temples, forever potential like the once and future king. Wishing and willing won't "relume" it, Othello's magical word at the end of the play. But every so often I call it up before my mind's eye, the way one might imagine a loved face from the past.

ANCIENT TRAVELERS in China, if they were making for Pendjikent, left Jiayuguan through its west portal. Ultima Thule, a more recent traveler called the prospect that confronted them, the point beyond which there's nothing more. Langdon Warner was the traveler, an American among the archaeologist-explorers. Curator of Chinese Art at Harvard's Fogg Museum, he had the scrupulous temperament of a man schooled in his rigorous discipline.

When he came to the major crossroads of his life, this acted on him both as a spur and a clog. Unexpectedly a bit of the romantic found its way into his makeup. Sometimes wild surmises crowded his brain, and he thought he would barter his all to possess a great work of art. So Warner looked in two directions, and doing his job while keeping his sensible and speculative selves in balance needed a firm hand on the tiller. But it needed something more, a dash of derring-do, and this overplus makes him worth going back to. I think of his story, and that of his fellow sojourners on the Silk Road, as potentially a version of mine. I don't call myself their equals, but I keep their example before me, hoping to follow it. You could say that in writing about them, I write about myself as I might be.

The old fort, Warner's jumping-off point, was still full of bustle a hundred years ago, the place where men cinched their belts before venturing on the unknown. He was bound for the Caves of the Thousand Buddhas, a treasure trove of paintings, statues, and manuscripts hidden for centuries beyond the Gobi Desert. He wouldn't be satisfied merely to see them; he wanted them for Harvard's Fogg Museum. But he was complicated and had his doubts about retrieving the past. Perhaps, he thought, that was synonymous with thieving. Whatever he thought, he found what he was after and took it away. Physically this needed iron will and a constitution to suit. Between him and his goal lay the ordeal of an icy winter. I traveled west by train and motorcar, swaddled in rugs; he endured the journey at ground level. In the book he wrote about it, *The Long Old Road in China* (1926), he makes you feel that it activated buried patterns in the self. Readers may think of the heroes of quest stories, Mozart's or Wagner's, and the trials they undergo en route to self-realization.

Warner realized himself as he discovered where his true loyalties lay. Was he a fortune hunter, a careerist avid of fame, or a scholar in pursuit of truth? The people he encountered on the way west likely challenged his Yankee preconceptions. Going out, he thought he knew what it meant to be human. Returning, he had to work this out from scratch. The experience of Asia was like sloughing his skin. For ten days he stared at the cave paintings, a spiritual upheaval. "The Holy Men of fourteen centuries ago had left their gods in splendor on those walls. Tens of thousands of them, walking in slow procession, [were] seated calm on flowering lotus blossoms, with hands raised to bless mankind, or rapt in meditation, or deeper still sunk in thoughtless Nirvana." But paradise had its obligatory serpent, personated by a trio of Mongols. One placed "his greasy open palm on a ninth-century wall painting," another "picked at the scaling paint with his fingernails." As they left, "their vile sheepskins rubbed a row of saintly figures by the doorway," taking the paint with them. "This was enough."

Warner knew what he must do, or rather he vacillated: he had a conscience. At last, however, he shut off his mind and acted. First fixing the crumbling pigments, he separated the paintings from the walls, packed them in felt, and cleared out for home. He was eighteen weeks on his way, by cart, train, and ocean liner, an exhausting journey filled with nights of remorse and black despair. What enormity had he committed? But each morning, when he looked at the paintings lashed securely between boards, his spirits lifted. So far from ravishing the land of its past, was he not performing an act of gratuitous kindness, saving for the future what would otherwise be lost? In a self-justifying letter to his wife, he glanced at Islam, a menacing presence in the country he was leaving. "How long before the Mohameddan rebellion that everyone expects? In twenty years this place [Dunhuang] won't be worth a visit." Better to rescue what he could before the idol smashers and the tomb robbers got there.

Posterity wonders, was he one of the latter? The Chinese put him on their list of "foreign devils," and Arthur Waley, the Sinologist who catalogued the Dunhuang paintings, called him a thief. But the story, fraught with complexity, needs more than invective. Perhaps Hamlet's phrase for the pirates who capture him and return him safe to his own country is apposite. They were like "thieves of mercy," he said, stealing it and at the same time conferring it. In fact Warner and the best of his colleagues—Sven Hedin, the Scandinavian who took risks because it pleased him; Sir Aurel Stein, the Hungarian Jew naturalized an Englishman and as valiant as any of them with Norman blood in their veins; Paul Pelliot, the superbly erudite Frenchman; the German Albert von Le Coq; Baron Otani of Japan—epitomize the mingled yarn of our life, good and ill together.

If my inclination were to prayer, I would light a candle to the scholar-explorers who reopened the Silk Road a hundred years ago. Pelliot, a Sinologist without peer, labored by candlelight through the vast library of scrolls in the Mugao Caves. He wanted to know the causes of things, the motive beyond others that impels men to do great deeds. Unaware that Stein had already been there, he thought their survival depended on him. Many of the most valuable manuscripts, including a Nestorian version of the Gospel of St. John, are now secure in the Musée Guimet in Paris thanks to Pelliot. He might have ended an obscure academic, but Central Asia, working its magic, added cubits to his stature. That is true of Warner, and if what he did in the Mugao Caves partly besmirched him, that is the fate of all who do the world's work

Hedin, the most daring of the great explorers, blotted his escutcheon by striking up a friendship with Hitler. Though a man of large soul, he missed the cloven foot, commenting perhaps on our incapacity to see into the nature of evil. He could have lived a comfortable life in Sweden, whose citizens are cared for from the cradle to the grave, but he knew there had to be a more bracing world elsewhere. "At the early age of twelve," he wrote in his autobiography, "my closest friends were Fenimore Cooper and Jules Verne, Livingstone and Stanley." *My Life as an Explorer* (1925) tells how he outpaced them. In Iran he ventured on a tower of silence, where Zoroastrians, not wanting to pollute the earth, laid out their dead. The sun dried the bodies, and vultures came down to eat them. At the university in Tehran, a professor of medicine and anthropology commissioned Hedin to procure him a trio of skulls. "I must have the cranial measurements!" he said, like Bela Lugosi in an old horror film. Hedin scaled the wall that encircled the boneyard, doing this "in the middle of June, when summer was at its height and the thermometer registered 106 in the shade." Undismayed by the "rank, sickening smell of decaying corpses," he cut off three skulls, stuffed them in his saddlebag, and brought them back to the devotee of science.

A type of the rogue male, he resembled Wilfrid Thesiger among more-recent explorers. Thesiger's heroes were the Arabs of the marshes and desert. Hedin, more nearly omnivorous, took the whole of Central Asia, both the land and its people, for his province. "I have been in love many times," he said, "but Asia remained my bride. She has held me captive in her cold embrace, and out of jealousy would never let me love any other. And I have been faithful to her, that is certain." Faithful, he might have said, almost to death. On May Day in 1895, "a spring-time feast of joy and light at home in Sweden," he found himself down to his last drop of water in the sterile wastes of the Taklamakan. This terrifying desert, compared to which the Sahara, said Stein, was only a cup of tea, lies across the Pamir Mountains in China's Wild West. Hedin stood alone on this ill-starred May Day, around him the prone bodies of his men, dogs, and camels, dying or already dead. He drank

Primus fuel and camel urine, said his farewells, and struggled on. Following his compass, he walked out of the desert alive.

Before the old year could beget a new one, he was on his way again, hunting buried treasure—the archaeological kind—in the ruins of ancient oases. The ruins or a piece of them are still there, a long, concave line on the desert's southern flank. To get from one to another takes grit and a dash of quixotry. Very few travel this spur of the fabulous road that runs north of Tibet and south of the Taklamakan. If you travel by camel, men reckon that you will need a month to get from Yarkan to Yutien, the largest of the oases. Your life depends on getting through.

Now that the dust of years has settled, Stein emerges as the best of them, the man above others I take as a model. He understood more than any how mastery of his craft—all the petty travails and life-threatening disasters that went with the work of exploring—depended on control of the self. When he was in the high country on his way back from Dunhuang, battling snow and fierce cold, his boots got soaked through, and his feet began to freeze. It was clear to him that gangrene would set in soon. He had scored an immense triumph in unearthing the fantastic cache of paintings, hidden for centuries in the Mugao Caves. Now the option was open to him to jettison his precious cargo and dash for home. A lesser man would have taken it. But he chose not to alter his deliberate pace, and for more than a month descended to ground level by yak, camel, and pony, all the while supervising his caravan of artifacts, fifty camels' worth. At last, having crossed into India, he found his surgeon and lost all the toes of his right foot. A stoic, he endured the loss without complaint and perhaps thought it a small price to pay.

His biography is mixed. Though equable-seeming, he never left off grudging his work. His sojourning life kept him in fettle, but its sum seemed to him a heap of discrete images, mysterious to the very end. He was still trying to piece the dots together when he died in Afghanistan. The first time he challenged the Taklamakan, he walked in the traces of a little country lane, an experience he writes about in the book that brought him to public attention, *Sand-Buried Ruins of Khotan* (1903). Drifting sand had filled the lane ages since, and only the boles of petrified fruit trees said that this had been an orchard. Peach, plum, and apricot once made the air fragrant; no more. A feeling of melancholy displacement took hold of him, "obliterating almost the sense of time."

But he lived on terms with desolation. The solitude of the desert harnessed his mind, and in "the womb of the Himalaya," he found his proper calling. Pursuing it, he acknowledged three masters, Alexander the Great, Marco Polo, and the Chinese Buddhist pilgrim Hsuan-Tsang. In the seventh century, this sojourning man took the overland route from China to India and back, setting down what he saw in his *Record of the Western Region.* By one of those odd conjunctions that crop up in history, Muhammad in the same years commenced his "new instauration," attempting to redo man and history. "All shall be changed" was the rubric. Implacably hostile to a quietist faith such as Buddhism, not least in the devotion of its bodhisattvas to the world and flesh, he sought to replace it with a religion of the sword. Though illiterate, he was hardly provincial, his merchant's life seeing to that, and the tenets of the religion he learned and taught were imparted, he said, by the archangel Gabriel. This revelation is the Qu'an or Koran. Communicated orally, it was written down after his death.

Muhammad is a sanguinary type of the great man, and the bloodletting of Islam in its beginnings seems an extension of his personality. How sensational is early Islam when put against the first centuries of the papacy; how crude Muhammad compared to Hsuan-Tsang. Absent his learned notetaking, said Frazer in *The Golden Bough,* "the ruins of Greece—they turn up everywhere in Chinese Turkestan, bearing witness to Alexander's long march—would be a labyrinth without a clue, a riddle without an answer." The gatherer of clues, helping Stein thread the labyrinth, became his patron saint. He made a good acolyte, following his own dream of learning like the Grail. He said: "I feel as if I could date a ruin by a broom, bootlast, or an old shoe." At the oasis of Niya in the Taklamakan, he was electrified to come on a pair of wooden tablets inscribed with writing like that "prevailing . . . in the first centuries of our era." Making contact with the far distant past, he had to know almost everything to recognize anything new. Near Kashgar he explored a subterranean sepulcher with niches in its walls. What were they meant for, unless to hold cinerary urns? But neither the Muslims nor their Buddhist predecessors practiced cremation. What then? In the heart of Asia, he had stumbled on a cemetery of Nestorian Christians.

THE PART OF UZBEKISTAN I am driving through has changed its personality, becoming flat as a piece of wallboard. But every so often, a clump of elevated ground breaks the monotony. A butte in the American West is like it, except that in this part of Asia, nothing goes up that high until you come to the mountains. I let my eye rest on the ragged surface of the limestone, then fall to the plain below. The height and then the drop-off suggest the course of a man's life, most of it a slightly undulating line like the floor of the desert, climbing abruptly to an emotional or physical peak. I have been thinking of Aurel Stein, and this, it occurs to me, plots the graph of his life.

Its high point occurred early. A generation before Langdon Warner, he discovered the Dunhuang Caves. On March 16, 1907, a day sacred to Clio, muse of history, he stood for the first time directly in front of them, hidden against the side of a steep valley surrounded by sand dunes and desert. "On the almost perpendicular conglomerate cliffs a multitude of dark cavities . . . (honeycombed) the somber rock face in irregular tiers from the foot of the cliffs where the stream almost washed them, to the top of the precipice." He thought of the dwellings of anchorites in early Italian paintings. But "the 'Caves of the Thousand Buddhas' were . . . tenanted not by Buddhist prelates, however holy, but by images of the Enlightened One himself."

There are almost five hundred caves, the first of them carved out in the fourth century A.D., the last nine hundred years later. Blowing sand, overwhelming them, saved them from Islam. Spreading eastward since the eighth century, it mutilated images of carnality wherever it came upon them. What would the haters of "our human face divine" have made of Dunhuang? In 1277, when the caves were sealed off, the iconoclasts were perilously close. But for six hundred years the desert protected them, and no one knew of Dunhuang's existence. The civilized world—I use the word deliberately—reclaimed the caves in the last years of the nineteenth century, when a Daoist priest named Wang, unlocking their secret, made restoration the great work of his life.

The caves are literally an art gallery, illustrating Chinese painting over nearly a thousand years. Despite the passage of time, the color on the walls remains vivid, mostly green, blue, white, black, and pink. The technique is tempera: atop the clay surface the artist spread and polished a cement-like substance, then applied paint made from mineral powder and metal oxide. Drying almost instantly, it stayed fast. Many of the paintings, more intense than my sense of the general run of Buddhist art, bear the impress of Greece. Alexander the Great "slept here," having crossed the Hindu Kush Mountains into Bactria, modern Afghanistan, in 329 B.C. He and his followers sponsored a new kind of art, truer to nature in depicting its subjects, their features, the folds of their garments, "that color on cheek or hair." Stein was prompt to observe this, remarking in many figures "the type of face, pose and drapery" he put a name to: "Graeco-Buddhist art."

The manner is new but the matter familiar. Legends of the bodhisattva, those self-sacrificing men and women who held off achieving nirvana to assist others needier than themselves; mix with Buddhist angels, the apsara, ethereal creatures of exquisite beauty. Tibetan-style mandalas, geometric in shape, represent the cosmos. Naturalism gets a hearing, a plow in the rain, musicians, a battle scene. One painting gives the likeness of Hsuan-Tsang, the bringer of Buddhism from India to China. Detained on his journey by the king of Gaochgang, far beyond the reach of imperial China, his protector, he gained his release by accepting a fantastic condition. He would lecture for a month to the king and his ministers on the Diamond Sutra, preeminent among Buddhist scriptures. The quid pro quo, honoring both the lecturer and his audience, breathes the same love of disinterested knowledge that distinguishes Stein. Muhammad is his opposite, a distinction with a difference.

One of the caves concealed a hidden door, and the monk Wang, prying it open, came on a smaller cave piled from floor to ceiling with scrolls and paintings. The manuscripts, more than fifty thousand of them, reached a height of nearly ten feet. One, printed on woodblock, was the Diamond Sutra, dating from the ninth century, the world's first printed book. Stein, learning of its existence, said it kept his heart buoyant for months. With assiduity and charm, he made the Daoist monk, simple but otherworldly zealous and this-worldly cunning, his friend. The tie that bound them was their mutual devotion to Hsuan-Tsang, celebrated throughout China, writes Jeannette Mirsky, Stein's biographer, as a sort of "saintly Munchausen."

The first fruit of their friendship, brought to Stein at daylight, was a clutch of paper rolls of the sutras, carried from India and translated, said the colophon, by Hsuan-Tsang himself. "The heavens had spoken." Wang, having lost his innocence, now collaborated with the man who had taken it. The wall blocking the hidden recess came down, and Stein entered the sancta sanctorum. By the dim light of a little lamp, he began to read, assisted by his invaluable secretary, Chiang. For more than three weeks, the two of them examined the inconceivable treasure, Buddhist texts in Chinese, Tibetan, Sanskrit, Brahmi, Sogdian, Uighur, Runic Turkic. To possess all this wealth, Stein paid the priest five hundred rupees toward the labor of restoring the caves. Then, his donkeys and camels loaded with manuscripts and paintings removed from the walls, he left Dunhuang for England and the British Museum.

Departing the caves, he thought that their guardian "now seemed to breathe freely again, and almost to recognize that I was performing a pious act in rescuing for Western scholarship these relics of ancient Buddhist literature and art which local ignorance would allow to lie here neglected or to get lost in the end." This was more than self-serving. The danger was real and not only from Islam. When he came back on a second foray, the authorities in Kashgar intervened to stop him. On demand he returned what he had taken, only to find that the art he meant to save didn't go to Beijing, as stipulated. It disappeared into air and has never turned up to this day.

CENTRAL ASIA FIGURES as a tabula rasa, scribbled on by such conquerors as Tamburlaine, Genghis Khan, Alexander the Great, and Enver Pasha. (The last wanted to found a Pan-Turkic state and died trying.) Like hairy comets, they flashed across the sky, then were quenched. Zealots who aimed to uplift the heathen revolved around them. Further out were necessitous natives, a multitude loyal mostly to their bread. But some in this story, both Asians and Europeans, feel an impersonal need to beautify their lives for beauty's own sweet sake. It seems important to remember them, paying honor where due.

Across the Pamirs in Western China, they let down water in pipes from the environing mountains to irrigate the low-lying fields. The result is a demi-Eden, made by hand. In the oasis town of Dunhuang, Mildred Cable and the French sisters, traveling there in the 1930s, saw a living carpet: "masses of pear, peach, and nectarine blossom . . . every bank crowned with blue desert iris." Poppy covered the ground with a veil like gossamer, "sometimes shaded with the faintest touch of pink to deep rose, and at other times scarlet streaked with silver-gray." In this same oasis, Buddhist monks brought forth a miracle of disinterested art, the Mugao Caves.

The three ladies, like the three theological virtues, bless the land they are part of. In their company is an eighteenth-century Englishman, one of the elect who dined with Dr. Johnson at the Turk's Head. Sir William Jones, known as "Oriental" Jones or "Persian" Jones, is buried far from home in the British cemetery in Calcutta. His home was Wales, but his heart beat more strongly east of Suez. The first Britisher to learn Sanskrit, he thought this ancient tongue an agreeable ancestor of the modern languages, "more perfect than the Greek, more copious than the Latin, and more exquisitely refined than either." Jones had an eidetic memory. When a school performance at Harrow needed copies of Shakespeare's *Tempest,* he was able to write out all of it without reference to the text of the play. A connoisseur of surfaces, he could see through the surface to the ghostly paradigm beneath.

His father showed him the way. Jones the Elder, a tutor of mathematics, introduced the notation for π: the ratio of the circumference to the diameter of a circle. His son's strong suit was languages, divided into groups: eight studied critically (English, Latin, French, Italian, Greek, Arabic, Persian, Sanskrit), eight intelligible with a dictionary (Spanish, German, Portuguese, Runic [Icelandic?], Hebrew, Bengali, Hindi, Turkish), twelve "attainable" (Tibetan, Pali [the early Indian dialect in which the Buddhist canon is recorded], Middle Persian, Deri [a Persian dialect spoken in Afghanistan], Russian, Aramaic, Ethiopian, Coptic, Welsh, Swedish, Dutch, Chinese). Jones, had he lived as long as Methuselah, might have reversed the confusion of tongues, not a good thing. He wasn't perfect and lamented the fall of the Tower of Babel, not knowing a fortunate fall when he saw one.

Many Europeans came to Asia as spoilsmen. The English, within a few generations of their arrival in India, were staking out huge chunks of it for the Crown. Some returned home disgruntled, unwilling to shoulder the white man's burden. Others stayed for other reasons, dreaming of naked odalisques waiting out east to receive them. Still others, sport for comedy, regretted the shuttered Sundays and unending drizzle of the land they left behind. They didn't care for people of color, their food and customs, nor the language, a babel of sound. Forster, who has a score to settle, tells about them in *A Passage to India.* They are like that St. Bernard, I mean the twelfth-century saint, who walked for a day beside Lake Geneva and asked at day's end where the lake was.

Russians like the czar's general, Nicolai Przhevalsky, heaped scorn on Asia and its people. He said a Chinese man was "a Jew plus a Muscovite pickpocket, both squared." But the opinionated man put humanity in his debt as he sought to discover what lay beneath the sands in Lop Nor. At the same time, however, he spearheaded Russian conquest in Asia, intending to make it a fief of St. Petersburg. The independent khanates fell one by one, Tashkent leading the van in 1865. Thirty thousand defenders couldn't hold off two thousand Russians, and Islam ever since has smarted at the mismatch. Samarkand followed in 1868, Khiva in 1873. The khan, attempting to forestall an attack, released a number of his Russian slaves, a magnanimous gesture, he thought, the slaves being his property. But the invaders, brushing it aside, turned their guns on the mud walls of the city and kept coming. Two years later they took Khokand, yielding, they said, "to the wishes of the Khokandi people." Merv fell a year after.

The inexorable advance of the imperial army was for the good of mankind, said General Przhevalsky. Carbine bullets and rifled cannon smoothed the way for civilization, "which would otherwise be very long in coming." That is hard to swallow but close to the truth. The slave trade was so much a part of local life in Khiva and Bokhara, according to the nineteenth-century traveler Vámbéry, that Turkomans "would not hesitate to sell into slavery the Prophet himself, did he fall into their hands." It was left to Europeans to rid Asia of this evil traffic, much in their favor. Not too much, however.

Russians claimed this was why they annexed the khanates. The English were only less brazen, and under the same pretext sought to stop the Russian advance. Sir Francis Younghusband, the perfect hero of *The Boy's Own Book,* was a glamorous player in this back-and-forth between Russia and England for control of the routes to India. When the Russians blocked Younghusband's entrance to Turkmenistan, he found another pass through the mountains. He said that was "always an easy matter in these parts." The bravado is part of his charm. Though deadly crevasses lurked under the snow, he trusted to the yak to carry him through. "Like the elephant which will not cross a shaky bridge, the yak knows by instinct the parts that will not bear, and snorting and sniffing along, he finds his way unerringly up a glacier." One must warm to a man who knows what the yak knows "by instinct."

But the boys' own hero grew older. In 1904 he stormed into Lhasa, wanting to add another jewel to the Crown. Behind him came a column of 10,000 coolies, 7,000 mules, 4,000 yaks, and cases of champagne for his brother officers. Tibetans shied from the British lion and the Russian bear impartially and did what they could to resist. British machine guns brooked no argument, however. Score: 628 Tibetans killed, 222 wounded. On the British side, none killed, a dozen wounded. The tally is depressing, and Younghusband a familiar type of Englishman, lording it over inferior peoples, swagger stick tucked under his arm. But it isn't enough to hate him: surprisingly one must love him, the most winning and resourceful of men. He is like the Chosen People, Handel's version. "Botches and blains! Botches and blains!" Handel hears them cry, calling down a plague on their enemies. Handel enjoys their bellicose bluster—not empty bluster either!—and the English have remained grateful, esteeming this composer above all others.

Peter Fleming, a traveler on the Silk Road in the 1930s, illustrates the unflappable manner, the more persuasive for the deliberate impudence that goes with it. In the company of Ella Maillart, a Swiss, he is headed west out of China when he meets a small donkey flying the Union Jack. Others would have been astonished; not he. The man on the donkey, a bearded Turki, bears a legend across his chest: BRITISH INDIAN POSTMAN. The mail, even at the ends of the earth, has come through. Taking over the postman's bag, Fleming and friend immerse themselves happily in three-month old copies of the *Times.*

He was on his way to Kashgar in China's Sinjiang Province, and he brought his self-assurance with him. Sinjiang is bigger than France, much of it terra incognita, but Fleming, anticipating a civilized venue, helped to create it. The British consulate in Sinjiang, an undistinguished building, now a second-class hotel, he named "Kashgar-les-Bains." Promptly light shone in darkness. George Macartney, an old China hand, presided over the consulate, together with his wife, Catherine, both blessed with tact, brains, and humanity. Like Fleming and others of that "kidney," they held the empire together.

Macartney (1867–1945), born of a Scottish father and a Chinese mother, grew up in London, leaving his mother behind in Nanking lest her color give scandal to English sensibilities. Matriculating at a French university, he became fluent in French, in addition to his English and Chinese—also easy in German and Russian and at least passable in Persian, Hindustani, and Turki. He sailed for India in 1887, the same year as Stein, wanting to serve in a consular post in the Chinese capital. He wound up in Kashgar, as far away as the moon from what he'd imagined, and stayed for the next twenty-eight years. The house in Kashgar, under his hand, became a heaven on earth, said Sir Clairmont Skrine, his biographer. Such names some of these Britishers had, another aspect of their imperturbable selves.

The biography sets Macartney apart from others of his generation in the consular service, the "cream of the public schools and universities." They "went to the East imbued with a sense of national superiority," which translated to "assumptions of racial superiority and of the divine right of the English people to rule over the colored races." In the Anglo-Indian world, including China, part of its orbit, "any stepping over the lines of caste and convention was not treated kindly." Macartney, sparing his blue-blooded colleagues, never mentioned his mother. Many in Asia, perhaps like that Chinese mother, differ from Westerners, not merely in color and physiognomy. In Northern India and the former khanates of Central Asia, they are predominantly Muslim, which translates to humble, even to self-abasing. They lack aggression and are satisfied to take the world as it comes. Macartney would never have called them inferior. But they live by non-Western priorities.

He is the exemplar of one kind of transplanted Englishman, more properly Britisher, and though he has nothing of Fleming's insouciance, he is not a whit behind him in intellect and sophistication. For him, as for Catherine Macartney, his wife, the East was a book of revelations. Reading it, they seemed never to surfeit. Married one day and bundled off the next to western China, she wasn't qualified for the pioneer's life, she said—"beyond being able to make a cake." Her remarkable memoir, *An English Lady in Chinese Turkestan* (1931), hints at gentility, but this lady pays more than she promises. Catherine and George Macartney called their home away from home "Chini-Bagh," or Chinese Garden. Ducks waddled about the lawn fronting the verandah. Inside were books and newspapers, long drinks, and a gramophone playing. The furniture was well polished, the comfortable armchairs covered with chintz. All this, a tabula rasa when they got there, was earned.

Among their guests were Owen and Eleanor Lattimore, he a famous scholar of Mongolian, later a target of Sen. Joseph McCarthy. They were spending their honeymoon on the Silk Road, Owen on the back of "a raking bay," his wife riding "a splendid black," and after many breathless, sticky days of desert, they found Chini-Bagh "an oasis of civilization." The description of how it was with them is hers. "At sunrise we rode past domed clay tombs and an encamped caravan and irrigated fields into the picture-book streets of the Turki city of Turfan. It is a blissful wandering life and full of beauty and elemental joys and we are greedily wishing it could go on forever."

Welcomed by the Macartneys, they reveled in "hot baths, clean sheets, dainty food, nice dishes, white-robed servants, a library of books, shady terraces and an enchanting garden riotous with fruit and flowers." These were things that went with being thoroughly human, and they seemed conjured up without effort. This affronted and mystified the discontented of the world. What was the key to British success? Dressing for dinner in Equatorial

Africa, British colonials built Tudor houses in upland Burma, played cricket in the Emirates and polo in Hong Kong. They wouldn't succumb to the heart of darkness. Their strict punctilio was both gratuitous and an act of mercy, and made a political statement. These were men and women living far from home, sometimes in straits, and calling themselves to order, they sought to set themselves free.

7

The Storks of Bukhara

Like the Time Traveler in H. G. Wells, I can move from past to present, enabled by language. Reliving time past, I have been traveling through western China. Now, quitting the Macartneys and their villa in Kashgar, I return to the long parabola I began with, from Kazakhstan to the Caspian Sea. My northwest diagonal from Shakhrisabz will bring me eventually to Bukhara. The sky is huge, dwarfing everything below it. Gripping the wheel of the car with both hands to keep myself awake, I watch the desert disappear, swallowed up in the rearview mirror. Only gray sachsara bushes break the featureless plain, and the tiny sand dunes that seem to lap it are like wavelets in the open sea. This is Transoxiana, known to the Arabs as Mavra-un-Nahr, "Beyond the Oxus." One of them called it fantastically "the Garden of the Commander of the Faithful."

Alexander the Great had to come with his A-game to conquer the people who lived here. He was at it almost two years. While he camped beside the Oxus, a pair of springs bubbled up next to his tent, one of water, one of oil. They are like the spring of oil that surfaced in Rome the day Christ was born, running all day long to the Tiber. Auguries, auspicious for good or foreboding evil, hitch on to all the great stories, and I wouldn't bet against what they say. Alexander on his barbarian side is monstrous, but the auguries tell for him, inclining me to back his Panhellenic dream, good for us all who are the legatees of Greece and the Western ideal it promoted. As to the bubbling springs, in my lifetime Soviet geologists, prospecting for oil in the valley of the Amu-Darya, found it near Tirmidh, the very spot where Alexander pitched camp.

Every so often blue-eyed babies are born in this wasteland, and Alexander's soldiers must have dropped their seed on the march. Soviet soldiers, bound for Afghanistan over the same road, will have done likewise. Low gray walls, announcing a village, interrupt the road they traveled. From a distance the village looks empty of people, though there must be a reason for the forest of telephone poles on the horizon. Closer to Bukhara, tall orange stacks send up plumes of yellowish flame, telling of natural gas belowground. Deduction leads me to conclude this, but other ways of reading the evidence are conceivable, and perhaps the stacks are totems honoring an unknown god.

Chasms made by old rainwater sculpt the hills, and a few stunted trees, searching out the water, have got a foothold on their sides. Cows and horses, only a scattering, graze the stubble fields, with here and there a lonely farmhouse dropped down like a marker in a board game. What designing hand put it in place, isolating a man from his fellows? Hunched over on a donkey, a solitary herdsman drives his sheep and goats home for the night. He and I are in the steppes of Asia, something like infinity.

I am twenty miles this side of Bukhara when I see the signboard pointing to a spur off the highway. I have been looking for it, and I take this side road to the little village of Kasri Orifon, one of Sufism's most venerated shrines. Bakhautdin Naqshband, the founder of an ancient order of Sufis, was born here in the early years of the fourteenth century. I have gone out of my way to honor his memory, and pilgrims from all over Central Asia are doing the same. One of my books calls Bakhautdin an Islamic Gandhi, but he is first of all a son of toil who worked with his hands. To me the appropriate comparison is to Jesus, son of the carpenter Joseph.

A *naqshband* is a carver of the wooden blocks used to print designs on cotton fabrics. Presumably the holy man fashioned these tools of his trade with hammer and chisel. He didn't distinguish between work and prayer, and neither do men of his order. They are contemplative, practicing the *zikr*, a litany reciting the different names of God, also techniques of perfect posture and breathing. But they favor a life of physical labor and make themselves skilled in a particular trade. The founder, skilled in veterinary medicine, spent seven years caring for animals, seven more mending the roads. More important than the odd conjunction, however, is the priority of the number seven. Bakhautdin and his coreligionists assigned it miraculous power. If you believed them, their mystical numerology was controlling for life itself.

It wasn't simply by chance, they would have said, that the founder was born in the seventh month of the year 1318, learned the Koran by heart before the age of seven, died at the age of seventy, and was carried to his grave by shifts of pallbearers, each of whom walked the expected seven steps. The imposition of numbers on the phenomenal world was meant to bring order out of chaos. Dante, not a man of the Middle Ages for nothing, is addicted to numerology from dread of the void. When he was writing the *Commedia,* the world was falling apart. In Western Europe the disastrous papacy of Boniface VIII had just ended; in the East a half-century later the reign of Tamburlaine was in full swing. These are portents of trouble, and the function of numbers was to address them.

The Naqshbandi complex I am bound for includes a pair of old mosques and a sixteenth-century *khanaga* covered by a huge dome. Parts of it are being repaired, and scaffolding partly hides the work in progress. But the elegance of the domed structure is evident despite the renovation, thanks in part to the unfortunate comparison with the modern buildings that have sprung up around it. I am reminded of an upscale shopping center in Anytown, USA. The tomb in the central courtyard is not much taller than a man. Pilgrims are circling it "withershins," in a direction contrary to the apparent course of the sun. They have made a wish and repeat the circle three times, their best chance that the wish will be granted. Inevitably an ancient mulberry tree is part of the scene, and barren women, crawling under and around it, hope to make themselves fertile.

Convention supposes that the Sufis were quietists, sitting idly by the side of the road, but in the nineteenth century they waged guerrilla warfare against the armies of czarist Russia. For many years, fighting for the independence of the Caucasus, they more than held their own, though the forces confronting them were hugely superior. The story is complete with heroes and villains. "Circassian sons of the mist," Lt. Arthur Conolly of the Sixth Bengal Native Light Cavalry called the former. (Conolly, an early reconnoiterer in the no-man's-land of the Caucasus, appears later in this narrative, meeting a soldier's violent death.)

To Circassians, Russian imperialists were the villains and still are. Russians, by the same token, knew their enemy as *basmachi,* a term of reproach connoting banditry and murder. But the *basmachi* knew themselves as lovers of freedom. They have never disappeared, nor have they left off fighting. In the 1920s, under the leadership of Enver Pasha, they were briefly a match for the Red Army. But God sides with the bigger battalions, and Enver and his comitatus died in the Pamirs, some say in a last suicidal charge. Many believe that he didn't die but hid himself and will rise to fight again, another version of the once and future king.

Noon is approaching, and out here in the country the air is parched. Not even a trickle of water moistens the irrigation ditches, and the skinny evergreen saplings planted around them seem verging on their end. Crocuses are blooming, however, only a modest pink but I am grateful. They have found a respite from the sun in the slightly shaded ground at the base of the buildings, and I take shelter there with them before I return to the car. My mind is beating on the unending struggle of right against might. But there are other ways to put this.

On the seat of the car is a month-old copy of the *International Herald Tribune,* saved for a news item that had got my attention and kept it. It reports a suicide bombing at Moscow's Domodedovo Airport, Russia's largest, claiming the lives of thirty-six people. The culprit, a twenty-year-old youth from Chechnya in the Caucasus, died in the attack but left a note in his Moscow apartment. The year 2011, it says, "will be the year of blood and tears." Unless Russia leaves the Caucasus, allowing it to become an independent emirate governed by sharia law, more attacks will follow. "Among us there are hundreds of brothers who are prepared to sacrifice themselves for freedom."

The shrill goodbye of the suicide bomber disgusts me, and a bath of cold water cools off my admiration for Bukhautdin and his brethren. Without giving much thought to political violence, I have always supposed it a necessary evil. How else were the Israelis to get rid of the British, or the East Indies their Dutch colonial masters? But this sojourn in Islam has changed my take on things, and I begin to see that "necessary" begs the question. Does violence ever achieve its end? Or does it recoil on itself, "falling on the other," like Macbeth's fruitless ambition?

My mind has been disquieted by the ideology of the Sufi woodblock carver, evidently equivocal, as I get farther into it, and its doubtful side sponsors other questions. For instance, how well does Bakhautdin sustain the comparison to Jesus? Does the hocus-pocus of his numerology really govern for life, and are the barren women crawling round the mulberry tree making themselves fertile or only exercising their bodies? Not least, how heroic are the apostles of violence, like Enver Pasha, who die fighting with their boots on?

Pondering these questions, I think of the words of a poet who was pious, though no Christian, who scoffed at superstition and hated violence with every breath of his being. "The day that dawns in fire will end in flame," Shelley said. Easy to ridicule, he was the Ineffectual Angel. I don't want to believe him, brought up as I am on Jefferson's tree of liberty that must be watered by the blood of patriots. Doubt is nagging at me, though, as I turn the key in the ignition.

COMING INTO KAGAN just outside Bukhara, I cross over railroad tracks, laid in a culvert beneath me. The tracks begin in Central Asia and end in St. Petersburg on the other side of the moon, and I wonder at the mystery of trains, how you board one in a familiar place and are transported through the night over vast distances to be set down at last in a place you've never seen before, nothing like the one you embarked from. Nineteenth-century Russians built this solitary train station outside the city to appease the emir of Bukhara, Abdallabad Khan. In his youth he thought trains an abomination but later changed his mind and, grown enamored of fancy-dress balls, journeyed from Kagan all the way to the czarist capital for the pleasure of having a dance.

His summer palace, reserved for the dog days, sits in a neatly landscaped park a few kilometers north of the city. As I draw closer, it looks to my eye like a huge pastry descended on by flies. The flies are vendors, buzzing and persistent. "No problem, mister," says one, when I push away his silk-on-cotton doilies. Without taking a breath, he thrusts out his other hand, piled high with small glass bowls, blue and green as always.

In the handsome white building the emir and his entourage spent part of each year, the Russians having levered him out of his winter quarters, where he lived at his own pleasure, into this more vulnerable place where he lived at theirs. He still enjoyed his creature comforts. The harem girls were quartered with him and had their own swimming pool, above it a viewing platform where he could watch them at play in the water. If one pleased more than others, he tossed her an apple. Before they cohabited, he had her bathed in donkey's milk, the smell of which got him going.

The Russians, alternating carrot with stick, sowed cultural confusion in Bukhara. Like the British imperialists, dressing its clients of the Hawaiian aristocracy in pompous uniforms heavy on gilt, they played a pathetic game with the emir of this once-fanatical theocracy. His annual visits to the Winter Palace in St. Petersburg were paid for by his patrons, who sent him off by private train, a gift from the queen. His son read Dostoevsky and steeled himself to be a soldier in the czar's army. In his lifetime and his father's, he lived between two worlds, one dead, the other powerless to be born. But only for a little while longer.

I sit on a bench contemplating the summer palace, Makhosa Sitoral Moki Hosa, "Palace of the Moon and Stars." Though well kept up, it is clearly deserted, and an air of melancholy hangs about the grounds. The shutters are closed, the shades drawn tight, but a cleaning woman perhaps has left one open, and I see that the glass windows are heart shaped. Czar Nicholas, a romantic, would have enjoyed that. In 1916 he was invited to come for a visit. He wanted to come but was unavoidably detained. The Red Army did come, and soon after the emir lost his power forever.

South of the harem pool, a notice directs visitors to the emir's zoo, not the attraction it used to be. Its major draw, the elephant, has departed for Moscow, but the peacocks are still there in all their self-importance. One sashays up to me, crying its hideous cry. Revolution has come and gone, but all that is lost on the peacock.

I approach Bukhara from the east, glad to be off the dreary stretch of road between it and the mountains. The emir's old capital, it is entered through the Ark, which dominates the main square known as the Registan. Both place-names crop up often in Asia, like "Plaza des Armas" in South American cities. Difference is more than sameness, however, and though *Registan* seems generic for the site it describes, the one in Bukhara has nothing of Samarkand's man-made beauty. Living up to its name, the "sandy place" is a colorless griddle reflecting back heat to the bronzed bowl of heaven. But the Ark, like a nineteenth-century city hall, towers over the sand, and once seen stays in the imagination. In mine it pairs with the great wall the Burmese built around Mandalay, hoping to keep out the English. Asians in Bukhara hoped to keep out the Russians, but in each case the old world fell before the advance of the new.

Yet no place on earth is less supine than Central Asia. I have returned to this part of the world, precisely because it hasn't fallen. Beaten down many times, it has always climbed up again. A truth my travels has elicited, perhaps the major truth, is that nothing vital ever dies altogether. Another way to put this is to say that what looks like death is transformation, a change into something "rich and strange," only ostensibly different.

WITHIN ITS ELEPHANTINE RAMPARTS, the Ark houses a small town, though nothing about it is welcoming to life. It seems hewn out of nature, not the benign nature that never betrayed the heart that loved her but the desert or the polar ice cap. Its main port, the west gate, is like a cave mouth in the face of a cliff. But the city it opens on has known man's civilizing touch for a long time. In the prehistoric past, Job of the Old Testament, venerated in Islam as Ayub, came to Bukhara and struck his staff on the ground. The Zarafshan River had begun falling—many centuries later it continues to fall, though it never dries up altogether—and Ayub showed the people where to find potable water. Medieval domes are built over the site, now part of the farmers' market. The inexhaustible river and the pools it replenishes seem Bukhara's appropriate insignia. Unlike the Ark, it stands for life.

With a caveat, however. The pools, excavated from stone in a later time to hold the water, answered an important need, but the water was rarely changed. The people drank from it gratefully, also used it to wash themselves and their clothing. Not surprisingly Bukhara in the Middle Ages became a byword for plague. Today the water has been sanitized, and you can bathe in it, they tell me, even drink it. "After you," I tell them.

In the heart of the old city, the gathering place called Labi-i-hauz (Tajik for "around the pool") looks like stagnant water but is mysteriously alive and of power to draw the people to itself. Ancient mulberry trees enshadow the pool, and on any afternoon a repertory theater of types assembles at water's edge, old men drinking tea, reciting Hadith (sayings of the Prophet), playing chess, numbering prayer beads, or hawking painted boxes. Not a few are merchants, their heads covered with caps and their chins with long beards, and they are adjourning for their "elevenses," the afternoon version, like shopkeepers in England. At the appointed time for prayers, they take themselves to the nearby mosque, its tower, crowned with bits of turquoise, visible from the west side of the pool.

Conveniently a painted *diwan* with a balustrade along two or three sides and a small table in the middle turns into a *chai-khana* or teahouse, accommodating some of these men. I have a ceramic image of two of them, both bearded and wearing turbans, one holding a teacup, the other an open book. Over their heads is a mulberry tree, its white berries of enormous size, and I imagine the old men murmuring their banalities or profundities beneath it. "What is life?" "Life is like a river." Sooner or later, every truth boils down to cliché.

Wise fools who live by their wits are an inevitable part of Islam's Commedia dell'Arte, for example, the famous pilgrim Hoja Nasruddin. A *hoja* made the pilgrimage to Mecca (hajj), and this one's statue stands on the pool's eastern edge. Grateful citizens put it there in token of his sense of humor. They had been scalped more than once by their neighbors, but he was too clever for that. Borrowing a pot from the merchant in the next stall, he returned it with a smaller one inside the bowl. The pot he'd borrowed was pregnant, he said—hadn't its owner noticed?—and it seemed only right that the offspring should go to him. The owner doesn't mind taking candy from a baby, and when he's asked to lend a bigger pot he's glad to comply. Time passes and he doesn't get it back, though. "I was going to tell you." says the Sufi. "It died."

I meet him or his cousin in one of the many stalls in the *shakhristan* or old town. So many stalls, hacked out of old madrassas, have been freshened up and handed over to the vendors! One of the madrassas depicts a phoenix and its mate on the portal, but this emblem of a way of life renewing itself seems sadly out of date. Once scholars of law, mathematics, and philosophy, including the Koran's, instructed their students in these dim interiors. Now, however, progress demands their removal. This transfer of property on the grand scale involves the state, sovereign in all such matters. Some think the state is out to promote commerce. I think it wants to draw the teeth of Islam.

They won't say so in Tashkent, the capital city. Instead they utter pieties, professing themselves devout Muslims. But like our American state, theirs is absolutely secular. It believes in no power greater than itself and is willing to accept no other authority, either on earth or in heaven. So the ancient madrassas must lower their flag. Money is to be made, and no more need be said.

Each stall is a cash cow, selling strings of colored postcards that ripple from the lintel like a shuffled deck of playing cards, below them shags of tobacco, drinking gourds, animal skins for wearing, saddles for riding. I picked the golden codgers who gaze from my study wall out of a bin piled with ceramics. Other bins hold needlework: friendship bracelets (a bit of cross-stitch tied round the wrist), pillbox hats decorated with velveteen and silvery thread, embroidered tablecloths called *suzaine,* elegantly festooned pillow covers. A complex of stalls becomes a self-contained neighborhood. If you need a blacksmith, he's waiting for you next to the baker and barber.

There is even a dentist, sitting cross-legged in front of his door. Laid out on a mat before him, the tools of his trade are fearsome.

American to my fingertips, I am the Grand Acquisitor, a label pinned on me by my skeptical wife. Bargaining is another matter, however, and on my liberal side, atrophied but still with a faint pulse left, I would sooner lose an arm than take advantage of those nice people, the poor. While I ask myself whether the piece of kitsch I'm looking at is worth it, one of them is picking my pockets. As he does this, he is asserting his love for my country. "America good!"

Most in the *shakhristan* favor a full-court press, and once you allow them to make eye contact, the game is pretty much over. But the carpet sellers seem different, not at all like the owner of the factory in Shakhrisabz. He is of the city, they are country mice in their psychology, and money isn't the bottom line. Though they have a product to sell, they don't seem especially eager to sell it. Thinking about the immense skill that goes to the weaving of those multitudinous threads, I understand why. Generally two men hold up a carpet, tilting it toward and away from the light so I can see it change color. I don't feel put off by their desire for my approval. They want me to see the permutations of color, for what they are selling is love.

I have a house full of carpets, but with me enough is never too much. When finally I turn away from the last carpet seller, he jumps up from his folding chair and indicates that I should sit down. I have said no to his carpet, but courtesy outweighs disappointment. His neighbors in the adjoining stalls stand round us smiling at me, disposed to be friendly. Their homely brown faces, seamed with work, are without guile. That doesn't mean they aren't sinners, but hiding what they are is beyond them. Though they want to have a conversation, neither they nor I know how to manage it. The Tower of Babel is the shadow that falls across us. St. Augustine says that a man would rather be with his dog than with a man of an alien tongue, and I believe him. But I would give much if I could talk with these men. As I get up to go, one of them puts his hand over his heart.

THE HOTEL BUKHARA PALACE is younger than me but has a look of instant senescence. Public housing in America is like it. The lightbulbs rattle when you unscrew them, the bathtub drain doesn't drain. Before I go down to dinner, I mean to have a preprandial stroll, but the lock on the door won't open to let me out of the room. I am about to summon help when I discover that I must press a button and lower the latch simultaneously. Turning the doorknob, I mutter, "Allah be willing."

But my laptop stares at me reproachfully from the nightstand beside the bed. First things first, it is saying, and wants to be "accessed," the way a cow with streaming udders wants to be milked. I regard it self-consciously, half-sneering, half-proud to be in on a young man's game. When I tap a few keys the screen brightens, and printed matter looks back at me, no streaming udders, only a single e-mail. How is it I'm not surprised it's from Ulug?

He is still in Shakhrisabz, dreaming extravagant dreams that mix with reality the way oil mixes with water. He has been on to the U.S. embassy in his nation's capital, asking that they tell him how much a year's study abroad will cost us. I like the way he puts it. A postscript adds: "At Harvard." I am to stand as his sponsor.

"Important I know when you return to America," he writes. "Am ready to accompany you but will need details. What airline are we flying?"

"Why you little so-and-so," I say to myself, typing curtly. "Am returning any day. Will message you from America." Is this likely to shake him? What odds will you give?

The Ark, seen from eye level, has the look of deftly woven fabric, like a basket for carrying produce. I imagine native women hoisting one on their shoulders. Massive columns at the corners might be the warp, holding the walls together. Ochre-colored like the baked landscape they rise from, the walls are the weft, an intricate weave of clay brick. But my domestic imagery is beguiling. In the square in front of the Ark, Charles Stoddart and Arthur Conolly, British colonials who'd offended Nasrullah Khan—they weren't aware that he thought himself Queen Victoria's equal—knelt down to die. Imams in the Friday mosque called *jami*, built at the top of the entrance ramp, watched with avidity.

The two officers spent their last days in the Zindon, a black hole behind the Ark closed with an iron grille. Almost worse than the snakes and scorpions were the lice infesting their bodies. Colonel Stoddart endured this confinement for three years before he died. Captain Conolly, as he had become, sailed from England to secure his release but followed him into prison. Khan Nasrullah, who delighted in tormenting them, a cat to their mice, might not have dared kill them except for the folly of the British army, simultaneously contemptuous of the Afghans and naive. The trap it stumbled into, when it retreated from Kabul on its way to India and was massacred to the last man but one, coincided with the imprisonment of Stoddart and Conolly. The khan, convinced by word of the Afghan triumph that he was dealing with a second-rate power, marched the prisoners out of their captivity and had them dig their own graves. Then, in the presence of a huge crowd, he had them beheaded.

Peter Hopkirk, in *The Great Game* (1990), his account of the Russian-British contest for control of the road to India, adds a poignant footnote to this story. Twenty years later a parcel came through the mail to Arthur Conolly's sister in London. It contained a prayer book that had evidently consoled him and Stoddart in the days of their captivity. On the endpapers and in the margins, a tiny hand recorded details of their long ordeal. The last of these entries ended in mid-sentence.

But the heart of darkness was also Bukhara-es-sharif, Bukhara the noble. On other cities, said the ancients, the light comes down from heaven, but it rose to the skies from Bukhara. In the ninth and tenth centuries, it gave the world a pantheon of disinterested thinkers, among them Avicenna the scientist and philosopher and Rudaki the poet. Muslims liken them to Newton and Shakespeare. How to assimilate these great men to the barbaric matrix that produced them is a problem. Evidently in Islam higher and lower, like good and evil, are less antitheses than complements. "Angel and brute man's wondrous leaven compose," wrote Rūmī. The convention I grew up with opposes man the thinking animal to the brutish lower orders, but the Muslim perception, possibly more acute, says that Avicenna and the rest are indivisibly both higher and lower.

Nasrullah Khan, known as "the Butcher," dwelt with beauty in Bukhara. Its sweet presence should have chastened him, but for reasons my psychology isn't big enough to cope with, it didn't. The history of Bukhara, like so much of Asia including the Indian subcontinent, is a tissue of unfathomable cruelty. Asians have a long memory, and I have heard people of color sigh for the good old days when the Union Jack flew from the governor's palace. With the governor, possibly a brute, you knew where you were. With the khan you knew nothing, except that his whim, striking terror in the hearts of his subjects, had no bounds. Tyranny a man can groan under and still live with, but with anarchy he can't live at all.

From the west facade of the Ark, the khan looked out on the street and on the tomb of Ismael Samani, founder of the Samanid line. Twelve hundred years ago, the Samanids inaugurated a golden age in Bukhara, and the tomb is its marvelous exemplar. The unadorned brick is strikingly plain, apparently nature's handiwork, not man's. This, of course, is part of its cunning. Though more than two meters thick, the baked terra-cotta walls have a volatile feel about them, and as the day dies and the shadows lengthen, they change in appearance, like that protean god who never holds his shape for long. The simple brick coffin that is the tomb's reason for being reminds us that even for princes "two paces of the vilest earth/Is room enough."

Much Islamic art and architecture finds a pattern in the Ismael Samani mausoleum. Its sense of strength comes from reining in, poles apart from the mindless letting go of the modern killers-by-suicide. Possibly the analogy is so sensational as to rob it of meaning, so let me, muttering a prayer, call it freakish and stick to aesthetics. The defining impulse I am trying for is evident in the refusal of the yellowing dome to get above itself, and in the humility of the miniature arches, feeling for earth like the Romanesque arch of the West. For an impulse opposed to the Romanesque, think of the great dome of St. Peter's, Rome, and the gothic arches of a church like Notre Dame de Paris, aching for heaven. These are the product of a different sensibility, a different kind of Christianity, a different vision of God and man.

Islam, being of magnitude, is necessarily many sided, like Christianity, and I find another side in the warren of shops and alleyways called *taqi-sarrafon,* just north of the Labi-i-hauz. In one of these shops, really no more than a hole in the wall, the garrulous vendor has elected me his partner in a game of intellectual ping pong. Weighing my saffron and spiced tea a grain at a time, he has an excuse to palaver. Ali is like his city, open faced with a devious heart, skeptical but intolerant, bent on salvation and given to sensual pleasure. Born in Herat over the border in Afghanistan, he talks up his birthplace like the Chamber of Commerce. "The cynosure of all eyes," it boasted half a million homes, twelve thousand shops, and six thousand hot baths. This was a city! "Let me tell you about its madrassas."

In what Ali says, true-to-life is less important than what the logicians call "satisfiable truth." He reminds me of those medieval scholars who put questions and answered them for the sake of exercising the mind. Is a man's fallen nature only sick, or is it dead? Does predestination occur involuntarily, ordained from outside us, or does it depend on foreknowledge? A world-famous physicist, Enrico Fermi, took great satisfaction in addressing questions like these. When he worked at Los Alamos, he kept running over rabbits on the road to and fro, and it pleased him to calculate, from the speed of his car and the mileage it covered, the number of rabbits in New Mexico. His colleagues, slightly bemused, spoke of "Fermi questions." I suspect that Avicenna, once resident in Bukhara, delighted in such intellectual sport for its own sake. At the same time and like his counterparts in the West, he took it seriously, play for mortal stakes. Perhaps much of Islam, its art and architecture, is explicable under the aspect of play. But all that is past tense.

Smiling at Ali, I hold out my tiny teacup, and he pours another dollop of tea. I am grateful for the tea in a land where my belly is always on the qui vive. Whenever food is put before it, sure to be a Trojan horse, it asks suspiciously, "Who goes there?"

Outside Ali's stall is Central Asia's oldest mosque, the Maghoki-Attar (Pit of the Herbalists), and one look at it is enough to make me swear off the generalizing habit. Clay brick and eggshell-colored, it casts down its eyes like a demure maiden, but no one would call this mosque humble. The majolica tiles on its corner towers clamor for attention, like the swastikas, an ancient symbol, on the arches. One scholar I read believes their four right angles represent the different stages of life. It isn't creeping with petty pace to the grave. The facade is wild with life, its writhing terra-cotta figures reminding me of rococo churches in Spain. Extravagance on such a scale raises questions. Perhaps it is saying that the surface is only surface, that is, unimportant, and you can do with it whatever you please. Underneath the surface is the meaning of life, and in this respect life is a river.

Defeating expectation, Bukhara's arches, though they don't soar like the Gothic arch, aspire to a point. Step by step its mihrabs are jagged. Simulating stalactites, they remember the cave where Muhammad hid himself on his flight from Mecca to Medina. The cave, like Islam, is multifold in sense, a dark declivity presenting things at their worst but also, as dark precedes day, the place where things begin climbing upward. The hero of the Hegira is a holy man whose dark heart is tumid with violence.

This man, who jumbles disparate things together but isn't a chaos, predicts the Muslim city. Bukhara is a medley of narrow, winding streets, few extending all the way through it, and of distinctive areas that feel closed off from each other, each with its own market and mosque. Compare the Byzantine city, Hellenistic in its origins, a chessboard of through roads and rectangular squares. Americans prefer the Byzantine model for its sense of order and proportion. But the Muslim city recalls the *discordia concors* or "discordant harmony" of an older psychology. Ella Christie, a traveler of sensibility, found that the cramped alleyways of Samarkand, as opposed to Venice's spacious piazzas, roused in her a livelier sense of reality. For that, we thank the proportions. St. Mark's, Venice, isolated in its grandeur, honors its Byzantine forebears. The Registan isn't isolated, or wasn't until Tamburlaine pulled down the old market. In its odd mixture of otherworldliness and mundanity—slender minarets and fluted domes mingling with the grave solidity of the environing madrassas—it is a bundle of contradictions, like life itself.

Cities on its scale, too big to be homogeneous, are more diverse but less finely tempered than their peers in the West. The Muslim aristocracy, both military and mercantile, was city-dwelling, unlike England's in the same period, and the cities it lived in exceeded in size anything in medieval Europe. Baghdad topped the list at three hundred thousand people, even Arab Cordoba reaching one hundred thousand in its glory years, around the beginning of the eleventh century. Typical Western cities, more properly towns, numbered just under or over sixty thousand, for example, fourteenth-century Paris and thirteenth-century Bologna. Rome in the same century was much smaller, only thirty-five thousand (G. E. Grunebaum, *Classical Islam,* 1963). The size of these communities limits their achievement, at the same time allowing for the uniformity of texture on which their more intense flowering depends.

Bukhara's most imposing monument, the Kalon, or Great Minaret, embodies this ambiguity of feeling and thought. First of all immense, it was once the world's tallest tower, until Kunya Urgench's exceeded it by a few cubits. Its complement, the Kalon Mosque, built in the fifteenth century, the interior finished early in the sixteenth, is able to house the city's entire male population. From the summit of the minaret beside it, four muezzins called the faithful to prayer, their cries echoing from the more than two hundred minarets in and around Bukhara. The Great One stood alone, rising forty-seven kilometers into the same atmosphere as Chartres Cathedral (built in the same twelfth century) and, on the other side of the world, Angkor Wat. But the Kalon architect, who labored triumphantly, died disappointed, "the flight of [his] fantasy" exceeding what he had made. All who try and fail because they are human will recognize a kindred spirit in him.

The minaret, tapering upward from its octagonal base, opens out like a collapsible spyglass. Its bands of lacy brickwork, one after another, terminate in a necklace of blue tile under the stalactite lantern. This blue majolica glaze gave the Timurid rulers—descendants of Tamburlaine—their great idea, and the Registan in Samarkand, incandescent with blue along the entire spectrum, is among its legatees. For almost nine hundred years, Bukhara's minaret has been both a watchtower and a beacon of hope. When exhausted travelers coming across the Kara-Kum Desert first glimpsed it, they knew journey's end was at hand. Impervious to earthquakes, it outlasted the Mongols. In the anecdote Genghis Khan bows in humility before it and, picking up his fallen hat, orders the Great Minaret spared. Of all that, Nasrullah Khan was innocent.

It had another name, the Tower of Death. On market days criminals suffered death "by jaculation," thrilling the ragtag multitude below. Made to climb the 105 steps to the top, they were sewed in a sack and thrown to oblivion. This aspect of Bukhara Nasrullah Khan took to heart. Initiating his reign with the beheading of his three younger brothers, he ended it by executing his wife and three daughters. He had them killed before his dying eyes, making sure they could never be other than chaste.

Surfeited with the khan and his fearful symmetry, I retreat to the grape arbor behind my hotel. It takes up much of the posterior courtyard, a gay place by night, bright with paper lanterns and music to dance by. This evening folk dancing is promised. I look forward to it passively, not caring to enter in or be got at. Go light on the verisimilitude, I'd tell them, if I were a pukka sahib.

The courtyard is a theater, chairs and little tables filling the mezzanine, the second story windows of the houses above and around us serving as the dress circle. Mulberry trees grow taller than the grapevines, lush Bukhara carpets hang from the windows, a scene faintly askew like an Impressionist painting. Happy faces in the crowd, grown slobbery with beer, salute the dancing girls in their gold-studded pants, gold hats, and shimmering tabards. The four-piece band is a string trio plus one. The mandolin, called the *rabab,* has six strings, the pair of guitars, a *dutar* and a *dombra,* only two. Bassing them, the drum or *doira* is like drums the world over, tying its ear to no tongue but its own. "Here's a dollar bill," I'd like to say to the *doira* man. "Go away!"

Much Uzbeki music is tuneless, but the West is a camel with its nose in the tent, and Tin Pan Alley tunes, golden oldies, have crept into the repertory. When the chorus line retires to the folding screen beside the stage, women in the audience get up to dance. They don't dance with men, only with each other, a creaky box step that resembles the fox-trot. Men in Central Asia dance only with men. Their dancing is more boisterous. In either case, however, the dance is formal. It doesn't release emotion, but faithful to another imperative, classically Islamic, it holds the emotions in check.

Bukhara's is the beauty of the spirit, according to a traditional saying, Samarkand's the beauty of earth. But this is too exclusive, and Bukhara makes a portmanteau where opposites jostle each other. Like fire and powder in Shakespeare's line, "which, as they kiss, consume," the explosion makes a third thing, decidedly worth having. Where the beauty of Samarkand is comprehended in a few intense foci, Bukhara's is dispersed. To get hold of the city, you must let it seep in by osmosis. For its beauty is everywhere, and its center is its circumference.

Shakespeare, describing an equivocal hero, calls him a "dove-feathered raven, ravening lamb," and the metaphor, an oxymoron, gives the sense of Bukhara. Depraved in morals like a beautiful woman gone to the bad, it gloried in gorgeous monuments that rise out of the most shameless sink of iniquity in the East. The nineteenth-century traveler Vámbéry said this. The only order it acknowledged was the axman's, a cat's-paw for the mullah or khan. The entertainments that pleased it most were cockfighting, gutter dentistry, and public executions. Against this embodied chaos, devotees of order proposed an "isotropic" world, the same in all directions. Something like that must be the point of the city's three "*kosh* ensembles," monumental structures placed opposite each other and describing a double or pair. The first pair, southwest of the Registan, compares and contrasts two sixteenth-century madrassas. Abdullah Khan was the builder, and one madrassa is named for him, the other, the Modar-i-Khan, for his mother (*modar* = mother). The difference between the two is obvious, but what the designer wants you to notice is sameness.

Readers may think of certain eighteenth-century buildings like Bath's Palladian Crescent or the line of palaces along the Neva in St. Petersburg. Partly we like to look at them because they repeat while varying the same pattern. Also these architectural wonders confess a passion for order, and that, it seems to me, is the primary source of their attraction, as if they are responding to something innate in our being. But the *kosh* ensemble, insisting on stasis, is less ordered than moribund. Where life, by contrast, is infinitely varied, this ensemble collapses variation in favor of a static world in which the rivers never run to the sea. I think it suggests an Islam from which poise is departing. That isn't the same as getting rid of mere messiness.

Bukhara's main pairing, a mosque and madrassa, stand side by side at the foot of the Great Minaret and look to me like sundered halves. Meeting expectation, the minaret has its mosque, a Friday or *jami* mosque. Colonnaded arcades, flowing like waves, support its little cupolas, almost three hundred of them. A plaza, the Poi Kalon, or Pedestal of the Great One, ties this Kalon Mosque to the Mir-i-Arab (Prince of the Arabs) Madrassa, among Islam's bravest monuments to learning. We might say of Harvard, judiciously lowering its immense self-esteem, that it is the Mir-i-Arab of Cambridge, Mass.

The madrassa takes its name from the friend and adviser of the Shaybani Khan who built it. Both friends are buried under the blue-domed *darskhana* or lecture hall, their tombs marked by the goat's tail and white flag of sainthood. Five hundred years ago, one or the other (my sources aren't clear) made a fortune in the slave trade. He was an equivocal saint. But guilt ate away at him, and the madrassa is his act of atonement.

Confronting it and its twin, I see an Islam verging on decline. Characteristically, classical Islam rejects perfect symmetry. (Readers may think of the unmatched towers of Chartres Cathedral.) Only Allah is perfect, and perfection is reserved to Him. But in this pairing of mosque and madrassa, symmetry is the seductive goal that beckons. It says that diminishing differences is better than aggrandizing them. This new or newly emergent psychology is like the art of trompe l'oeil, not more ordered than nature but evacuated of it. Against the natural world, always a little disheveled, it prefers a kempt and airless world of formal landscapes so severe they hardly breathe, or of dead languages that would rather be dead than suffer a solecism.

Bukhara's third *kosh* ensemble, two madrassas that face each other northeast of the Great Minaret, bears out these generalizations. One looks to the past, the other to the future. My reactionary viewpoint says that the older one most merits attention. Ulug Beg, Tamburlaine's extraordinary grandson, an architect, astronomer, and cultural hero, created it in 1417. The second structure, the work of Abdul Aziz Khan, dates from two centuries later. Completing the *kosh* ensemble, it yearns for a less comprehensive psychology than its predecessor's, a psychology in which variables, if any, are few.

The idea of an ensemble could not have occurred to Ulug Beg. His building is autonomous, suiting a free spirit. Words inscribed on the entrance portal put him before us: "It is the sacred duty of every Muslim man and woman to seek after knowledge." This gives the quietus to conventional notions of benighted Islam. My reading of classical Islam suggests a mingled yarn like the medieval Christian, often nay-saying but always inquisitive, rational but emotional, on the one hand St. Thomas, no thinker more subtle, on the other St. Bonaventura, whose illumination is of the heart.

But classical is poised, and now the poise begins to falter. An image for what is happening is that of a sea captain battening down the hatches, fearing disorders to come. As the fear waxes, Islam, new style, seeks to true up all the lines, denying the chance for exceptions. Abdul Aziz Khan's completing of the ensemble begun by Ulug Beg offers an illustration. In its mode of reading the world, stricture and codification are up front. It aims to replace the all-acceptive psychology that lets all the creatures into the Ark.

Meanwhile, atop the Kalon Mosque across the plaza, messy life is supplementing and correcting the breathless order of art. Thrusting up from the mosque's western end, the huge blue dome seems to support a cylindrical pile of black rubbish, enough to fill a dump truck. I am looking at a stork's nest, left over from the time when flocks of the great birds migrated to Bukhara from Egypt. They came back every year, bringing good luck. But the Soviets, those connoisseurs of a sclerotic order, put a stop to the annual migration. Draining the pools, they took away the insects and the stagnant water, just right for a stork.

8

Khiva and the Pot of Basil

The desert has a new skin west of Bukhara. Sloughing its old one, it teems with noisy life, birdcalls in the near distance, gophers and foxes flitting across the sands. Deeper in are lowing cattle, heard before seen. A beaten path, obviously trod by man, leads toward them but breaks off, whisked away by magic. The calcareous soil turns sandy, its color changing from grayish white to red. Clusters of huts materialize, squatting on the desert floor like "black houses" in rural Scotland, low structures that merge with earth, the sod a blanket laid on their roofs. All this detail seems to argue a controlling presence in things, remembering the poet's "mighty maze but not without a plan." Perhaps, however, there is no plan, and I am only rehearsing that old epistemological rag, the Christian version I was raised on.

Perched on a sand dune is a hand-lettered sign, pointing vaguely westward. Wanting to read it, I turn the car in that direction. The sign is like a bottle in the water, some forlorn castaway's. This may be more of the activity I'm prone to, dreaming a form on the void, though I can almost see the man who wrote the sign, a remittance man on his last legs. The footprints disappearing in sand belong to him. His canteen is nearly empty, fever hollows his cheeks. On a ribbon around his neck is a monocle, souvenir of better days. Looking at his map, he scrawls the message: "Amu Darya 60 KM."

The great river divides Uzbekistan on the north from Turkmenistan on the south. Alexander the Great crossed it on his way to the conquest of Asia, and I am close on his heels. But I want to interrupt my journey and drop a line in the water. Catfish, known as *lakkh,* live in the water, growing, I have read, up to two meters long. Some weigh more than 120 kilograms, going on

300 pounds. The river that nourished these monsters was deep, fast flowing, and nearly a mile from bank to bank. Alexander couldn't drive piles into its sandy bottom; he couldn't construct a bridge or transport his men by ferry, his enemies, the Sogdians, having destroyed all the boats. But he had a fertile brain and a stout heart. Emulating the Persian Emperor Darius, who had defeated Nebuchadnezzar by crossing the Tigris on inflated animal hides, he filled his tents with straw, stitched them up tight, and got the army over the river on their skins.

Alexander's Patroclus was Hephaestion, a soldier like himself; his Helen a Bactrian princess, Roxana, said by the Macedonians to be the East's most beautiful woman. Each side of him, the ham-fisted male and softer female, play into his story. In retaliation for 2,000 of his own surprised and killed by the Sogdians, he massacred 120,000 of them. But surveying the land with an eye to enhancing it, he founded many more cities than other conquerors destroyed. When his friend of friends, Hephaestion, died, he crucified the doctor who had ministered to him, and his soldiers rued the way he drove them, even to the ends of the earth. But few before him had ever penetrated to India, a fairy-tale land, and he gave it as a gift to the meanest of his men. So his nature was bifold, a "concordant discord," one part modifying but also validating the other. Nothing in the sands recalls him, or the Turks, Sogdians, Scythians, and Mongols who came later. All are gone where time keeps the hours. But Alexander, mingling two parts in one person, has more "thickness" than his successors, a reason he still lives in our minds.

Our industrial society, creator of rubbish that never dies, has its legacy too. The scurf of modern life litters the desert beside the highway, abandoned tires, plastic bags, throwaway cans that crush if you squeeze them, a Styrofoam cup. The desert seems lonelier for these hints of our civilization, or am I "anthropomorphizing" the world in our image and likeness, a habit of intellectuals who endow it with feelings it can hardly possess? Wanting to relieve the emptiness, I pop a CD of Uzbeki music into the player. I am looking for ruins, a crop that doesn't fail in this land that's older than time, and the music suits my brooding on last things. Ruins bid me think of my end. Like good works to the elect, though, they constitute the visible sign of salvation to a traveler in distant lands.

Today I hope to be saved. I am heading for Khiva, or what is left of it, partly a ruin, partly reconstructed. The desert outside Khiva, known as the Kyzyl-Kum, is scantily clothed with saxaul shrub and brown grass. In spring a soft, rank-smelling weed puts out blossoms, but they die and rot within days. Beneath this disagreeable plant lurk scorpions and tarantulas, even serpents, some the size of a man. "Look like the innocent flower," says Lady Macbeth, "but be the serpent under it," a good rubric for the desert. Strewn about it are the corpses of camels, left to rot unburied.

In daytime the sands, agitated by the sun's burning heat, throw up images of trees and water. The traveler who is beguiled by them may wander aimlessly for days, until he and his horse sink exhausted to die. And yet there is something "witching" in the long marches across the glowing cinder. The word is J. A. MacGahan's, the *New York Herald* correspondent who wrote a book about the fall of Khiva (1874). To get his story, he had to cross a pair of deserts, a tale in itself. "The dreamy, weary noon reposes, the fresh cool of evening when you throw yourself on the sand and watch the stars come out, and the round red moon slowly rise"—all this induced a sense of freedom from the humdrum of daily life. MacGahan, like the Sufi mystic, said the silence was sublime.

Further east he crossed the heartland's other great river, the Syr-Darya. Tamburlaine and his huge army, en route to China, had got that far, battling the savage winter that took his life. But spring was in the air as MacGahan approached the river, and everywhere the Kyrgyz herdsmen with their tents and camels were on their annual migration northward. Wildflowers had begun to bloom as he entered the Kara-Kum Desert, twin to the Kyzyl-Kum he had yet to experience. Slowly he plodded on until at last he saw, from the top of a dune, "the dark-blue waters of the Aral Sea, lying in the midst of the waste of yellow sands, and glimmering in the sun like a turquoise set in gold."

Matthew Arnold indulged the same romantic strain, appropriate, he thought, to its subject, in the ending of *Sohrab and Rustum*. Father and son die together beside the Oxus, but the majestic river floats on, seeking its destination. "At last, / The long'd-for dash of waves is heard, and wide/His luminous home of waters opens, bright / And tranquil, from whose floor the new-bath'd stars / Emerge, and shine upon the Aral Sea." The stars don't emerge from the water, they only seem to, and this is appropriate as well, suiting its magical power.

The land beside the highway is alive, much of it cultivated with cotton. But I see a long phalanx of rice paddies, always restful to the eye, even moving, especially if men and women are out in the fields. They are pale and diminished against the viscous green of the landscape, in which they are submerged like fish in the sea. But they are working with a will, to my sense on the side of life, not against it. Storied cities have taken root in the paper-thin soil, arid except when the river floods and renews it. They flourish for some centuries, then sink back nervelessly. Khiva repeats this pattern with a difference.

People have lived hereabout—in Khorezm, the name of the surrounding country—for six millennia, sustained by the silt-laden waters of the Amu-Darya. Rising every year, they bestow a fugitive life on the red sands and black sands that hem the river in like a mirage. This transient smear of green guarantees a permanent population grouping together somewhere in the vicinity. Since the end of the sixteenth century, Khiva has been the capital of Khorezm, though it is relatively small, rarely bigger than forty thousand people. Today it is less a real city than a museum. The inner town, "Itchan Qala," is the hole in the doughnut around it. Its walls, more than forty feet high, enclose a cross-section of Islamic architecture. Under the Samanid dynasty (892–999 A.D.), an architectural renaissance flourished in Khorezm, penetrating eastward into Transoxiana and Afghanistan. Bukhara and Samarkand bear its impress, notably in Bukhara's simple and memorable tomb of Ismail Samani. One of Islam's great triumphs, its dome sits on the squinches, the concentrically wider arches that accommodate its round superstructure to a square base, as if placed there by nature. The glazed wicker of the walls, almost a replica of the sun gleaming off them, seems to have dropped down from heaven. This swapping back and forth of art and nature is evident in the Itchan Qala wherever I turn.

But where does this style come from? What inspired the cruciform mosque, like the Friday Mosque in Isfahan, the high vaulted niches in each of the four walls of the court, the revetments (retaining walls) of glazed tiles, the domed tomb chambers like Tamburlaine's? I think I have an answer, worked out in making the book. When I went to India for the first time, I found it hard to match its unique-seeming architecture with anything in my previous experience. It appeared to spring from air, and I needed a missing link to account for the continuities I sensed but couldn't pin down. The link, I see now, was Persia, going back to the Achaemenids and Darius the Great. In the sixth century B.C., he conquered Northern India. An empire list exhibited at the royal palace in Persepolis and mentioning the River Indus pinpoints this early date.

Two centuries later Alexander the Great reached the northwest frontier and conquered much of the Punjab. The principal legacy of these European invasions is the art of Gandhara, now Pakistan. Darius spent the winter of 517 in Gandhara, preparing for the Indian war. The Achaemenids named this easternmost acquisition the land "beyond the mountains." Indians themselves called it Gandhara. They were cousins of the Persians, they seem to have thought, and after Persia disappeared as a great power, India became its logical extension. Something like the same changing of the guard describes the transfer of real and noumenal power from the First Rome to the second and third. When Persian, Greek, and Indian culture flowed together, a hybrid resulted, Greco-Buddhist art.

Gandharan sculpture represents the Buddha in human form, and depicting stories of his life (*jataka*) suggests real people, not types. Asoka the Great (c. 272–32 B.C.) gave it its chief impetus, fostering an art more clearly derived from nature. Historians have a name for the piece of India/Pakistan/Afghanistan where it flourished: the Kushan empire. Straddling either side of the midcourse of the Oxus, it stretched from Delhi to Khorezm in the early centuries A.D. At its peak, in the second century, it encompassed Sogdiana, Bactria, Pakistan, Northern India, and possibly Kashmir. To ancient writers it seemed as powerful as Rome and Parthia. The art it created, blending Indian and Hellenic strains, seems to me astounding. Why is so much that is wonderful almost unknown to the world?

For example the gold reliquary of the first century A.D. discovered in eastern Afghanistan. Buddhas and bodhisattvas encircle the reliquary casket, 6.5 centimeters high. Corinthian columns separate them, each supporting an arch. Between each arch is an eagle on the wing. In a frieze depicting the Buddha's previous incarnations, six nubile young women dance happily with one another. Other sculptures, chiseled from red sandstone, show young men and women engaged in erotic play. In a masterful rendering of a Bacchanalian scene, a courtesan with great thighs and swelling breasts falls to the floor in a near-drunken stupor. But this powerfully sensual work is remote from grossness, and in all that I have knowledge of, tact characterizes the art of Gandhara.

In different manifestations, some architectural, others simply objets d'art, most taking off from religion but at the same time superbly mundane, Gandharan art continued on its course for hundreds of years. All the while Islam, a different kind of art committed to the abstract, was moving inexorably eastward. Kushan artisans must have known what was coming their way but worked on serenely right up until the stunning appearance of the new dispensation in the late seventh and early eighth centuries. Then, within a hundred years, the activity of the artists, Buddhist and Hindu alike—and their kindred spirits the monks—ceased to be.

THE ARTISTIC RENAISSANCE that washed up in Khiva is described by a common aesthetic. I call it Persian. I want a new synthetic term to describe yet another new incarnation, not the same as Greco-Buddhist art, and *Persian* fits the bill. Persia (Iran), waxing and waning in size and power over the centuries, has always been profoundly "irredentist," casting covetous eyes on its neighbors, and its impact on the culture of Islam is immense. Not content with their land, it wanted to replace their mind-set with its own. This accounts for the ubiquity of the Persian style. I detect it in mosques, madrassas, covered bazaars (*tok*), forts (*arks*), tombs, bathhouses (*hammam*), shopping arcades (*tim*), and caravansaries (*rabat*)—Sultan Sanjar built a huge one in the desert between Samarkand and Bukhara—also in manuscript painting, calligraphy, carpets, and ceramics. An appendix in Henri Stierlin's *Islamic Art and Architecture* (2002) lists and describes some of these buildings and works of art. First appearing about 900 A.D., the Persian style strengthened over time, persisting into the eighteenth century. It reached its terminus ad quem in the reign of the Persian usurper Nader Shah, who seized power in the 1740s. A few "outliers" bring the style in its decline forward as late as the twentieth century.

Tamburlaine, like his son Shah Rukh and grandson Ulug Beg, is a devotee of this style. Not a mere killer, he was determined "to build a Masjed-i-Jami [Friday Mosque] in Samarkand which should be without a rival in any country." The mark of Persia is on it, as on the columned porches called *talar,* a reminiscence of the Achaemenids, and on the elongated entrance portals, tall enough to catch the prevailing winds and distribute them through the buildings below. The *iwan,* a barrel-vaulted hall, opens on a courtyard and, when multiplied by four, makes a design critical for the future. The squinch, its interior corners indispensable to the repertory, cradles the weight above them while concealing its function. Surfaces that reflect the Persian style are frequently adorned with tile work, mingling lapis lazuli and turquoise ("color of the Turks") to create a third color called, not surprisingly, "Persian blue."

In Khiva the staple tiles are greenish-blue, in Samarkand blue, in Bukhara brown. But wherever the eye moves, exuberant color is the rule. Its use in Khiva's decorative art is first of all to brighten abstractions, geometric or star-shaped, as in Samarkand, whose ruler, Ulug Beg, was a passionate astronomer. Color is more than natural in the stylized flowers called *girikh* and the elegant calligraphy, either the square Kufic script or the scrolling and foliated Thuluth. The finest tiles are enameled; a step down in quality is the luster faience or glazed terra-cotta. A name worth recalling among architects working with enamel brick and mosaic faience is Qavar ad-Din of Shiraz, one of Islam's great men.

That all these specimens of artistic cunning should have coalesced in Khiva was hardly inevitable. In the beginning it functioned merely as a caravan stop on the Silk Road, funneling traffic north to Russia via the Caspian Sea. Almost until modern times, huge strings of camels, some numbering as many as four thousand head, slaked their thirst at its oasis before resuming the endless journey. Closing my eyes for an instant, I can hear the tinkling of their bells. An easterly route, skirting the shrine of the Sufi master Bakhautdin Naskshbandi, led the camel train to Bukhara. There a spur of the great road went north into Mongolia, after that on a long, sloping diagonal to Beijing. Merv was the major transit point to the south, and Kunya-Urgench to the west. (The latter has nothing in common with Urgench, my way station to Khiva, except the name.)

But Khiva was never more than a minor entrepôt, and as the Silk Road withered, its reason for being became problematic. Over the centuries it ceased to be known as a welcoming respite, segueing into a locus for nomads and wandering cutthroats. Soviet archaeologists changed that. Their intervention might have been calamitous, as modern restoring often is. Think St. Paul's–outside-the-Walls, one of Rome's principal basilicas until the fire of 1823 left only its mosaics and the triumphal arch. The church, sparing no expense, put it back together but lost much of its medieval soul in the process. Khiva's restoration runs this risk, and those who say it is too perfect are right. But Khiva would have succumbed to the desert had the heavy hand of the state not forced it to put on a semblance of its former self. So two cheers for the Soviet archaeologists. Modern Amphions, they commanded the tumbled walls of the city to rise.

That Khiva came into being in the first place is owing to nature's casual goodwill. In the dim past, says tradition, Shem, son of Noah, athirst in the desert, stumbled on an oasis, the same one I'm after. "Khei-vakh!" he cried. "What wonderful water is in the well!," and founded the first version of Khiva. Within its narrow circuit of mud brick, the ardent spirit of Islam, a wonder-working djinn, achieved a stunning crystallization. Uttering the right words as it waved its wand, it brought a complete city into being, looking now as it must have looked a thousand years ago.

Ármin Vámbéry, a connoisseur of things past, saw it at a distance in the later nineteenth century, "surrounded by gardens and surmounted by its many towers and cupolas." The young Russian officer Nikolai Muraviev, sent out from St. Petersburg to reconnoiter, remarked on its same prosperous aura a century before. He remembered the golden ball that crowned the blue-tiled dome of the mosque and gleamed as the sun reflected off it. My take is somewhat different. To me Khiva seems a place where men's brows are furrowed, intent on study or gain, and the closely packed buildings call to mind lower Manhattan just above Battery Park. A disproportionate number of these buildings are madrassas or colleges—I count sixteen; my guidebook says twenty-two—befitting a center of Muslim theology. The people who lived here loved learning more than nature. Today it seems that nobody lives here. The modern city, shorn of its greenery and without the glad sense of nature's breezes that blow where they list, feels as if a vacuum cleaner has sucked out the air and a glass dome been lowered over the buildings. In no city I know are the component parts so precisely fitted or so exquisitely clean. A Disney World might have been dropped down in Central Asia. But that sounds dismissive, and despite the antiseptic look, Khiva is the real thing.

I concentrate on that part of it enclosed within the Itchan Qala, and for convenience's sake locate its major monuments along the city's major axis. That is or was Karl Marx Street, running between the east and west gates in the wall. Inside the west gate, the sawed-off tower should have been grander, judging from the enormous base, but the money ran out or energy flagged. Some say the khan declined to complete it when he realized that his new minaret would look down on his harem and the muezzin look in on his wives. What is left of this Kalon Minor minaret is a stump, like the foot and ankle of the Emperor Constantine in the museum atop Rome's Capitoline Hill. It seems a survival from the antediluvian age. "There were giants in the earth in those days."

Facing the minaret across Karla Marxa Ulitsa is the Kukhna Ark, "Old Citadel," a twelfth-century fortress where the khan lived with his concubines and his stable of boys. The boys, called *bacha,* were dancers and sexually went both ways. When the women bored, they were summoned as replacements, entertaining both their master and his guests. He had more than one residence and liked to go a royal "progress" from one to another. In the Tash Khauli (Stone) Palace, his four legal wives, female relatives, and Persian serving girls were quartered together. He had the pick of the lot.

AMONG THE BUILDINGS the Persian style created in Khiva, the Tash Khauli Palace is exemplary, generous in form, even lavish. To me it suggests a huge accordion, expanding into three courts and parceling out its functions among them. The smallest, Ishrat-Khauli in the southeast corner, was for ceremonial occasions, like formal banquets. Arz-Khauli in the southwest corner dispensed justice and needed a pair of gateways, one for acquittal, the other for those condemned to die. The harem was accessible through the third and largest court via a secret corridor, the *dolom.* Only the khan could walk that way. What did that do for his libido? His sense of himself? Color and design figure importantly and were meant to dazzle his eyes. Blue and white majolica tiles cover the walls of the palace's five north-facing *iwans* and the pillars that hold up the vaulted ceilings. Like nature this style abhors a vacuum.

The palace spread itself in 150 rooms, each with its lofty ceiling and so configured as to catch even the most fugitive breeze. The famous khan who built it didn't care to be uncomfortably warm. Wanting to get forward with the work, he executed its architect when he failed to finish in the two years allotted him. In the event the job took eight years and many more lives than one, most of them slaves. The interior is brightened by China blue tile, a vitrified ceramic, work of a master. Carved wooden pillars that stand on carved marble bases support the handsome painted ceiling. Beauty springs from license; beauty and license are yoked together. Consummate artistry complemented by our darker side seems a hallmark of the Persian style.

I walk the long southwestern diagonal that leads to the earliest known building in Khiva, the tomb of the Sufi master Sayid Allah ad Din (died 1303 A.D.). Like the Tash Khauli Palace, it transcends its explicit purpose, and a mosque is attached to the mausoleum. *Austere* is the word for this funerary complex. But majolica tiling lightens the place of death, and it isn't easily pinned down. Focus should go to the interpenetrating of opposites, close to the heart of Islam. Despite the character often assigned it, it isn't "dichotomous" but, like any considerable culture, mingles black and white to create a third medium, different from either. Khiva was under the Golden Horde when the tomb was erected in the first decade of the fourteenth century, and it illuminates a side of the Mongols not always honored. Infamous in war, in peace they were masterful builders.

As I move back up the dusty street toward the East gate and the Tash Khauli Palace, I become aware of the Allah Kuii Khan caravansary blotting half the sky above my head. Today this two-story hostel as it was is the Univermag, Khiva's low-budget department store. There is symmetry in that, the present resuming the past with a difference. Not just coincidentally the madrassa that bears the khan's name, dating from 1882–83, constitutes one-half of a *kosh* ensemble, the portent of decadence to come. Its partner, directly to the south and completing the ensemble, is the Kutlugh Murad Inak. The portals of the two buildings, facing each other on either side of a square, are taking order with nature, hoping to make it like art.

The war correspondent J. A. MacGahan was present at the fall of Khiva and lets us feel what this meant. The hour was midnight, and he stood on the roof of the Tash Khauli Palace. "The silent, sleeping city lay bathed in a flood of moonlight. The flat mud roofs [of the palace] had turned to marble; the tall slender minarets rose dim and indistinct, like sceptred sentinels watching over the city. . . . The exterior walls . . . with battlements and towers . . . [looked] in the misty moonlight as high as the sky and as distant as the horizon." The city has been transformed, no longer real "but a leaf torn from the enchanted pages of the Arabian Nights."

Far from enchanted, the city was hunkered down behind high mud walls, battlemented with round buttresses. A ditch half filled with water encircled it. The Russian besiegers saw the tips of trees and spires of minarets standing over the walls, most noticeably the badgirs—wind tunnels—reflecting the sun's rays like porcelain. The badgirs, located invariably on the south side of the houses and facing north, ascended from a high porch eight or ten feet above the surrounding walls, driving the wind down the way a wind sail does aboard ship.

MacGahan, among the besiegers, remembered the ragged inhabitants bowing fearfully as the victorious Russians entered the city. He found it a miserable place, and so, very likely, it was. But imagination, set to work on some of the buildings, is able to transform them. The Kukna Ark, oldest of Khiva's palaces, belongs in the Bad Lands, or the Sahara of the French Foreign Legion. How anyone got in when the gates were shut, especially with guns pointed at them from above, is the stuff of an old black and white movie. Eduardo Cianelli stars as the Mahdi. The mud-brick walls, bulging with their semicircular towers, follow a pattern of defensive fortification that goes back to Alexander the Great. If they held off the enemy in his day, the khan supposed, they would do the same for him, and he and his elite waited in confidence for the relief column to appear over the sands. But they didn't reckon on gunpowder, and it blew the walls down.

The underground pillars of the Ark's Djuma Mosque are antediluvian but have been rebuilt many times. At least nine rows of them occupy the cavernous hall, pierced by a skylight admitting a few rays of the sun. They stand in semidarkness, and I reach out to touch them, like a child craving assurance. The flat wooden roof, resembling a chair caned with rattan, is crossed at right angles by heavy beams that filter the light. All the pillars are carved, each one unique, and ascend from stone pedestals. A petrified forest, it seems to go on forever, like Istanbul's Underground Cistern, where defeated Byzantium waits for time to restore its old glory. Since this is a mosque, it has a mihrab, the carved niche in the wall facing Mecca. Dead white and lacking ornamentation, it is simplicity itself, unlike the pillars around it.

Kneeling in its concave recess, the khan spoke to his God. Vámbéry, watching surreptitiously, said he revealed in every feature "the debauched, worn-out, dull-minded, inhuman tyrant; his eyes . . . sunken, his lips of a pallid white." Sycophancy was the road to his heart, and he bestowed brightly colored silks, divided in four groups called "heads," on his favorite toadies. That these were rewards was clear, but for what? Vámbéry got his answer when, one day, a hundred horsemen galloped into the city, each with a sack thrown across his saddle. In the presence of the khan, they removed the sacks, and taking hold of the two sides of the end, spilled the contents on the ground the way we spill out potatoes.

"But these were human heads, the heads of slaughtered enemies, which were rolling at the foot of the official who wrote down their number." Kicking the heads into a heap, he handed each horseman a receipt, redeemable for a special suit of honor. The suits or heads varied from four to twelve or twenty or forty, "as the case may be." The more heads, the more elaborate the honor.

At the eastern end of the Ark, the parapets, pushing out from the flat surface of the wall, might be occasioned by the groans of malefactors, paying their debt to society. My description, though fanciful, can't be far off. Vámbéry, inspecting the *zindon,* or jail, saw eight of its inhabitants, old men, having their eyes gouged out while their tormentor wiped his knife on their beards. Capt. Frederick Burnaby, the British cavalry officer who wrote the thrilling *Ride to Khiva* (1876), wondered what happened if a culprit stayed firm in his denials of wrongdoing. "We beat him with rods," said the royal vizier, "put salt in his mouth, and expose him to the burning rays of the sun." Sooner or later, he tells them what they want to hear.

I divert the course of my narrative to salute Captain Burnaby, a man strong enough to carry a pony under each arm. Educated at Harrow and fluent in French, Italian, German, Russian, and Spanish, he used a working knowledge of Turkish and Arabic to get himself a billet in Central Asia. War was his meat and drink. When things quieted down in Khiva, he moved his restless giant's frame to Africa and friendship with Chinese Gordon, soon to find a hero's death in Khartoum. On January 17, 1885, he died, at the age of forty-two, fighting in hand-to-hand combat in the Sudan. He and seventy-five of his mates are buried under the sands, around them the bodies of eleven hundred of the enemy.

SURE TO MAKE A STRONG MAN SHUDDER, Khiva's slave market lies at the other end of Karl Marx Street. Central Asia's largest, it traded in human flesh, including the flesh of kidnapped Russians, for three hundred years. Entrance is through the east gate, a long, vaulted passage lined by recessed cells and closed off at intervals by enormous carved doors. The outer gates served as bulletin boards for posting public decrees, also as the site of executions and the punishment of runaway slaves. Their ears nailed to the gates, they stood there to the common gaze, objects of derision, not pity. Impalement was the fate of some, those who suffered it often taking two days to die. The khan thought smoking and drinking alcohol immoral, and offenders, if convicted of either, had their mouths slit open from ear to ear. This created a permanent grin like our symbol for happiness.

Well into the nineteenth century, long after William Wilberforce persuaded England's Parliament to abolish the slave trade, it continued to flourish in Khiva. The trade was lucrative, Russians making the best candidates for servitude. They were big-boned and said by Muslims to be naturally servile. Slavs were synonymous with slaves. In 1840 Richmond Shakespear, another of those intrepid British officers whose gallantry covers many of the nineteenth-century's sins, freed Khiva's Russian slaves and most of the others. In my imagination, however, I remain imprisoned in one of those dank cells off the tunnel. Coming out of darkness, I feel my feet on the sand, sun-drenched and blood-soaked, where spectators are waiting to turn thumbs up or down.

Beginning in the reign of Peter the Great, Russia sought to get rid of this unspeakable place. It sent a military expedition in 1717 under Prince Bekovich, who responded agreeably to the khan's suggestion that he billet his men in the surrounding countryside. That way they'd be less cramped for room, said his solicitous host. All had their throats cut, and the head of Bekovich went back to the czar. This brew of cruelty and deceit and the pleasure taken in them stabs the heart of Central Asia.

The brew might have bubbled for many years more, but in 1840 a pair of British officers, courageous beyond thought, demanded that the khan set free Khiva's slaves. The Russians had sent their own emissary, Captain Muraviev, in 1819. Riding through the city's narrow streets alone, he was appalled when fellow Russians, kidnapped long ago, crowded about his horse's flanks and begged him in whispers to bring them home. The memory of those pitiful souls haunted the young officer for the rest of his life. But his mission was a failure.

Following in his tracks, Capt. William Abbott set out for Khiva on Christmas Eve, 1859. His journey across the desert coincided with the long-awaited Russian attack on the city, intended solely, if you believed St. Petersburg, to free its three thousand Russian slaves. The thirty thousand Persians and Kurds imprisoned with them were a gratuity. But snow and unprecedented cold took a dreadful toll on the Cossacks and their ten thousand camels. Vermin covered the men, scurvy winnowed their ranks, the camels died at the rate of a hundred a day. In the early winter of 1840, General Vasily Alekseevich Perovsky gave the order to turn back. Before the army reached its starting point, seven months after leaving it, a fifth of the men had died without having fired a shot.

Abbott, unaware of the disaster to Russian arms, only of the Russian threat, carried a self-serving message from his superiors. Were the khan to free the slaves himself, he would explode St. Petersburg's pretext and spare his city from being put to the sword. But as Abbott entered Khiva in his

British regimentals, he got news that seemed to undercut him and his mission. A pair of Europeans, nationality unknown, had been there before him. Tortured with red-hot skewers, their throats slit, they had been thrown into the desert, food for jackals. The khan no doubt enjoyed dangling the prospect of such a fate before his visitor. Otherwise he did nothing, content to watch the running sands in the glass.

Meanwhile England, growing restless, dispatched a second ambassador to light a fire under the first. Lt. Richmond Shakespear was twenty-eight and not a man to take no for an answer. Incredibly Shakespear succeeded. The khan issued an edict, and this British political officer who had never been to war was suddenly in charge of three hundred males, eighteen females, and eleven children. The men who were to be freed had been slaves for ten years on average, the women seventeen, long enough to roil the negotiation. Some of the khan's subjects, having paid twenty pounds and more for a well-built bondsman, declined to surrender him. Heated representations followed, and person by person Lieutenant Shakespear whittled down the number of those still being held back. At last he reduced it to one, a young girl.

Her mother was distraught at the idea of leaving this child behind. The lieutenant, though sympathetic, knew that his delicate mission, and with it the freeing of so many, might founder on the issue of one. But he decided he must make her an issue. I imagine him remembering his schoolboy Cicero. "Civis Romanus sum," he said he was, a servant of the world's greatest power. The girl must be set free! She had no desire to leave her home in the palace, his palace, the khan retorted. Shakespear said she was too young to decide that. Furious but frustrated, the khan turned to his vizier. "Give him the child!" Shakespear had seldom seen a more beautiful girl, he wrote in his diary. He supposed she had been destined for the khan's personal use.

Like Xenophon he led his band of survivors, now 416 in all, out of the wilderness, in his case as far as St. Petersburg for an audience with royalty. Khiva's ruler had stipulated that he achieve this, a condition of emancipating his captives. The czar thanked him profusely and called off the invading army. In private he was incensed at the Englishman's intervention. For as England had counted on, it meant an end for the time being to Russia's designs on the independence of Khiva. Back in London Shakespear was knighted by Queen Victoria, a girl on the throne even younger than he was. Abbott, the bridesmaid in this story, had to wait for his reward. In time, however, he became a general, and a town in northern Pakistan, Abbottabad, bears his name.

Early in the twenty-first century, the terrorist Osama bin Laden ended his life there, run to ground by American soldiers.

THE KUKNA ARK bore impassive witness to the slave trade in Khiva. For posterity, though not for the wretched protagonists, the misery is palliated by the art that went with it, an unexpected increment. Artisans of high quality worked on the Ark, tiling the facade and inlaying the interior walls or incising their plastered surface. The carving and painting of the plaster is ganch work, one of their notable triumphs. Estimating the skill that went into it, I am witness myself to the startling conjunction of beauty and horror. The effect, or the cause of the effect, is like that of Keats's macabre poem, "Isabella; or, the Pot of Basil." Under the luxurious plant, fertilizing its growth, is the skull of the heroine's dead lover.

Khiva's artisans, chiseling the wood on the doors, aimed to reveal the spirit within. They weren't elaborating, in theory, at least, but setting the spirit free. The statues of Michelangelo honor this aesthetic, and the work of both in its reading of the world is Platonic. It says that what is important lies under the surface, not perceptible to the senses: sight, hearing, taste, or smell. Willingness to equate the surface with "superficies," things of little account on the way to some better thing, seems a key to much cruelty. "If I gouge out your eyes," the torturer might tell his victim, "I don't hurt you where you really live." The proposition that what's up front doesn't count holds for Islam and for Plato and his epigones too.

But how to explain the immense beauty of Islamic tile work and ganch work? Perhaps the artisans were giving a loose to their spirits, decorating with abandon while supposing that what they did was merest decoration. The idea affronts me, but I put it out as a hypothesis. I find the coffered ceiling in the khan's throne room amazing, but perhaps he, unlike me, had no eye for superficies. When winter arrived he quit his civilized interior, setting up his yurt on a raised brick platform in the courtyard. Outside in the weather, he remembered where he came from.

Equidistant between the east and south gates, the Islam Khodja Madrassa and minaret is tiled in bands of red and turquoise, the minaret itself rivaling in height the Kalon or "great" minaret in Bukhara, Central Asia's tallest. Edgar Knobloch, the archaeologist, calls it the last significant architectural achievement in this part of the world. In back of it, to the west, I find Khiva's most nearly perfect structure, the Pakhlavan Makhmud Ensemble. Its cupola rises from an octagonal base over a rectangular main chamber, a faithful replicating of the convention we meet in Samarkand. Green is the Prophet's color, turquoise—green and blue mixed—is the color of Khiva, and the turquoise tiles on the tomb's central dome are its ne plus ultra. It is named for the city's patron saint, a poet and philosopher and, incongruously, a champion wrestler. He was Pakhlavan Makhmud, the Hercules of the East, and when he died in 1325 he entered local folklore as the perfect melding of intellect and physical prowess. Strange to think that this long-ago Muslim should have embodied Thomas Jefferson's ideal American, an Aristotle in mind and a Greek god in body.

His tomb stands on the south side of my east-west axis, behind the Djuma Mosque and minaret. First of all it honors Islamic convention, a classic dome on a cube. The dome is solid blue, its cylindrical "chassis" paler blue and white in a herringbone pattern. To the left rises the minaret, topped by a little blue dome and finial, this one like a Buddhist stupa, or you may think, as I did, of a tinkling bell on the dinner table turned upside down. Convention outdoes itself in the necklace of color under the bell—blues, whites, and browns succeeding each other—and in the long column flaring outward like a cobra's neck as it descends. The ensemble is a necropolis, whose nest of grayish-white domes in the foreground suggests a launching pad of graves. Gathering strength as they cluster together, they spring the big dome skyward.

In all this there is nothing of hagiography, though the ensemble celebrates a virtuous man. The worship is entirely in the color and form. No flowers, not real ones nor their likeness in paint or plaster, decorate the graves. Art in Khiva isn't always that austere. Some of it, Matisse-like, represents vegetables and flowers, a case of art following nature. This is unusual in the decorative arts of Islam and suggests the impact of the Persian takeover in the mid-eighteenth century. Evidently the more natural-seeming aesthetic favored by the usurper Nader Shah met a friendly reception.

Here the position, mine anyway, gets ticklish. To my sense the Persia just now before us isn't equal aesthetically to the Persia of the great days, coming down to the seventeenth century. I don't want to leave it at words. *Great* means the polychrome decoration on the Friday Mosque at Yazd, completed in 1327, and its stunningly tall *iwan-pishtaq* at the entrance, every inch covered with exquisite mosaic tile. Or it means the Isfahan Shah Abbas created in 1598 and later, its Maidan or vast open square, a stage across which the Mosque of the Shah and the Lotfollah Mosque, each with its gorgeous dome, confront each other like knights at barriers. The Persian style in its late manifesting isn't up to this and seems synonymous with old constraints loosening.

Most would cheer an improvement. But my possibly backward-looking intelligence thinks it is announcing a latitudinarian Islam. I find the loosening unfortunate, like the pictorial art it produces. Its aesthetic isn't tolerant, a conventional misunderstanding, but eclectic, where anything goes. Compare for the difference the Gur-i-Emir, Tamburlaine's mausoleum in Samarkand. It departs from the norm, even radically, but don't call it eclectic. Its art is ecumenical, meaning comprehensive.

Displacing the comprehensive creations of the greater past, eclectic is the word for latter-day Islamic art. It bespeaks a state of mind that declines to judge, having no point to depart from. *Laodicean* is a word for this, definitely pejorative. The art it sponsors might be anybody's, whereas the geometric forms in the Pakhlavan tomb are the work of an artist whose like we won't see again. Like the classic art they exemplify, they don't represent, though they may evoke. My candidate, possibly whimsical, for what they evoke is cell structure. And why not? That would give us the common form underlying all the varieties of life.

The absence of the human face divine, vexing to me elsewhere, is not felt as absence in Khiva. Its classic art exists on another plane—no need to call it higher or lower—where flesh and blood seem less persuasive than the abstract verities they betoken. The Islamic art before me—emphasis on its blue and white tile work—is neither Judaic nor watered-down Christian, nor does it reflect the too-easy syncretism I find myself prone to. Shrugging off comparisons, it isn't better than Western art but indigenous in its reading of last things, that is, incomparably itself.

MOSTLY MY SENSE of buildings in the Ark is hazy; I'd call them general issue Islam, hard to tell apart. But the large Djuma or Friday mosque separates itself out. In form it is "hypostyle": its enclosed space divided into separate units by the more than two hundred wooden pillars that hold up the roof. Some of the pillars date from the eighteenth century, others, going back eleven hundred years, are left over from the first mosque on the site. You can climb to the top on the eighty-one steps of the minaret's interior staircase, blessedly cool after the heat of the desert. The dates of these buildings, many of them relatively recent, come as a surprise. Khiva looks medieval to a cursory eye, and lovers of things past may take the wish for the deed. Its appearance is, however, calculated by the restorers. All the monumental buildings, mosques, minarets, *khanakas* where the Sufis recited their *zikr,* madrassas, caravansaries, are the work of a powerful nineteenth-century ruler, Allah Quli Khan. The stunning blue tiles in the harem of the Tash Hauli Palace are his or his artisans'. But the art and architecture he favored is essentially that of the seventeenth and eighteenth centuries, a late version of the "Persian style," and its omnipresence makes Khiva appear seamless.

The great style had a long gestation. There is much to admire before it, but the colossal labor of the Achaemenids, principally Darius (524?–486? B.C.) and Cyrus (424?–401 B.C.), both called "the Great" and both builders on the grand scale, survives largely as ruins. Inevitably the wreck of Ozymandias in Shelley's poem will come to mind as you stroll amid the palaces of Persepolis. The new departure called Persian must be later than this, and cultural historians date it to the lifetime of Muhammad. It isn't found in his native Arabia, however.

Its origins are eastward, in Mesopotamia, the storied sliver of land between the Tigris and Euphrates Rivers. Here the Sassanids (226?–641 A.D.), the last native dynasty to rule in Persia before the Islamic ascendancy, created prototypical works such as the palace at Ctesiphon, on the Tigris downstream from Baghdad. Its great vaulted arch rose more than a hundred feet, prompting future builders to imitate and refine it. The succeeding dynasty, the Abbasids (750–932), saw that the arch of Ctesiphon needed something more for the sake of completeness, and to this conch-shaped *iwan* (to give it what became its technical name), it added an attendant courtyard and flanking madrassas. *Pishtaq* is the umbrella term for this centerpiece with the arch in the middle.

The madrassas connected to it go up two stories and are honeycombed with rooms for students and professors. At their corners four paired *iwans* face each other around the courtyard in the center. The courtyard is critical and distinguishes the Persian style from that of the Ottomans, great in a different way. Constantinople, dispensing with the courtyard, puts its emphasis on the facade. It is paradoxical but true that Turkish art, influenced by Byzantium, is more nearly Christian. In the art I am describing, the enclosed opening has an unmistakable profile. It doesn't ascend to a sharp point as in the Gothic arch, nor is it rounded as in Romanesque. It tapers like a swan's neck, as if squeezed between forefinger and thumb. It is the Persian arch.

Ulug Beg's madrassa in the Registan, Samarkand, is the gold standard for these Koranic schools, but Khiva offers sufficient examples, such as the Allah Quli Khan, built 1882–83. To its basic foundation, other times and rulers added their own sense of what constituted an ideal whole—like parks and running water, harking back to the Achaemenid past. Under the Abbasids they enfiladed their palaces with gardens in the *chahar bagh* manner, an exact cruciform, the four parts separated by the four rivers of paradise, in the center a pool for ablutions. A superb example is the fourteenth-century gardens of the Generalife in the Alhambra, Granada, Spain.

A roll call of dynasties led by angry men participated in the making of the all-conquering style, among them the Seljuks, persianized Turks; the Ghaznids, a mighty power in the eleventh century under their Sultan Mahmud; the Mongols, not merely barbarians but imposers of a Roman pax on Central Asia; the Timurids, descendants of Tamburlaine; and the Uzbeki Shaybanids, who overthrew the Timurids but completed their work. It is "passing strange" that periods of artistic flourishing should coincide with murderous hammer blows, even seem to require them. Keats was on to a cold truth in the Isabella poem he came to dislike, perceiving that decay and its predecessor violence are the condition of health-to-come. When Shakespeare's character sees new life peering through the hollow eyes of death, he is hurrying together a train of thought that runs: the man dies, he withers to his bones (a skull), and through their decomposing life renews itself. The new cycle that begins doesn't always begin on cue. Sometimes the Middle Ages overstayed its welcome, and the Renaissance was slow getting out of the gate. Sometimes a new cycle, reaching certain high points, sustains them for long periods of time. One such period is the golden age of the Persian style, from the tenth through the thirteenth centuries. The style itself, not so radiant as it was, lasted longer, from 900 A.D. to the early eighteenth century, when floral decoration began to titivate the work of art. We may think of the Silver Age of Rome, after its Age of Gold, the time of Horace, Virgil, and Ovid.

The Abbasid capital, Baghdad, further upstream on the Tigris, astonished its subjects in this golden age with gigantic mosques, singular for their "ziggurats" (like the Tower of Babel), spiraling minarets that look ahead to Borromini's spire of Sant' Ivo in the Campo Marzio, Rome. (I don't speak of influence but fellow feeling.) These structures assault the heavens, part of their artistic intention. Islam is distinguished by its art of the miniature, "multum in parvo," but its prevailing impulse goes the other way. Generally its monuments, whether mosques or mausoleums, have a tropism like the sunflower's. The Gur-i-Emir is exemplary, directing the eye upward to its great bulbous dome. A double skin creates a second dome under the first, the space between them left vacant, and this is characteristic of the new style. Inside the mausoleum the eye, looking up, is brought to a stand, confronting a lowered heavens more suiting a funerary chamber.

Some examples of the Persian style are decorative only, like the glazed polychrome tile called *kashi.* The *chatri,* a domelike helmet seated on a pillar, is decorative. (The pillar doesn't need a hat.) *Chatris* are conspicuous on the facade of Humayun's tomb in Delhi, built by a Persian architect. *Muqarnas,* small concave receptacles, often decorate the facades, *mihrabs,* and inner skin of domed buildings, like the Tilly-Kari Madrassa-Mosque in the Registan, Samarkand. Clad in gold, they are like overflowing honeypots, shimmering in the sun. Theirs is the beauty that needs no excuse but itself.

Sometimes, however, form supports what it adorns. The flaring tops of the minarets to either side of Ulug Beg's great madrassa in Samarkand are all interlacing *muqarnas,* a feast for the eye. But more than that, they are squinches and hold up the platform above them. In Timurid buildings, their architects tutored in the Persian style, calligraphy beautifies. That is the primary function of the elegant cursive script—*thuluth* or *naskhie*—on the high drums that carry the domes of the buildings. But obviously the calligraphy informs us, a reason for being of the more angular and stylized Kufic script used for inscriptions and Koranic texts. Or let me boil this down and speak of one reason, for generally utility and its more disinterested cousin go hand in glove.

The tally of exotic terms denoting aspects of the Persian style is long, and I needn't recite it all. But before breaking off, I must comment on nature's gradual intrusion in what used to be an art of abstraction. In the later centuries, the classic style is enriched or debased—readers will decide for themselves—by flowering vines whose tendrils obscure what they fasten on, until at last nothing of the surface is left unadorned. The artistic composition begins to be populated by birds and animals, like the leonine creatures on the prowl in Samarkand's Shir Dor Madrassa, or the pair of simurghs, Persia's sacred bird, above the arch of the *pishtaq* in the seventeenth-century Nadir Divan Beghi Madrassa in Bukhara.

All this has its interest, and I grant the birds and flowers considerable charm. But like the Churrigueresque style of eighteenth-century Spain, the later art of Islam is overdecorated at least. It speaks to me of the horror of a vacuum. I am looking at a goblet from the Tash Khauli Palace, 1830–32, or rather at a goblet carved from a wooden column, with a bulbous bottom and tapering neck (illustrated in Markus Hattstein and Peter Delius's *Islam: Art and Architecture*, 2004, page 445). Atop it is a crown from the sides of which panels extend down, mimicking its shape. Between them the hollowed-out wood, like the goblet but inverting it, suggests the stately shape of swans. Every particle of this object of art is covered with the most meticulous tracery, exquisite but in danger of dying "of its own too much."

Abstract is preferable to realistic in the art of Islam, and its syncretic side, lumping the two together, takes away more than it gives. But the realism, at least in some enormously affecting miniatures, from Persia, from India, and in the ornamental art of *pietra dura* isn't naturalistic, much less photographic. At its best it glows with a vision that seems transmitted from inside out rather than the other way round. Remembering Byron on Shelley: "like an alabaster vase lit from within."

9

Ashkabad, City of Love

My destination is Ashkabad, the capital of Turkmenistan, a new country carved out of the erstwhile Soviet Union. Of old a nomad encampment, it has metamorphosed overnight to an Asian-style Las Vegas. To get there I cross the border and pick up a plane at Dashoguz. The choice between lounging in a reclining seat and navigating the Kara-Kum Desert by car isn't a hard one. In no time at all, I am at journey's end and watch from the window of my plane as we land. The heavens themselves, pinkish with reflecting neon, seem to know that something modern this way comes. I catch a glimpse of tentacle-like structures on the horizon. Then abruptly the Emerald City of Oz is on me, except that all the buildings are white.

Behind a screen the Wizard, who is also Turkmenistan's president, is manipulating a movie projector. The images it projects are exclusively of him. In one he is a modern man in suit and tie conducting the business of state, in another Turkman Bashi, "the leader of the Turks." This requires a faintly medieval getup consisting mostly of a long, belted gown and leather surcoat. One hand is extended, the other, à la Tamburlaine, holds an orb. The cynosure of all eyes isn't a young man, but his hair, when you see him on screen, is black. He is generally grinning in the hope his grin will engage you and looks a little like Dean Martin. Call him Dino. Though crazy, he was dangerous, and only since his death have people in his country ventured to lift up their heads.

The leader of the Turks is or was Saparmurat Niyazov, who went to translunar paradise in 2006. His successor as president, Gurbanguly Berdymukhammedov, is also a despot whose image, like Caesar's, appears on the nation's new coins. Off with the old, on with the new. Even so, the new man is less into personality and has been whittling away at its cult. The days of the week and months of the year are no longer named in honor of Turkman Bashi and his family, and his most imposing monument is being removed to a less conspicuous corner of the city. This is the Neutrality Arch, so-called to reflect the above-the-battle pose of President Niyazov, who hoped to play off Russia and the United States while accepting large infusions of cash from either.

I liken the arch to Sanders Memorial Theater at Harvard, a neo-Gothic survival, the pride of its pretentious time. Looking at it led an uncomfortable but polite French visitor to exclaim, "Voila, quelque chose!" Sanders Theater is rock-ribbed, but you can see through the Neutrality Arch. It stands on a white tripod, 246 feet above the ground, suggesting a rocket ship ready for takeoff. Confronted with it for the first time, I thought of the Eiffel Tower, in the same picture-postcard class. But the arch's chef d'oeuvre is in a class by itself. This is a golden statue of the leader, 39 feet tall. Perched on a globe at the pinnacle, he welcomes the world with out-flung arms. Always facing the sun, he rotates nonstop and like a Hindu god manages to embrace all four points of the compass, though he has only two arms. Mountains, sea, and desert surround him but he appears to dwarf them, the Caspian Sea on the west, the Kopet Dagh Mountains to the south, everywhere else the Kara-Kum (Black Sands) Desert.

Despite the effort to sweep the more flamboyant past under the rug, Turkman Bashi won't go away. Maybe that is appropriate, his singular self being the principal reason for visiting Turkmenistan. He has the weird charm of totally useless things, like the Chinese empress's stone boat that can never sail, moored at lake's edge outside the imperial capital, Beijing. Ubiquity is of his essence, and his image shows up everywhere, on wristwatches, bottles of perfume, vodka, the national drink. His dilated eyes, like a medieval Pantocrator's, are always on you when you look in their direction. I am aware that they are bent on me as I leave the hotel my first morning in town.

The maniacally happy face hangs from the facade of the large building across the street, a model of the White House, all marble. More white buildings line the wide thoroughfare, and Corinthian columns, like soldiers on parade, line up in front of them. This is desert country where water is scarcer than the proverbial hens' teeth, but it gushes with abandon from fountains on every street corner, the ultimate in conspicuous consumption. (The Arabs in the Emirates are like that.) There is a lot of oil and natural gas underground in this country, many billions of manats' worth, and wasting it on cascading water or vast stores of marble is how the dictator put it to work. The manat is the nation's currency, 14,500 to the dollar. That is the black market rate, the only rate worth quoting.

I can guess what will happen to the oil and gas, now that Turkman Bashi is gone. Foreign companies, mostly American, will reach a trade agreement. It will let them drill wells and pipe the underground gas across the Caspian Sea into southern Europe. This end-run around the newly awakened Russian bear will cut out its giant gas company, Gazprom, the ruler of the roost in Central Asia. Its control translates to power, and one reading of the national interest, America's, is that wresting power from a potential enemy is good politics and sound economics. Meanwhile the people of Turkmenistan look up like hungry sheep and are not fed.

Partly they have themselves to blame. To make the leader disappear, they had only to close their eyes. Shutting out the sound of his voice was harder. No doubt they could have held their hands over their ears, though not a practicable defense against the government's TV. A single channel beaming messages 24/7, it reaches the people via satellite dishes attached like little pasta ears, *orecchie,* to the building wall outside the windows of their apartments. This device seems modeled on the small TV sets high up on the wall in American doctors' offices. They show sitcoms around the clock, with a lot of canned laughter, and can't be got at by human hands. The people in the apartments can't choose but hear what their leader has on his mind. The *onecchie* see to that. His name is different now, but his message is the same. Big Brother Is Watching. Or Listening.

Outside town the military police, guns in their unflapped holsters, man checkpoints at intervals of less than a mile. Every vehicle coming or going is stopped. Nothing seems to happen, and I haven't seen anyone pulled out of his car. But the constant surveillance begets a psychology. In the police state, the inhabitants are inmates and learn to police themselves.

It is still early morning in Ashkabad, and I am treated to a calendar-art sunrise. Rifts of color divide the sky in sections, pink, gray with an underside of white, light blue between them. Even in this wacko fantasy world, the natural world still does its appointed thing. Man, however fertile of invention, can't roll back its beauty, and though I know it has no moral suasion, despite what preachers and many teachers assert, perhaps its unforced generosity will save us. Glamour as a means of grace.

I am walking straight north on prospect Saparmurat Turkmenbashi, the biggest north-south artery in town. In front of me at the edge of the city is the desert, and if you see it from the air, it lets you know that Ashkabad is only a blip on the map, perhaps not as permanent as Sanders Memorial Theater. This here-today-gone-tomorrow sense puts in perspective the grandiose vision of the leader of the Turks. I know and the desert knows that his magic kingdom is made of papier-mâché and won't leave a rack behind. His outlandishness suits impartially the style of Fascist and Communist building, the matrix Ashkabad comes out of. Its construction reflects a psychology in concrete and steel. Though the materials are hard, the idea of what to do with them is squishy, lacking substance. An example to raise eyebrows is the autobiography of the leader, a physical book as big as all outdoors. No one thought before to make a book a building, and the absurdity suits its subject, "a clown in regal purple dressed." On the principle that a picture is worth a thousand words, the book is opened to a huge photograph of Turkman Bashi. The pages before and after are empty and can't be turned, or they are like the bindings of make-believe books in a gentleman's library, genuine simulated leather with nothing beneath it.

One of those quirks the mind is prone to leads me to Grant's Tomb in uptown New York. Then the mind jumps to President Grant, who wrote an autobiography too, having debts to discharge. He incurred them by trusting scoundrelly colleagues who'd bilked the country on his watch, and though dying of cancer, he agreed to do the book, feeling honor bound to pay back the money. No one knows what made President Niyazov write. Pop psychologists might say he had the need to show himself in his true colors.

I'd like to hear them on the Tower of Independence. Bigger than the book that wants to be a building, it commemorates with flourishes the day in 1991 Turkmenistan achieved its national identity. Atop the revolving restaurant on the roof, I picture a hot-air balloon leaking slowly over the city. Bone dry, it tells of the desert waiting around the corner. The underwear I washed and hung in the shower before turning in crackles like a pair of mandibles when I put it on in the morning. That isn't how I want my underwear, and on the list of places I'm not likely to return to, this one ranks high. But had I been to one of the circles in Dante's *Inferno*, I'd do my best to write down the details.

MY IMAGINARY CLOCK has almost struck the dinner hour. Normally this is up there with the happy hour when the price of cocktails drops by half. I am a sensualist (also by turns an ascetic), and devoted to pleasing my palate. But the décor on the walls of the hotel makes food and drink seem less urgent. Images of Turkmen Bashi begin just below the ceiling, extending to the dado above the floor. A particularly revolting specimen hangs over the entrance to the restaurant, warning me off as I prepare to enter. It seems to convey Dante's minatory words above the portals of Hell. "Abandon all hope, ye who enter here." Averting my eyes from the accusing eyes that have found me, I leave the restaurant behind and go through the revolving doors to the street. Just around the corner is a mom-and-pop eatery, ordinary cinder block, dispensing with the white marble facing. "Plain honest food!" I tell myself, and head in its direction.

Knowing what was good for me and what wasn't, I had sworn off dining out in former Soviet client states. No more cold diced beets for breakfast, topped with a dollop of synthetic whipped cream. No more brown wine from Moldavia, a province of the old USSR I don't intend to visit. The best way to cope with restaurant food in Central Asia is to clamp a padlock on your mouth like Papageno in the opera. But the good I mean to do I don't always do, and when the waitress pulls out a chair, I sit down.

They have different kinds of plov laced with mutton, mutton chops, a mutton casserole, and cutlets of diced mutton, covered with bread crumbs. A large pot of *shurpa,* bouillon made from mutton, is seething on the hob. I go with the *shurpa.* Would I like a cold glass of *kumiss,* an acidic drink brewed from mare's milk? Having had a surfeit of coarse vodka and coarser wine, I go with the *kumiss.* The waitress, who hopes for a big tip, is unusually attentive. Without my asking, she sets a platter of fresh fruit on the table, pale green melon, rosy apples, juicy russet-colored pears, folds her hands across her apron, and smiles. Ah, *perfide!* Picking up my knife and fork, I fall to.

Later, too late to make a difference, I deconstruct the menu. The meat will have been tainted long before it came to the table, the milk was unpasteurized, and the fruit, if it didn't come from a can, came from fields where you wouldn't care to walk barefoot. When I lived in London just after the War, I didn't have an icebox but kept my milk, butter, and eggs in a pitcher of cold water sitting on the window ledge of a north-facing window. This arrangement worked well enough, and the perishables never went bad. People in

Central Asia don't see the need to bother, their bodies from early on having learned to accommodate every noxious germ known to man. Live and let live.

Visceral quivering, slight at first but not going away, was the first sign of trouble. No more Third World, I said, antedating my New Year's resolutions. I had just enough warning in my bowels and reins to push back the chair and dash for the toilet. A subset of Fraser's Law holds that civilization begins with adequate plumbing, and on this count, Central Asia is still at the starting gate. But the primitive men's room, if little more than a hole in the floor, saved me for polite society. White of face, I returned to the restaurant, settled my bill, and headed for home.

I got through the night by pressing a wet hankie against my forehead (no facecloths in Asia's bathrooms), all the while reciting a line from the Bard. Scribbled in my phylactery, it said that "time and the hour run through the roughest day." Experience has approved this hopeful saying before and perhaps would approve it again. Time did run on, as promised, and early in the morning I cracked the door of my room and rejoined the world. For a long time after that, thoughts of mutton made my stomach heave. But I remembered a restaurant in midtown Manhattan that served mutton to kill for. It came to the table on a silver salver, and the venerable waiter who brought it offered to uncover, taking the meat from the bone with deft fingers.

This lovely experience occurred in my country, no better place on earth! God Bless America! What had ever possessed me to leave? I know the answer to that one. *Sojourner for Truth* is the name of my vessel, and standing on the quarterdeck, I am going down with the ship.

A SANDWICH BOARD in the hotel lobby advertises a tour of the sights. It sounds painless, and I decide to be on the bus. Reception directs me to the concierge, who is also the bellhop. "I am Sanjar," he says, escorting me out to the curb. "No bus," he says apologetically. There isn't a car either. What he has is a "put-put," a motorized bike built for two.

I ride sidesaddle, both arms gripping the driver, while the wind that ruffles my hair blows away the cobwebs. The sun is high in the heavens over the roofs and smokestacks of Ashkabad, but it doesn't look like a hive of industry. It looks as the lowing herd is winding over the lea. "Are the people going home?' I ask my guide. Sanjar jerks his head around his shoulder. "Sunday market. I show you later."

He is named for one of the ancestors, famous for mass killing, a popular line of work in this part of the world. But in Sanjar the younger, the tide of hormones has ebbed, and this mild-mannered young man is all talk. Mostly he wants to talk about his city. There is the new industrial park, named for the ex-president. Pass on that, I say. Ditto for the oil refinery. "How about churches?" I ask him. "You want church?" he says, smirking. "Put yourself in my hands!"

The Russian Orthodox church takes up half a block behind the main drag, Prospekt Magtumguly. Its dull redbrick exterior isn't inviting, the interior smells of must, and the walls are lined with sentimental nineteenth-century paintings. Only a while ago, the church remembered the vanished age when Communism ruled and the practice of religion was forbidden. Now religion is sanctioned once more, and the church has put its head back up, but something about it is off key. Like British churches in the East, it tells of homesickness, a condition that enervates. It is a sickness, after all, slackening the tension that holds things together. Seeking to re-create the old and familiar, British colonial churches never got it quite right, and this Russian Orthodox church is like them. It feels uncomfortable, as if its clothes don't fit.

But a wedding is in progress, and we sit down to watch in a vacant pew to the rear. The bride is veiled, not a flimsy drapery that tantalizes but a veil like a visor hiding everything behind it. In a whisper Sanjar tells me that the groom has never seen her face, not even on the day he and she agreed to marry. Of course they themselves had little to do with it. His father and hers stage-managed the entire business, the date, the dowry to be paid, the nature of the wedding reception. Not vodka, Moldavian champagne.

Surely the young people themselves are up in arms at this? Yes and no, Sanjar says. The groom is chafing at the bit, he adds slyly, and who's surprised? Sex is the catnip that brings him to the altar; otherwise why get married? But the imams look at life differently and want him to follow their lead. "Wisely and slow."

"Maybe the imams have a point," I say.

"But we're flesh and blood," Sanjar says, protesting.

"That doesn't mean we're animals," I say, warming to this debate that has no winners or losers.

Swiveling his head around, Sanjar winks broadly. "Let me tell you about my friend Kashka. Pouf!" and lifting his hands from the handlebars, he claps them together.

"Don't do that!" I say.

"If he doesn't have a woman five days out of seven he'll go up in flames," he says.

"Your friend ought to get married," I tell him.

Sanjar nods his head in agreement. "But the woman of his life has to be special," he says. "So what does he do? He gets his mother to act as his agent. She invites the young lady he's got his eye on to come to the house for tea. 'Just the two of us,' she says. 'My son has to work.' This tells the girl she has nothing to fear."

"You're not saying his mother is a pimp!" I ask him.

"What kind of person am I!" he says huffily. "But here's the beauty of it! As soon as the girl walks into the house, she drops her veil. This is the moment Kashka has been waiting for. Through a keyhole in the closet door, he sees her uncovered face. 'She has sheep's eyes and is lovely,' he thinks. 'But she isn't moon-faced! And where are her hips? A woman without hips? I'll offer 200 rubles, not a penny more!'"

"He ought to be ashamed!" I say indignantly. "The woman's worth depends on what she looks like, is that it?"

"Even worse, he calculates her value in rubles!"

"Hold on!" Sanjar says. "It's called striking a bargain. You say how high you're willing to go. 'Nay!' says the girl's father. He ups the ante. 'You must be insane!' says the suitor. And so on until they reach an understanding."

"Marriage isn't like that," I say. Having been married more than once, I ought to know. "You think about what you're getting into. If you have anything upstairs, you've got more than a pretty face on your mind. You're thinking of the years ahead. Right?" I pause, wondering if this is true, and coughing self-consciously, continue. "As for the woman's beauty, that will fade over time, be sure of it."

"Cheer up!" Sanjar says. "There's plenty of fish in the sea."

"But the man," I say, "even a man like you will still love and cherish her. Or he will if they've made a proper marriage."

"What about the woman?" he asks me.

"She's taken a vow to love and honor," I say.

"And obey!" he says, adding, "You're a romantic!"

Shakespeare's sharp-edged comedy of Beatrice and Benedick comes to my mind, a tale of adult lovers and the young romantic couple who set them off. "Sweet," says the young man—I cast him as the foolish tenor in what seems to be a piece of froth called *Much Ado about Nothing*—"Sweet," he says, "let me see your face." He hasn't seen the woman who stands deeply veiled at the altar, a substitute for the cousin he thinks he has jilted. This fickle young man doesn't know who she is unless he sees her face! But see her "you will not," says her shrewd old father, "till you have taken her hand." First he must seal the bond of marriage, inevitably a leap in the dark. Shakespeare was as "lusty at legs" as any man but had an eye all the same to "cold gradation and well-balanced form," another phrase from another play worth a note in the phylactery. The Islamic world, our world too, used to be versed in such matters.

It is only fair that Sanjar decide where we go next. He doesn't say so, but I get the idea, and when he nominates the apartment house towers, first of their kind in Central Asia, I agree to have a look. The towers don't have broken windows or door frames out of kilter, like new construction in Brezhnev's time, but they put me in mind of a man who has aged prematurely. He was living in the world of *Lost Horizon,* inside the air-controlled cocoon, and wouldn't listen when they told him not to go out in the cold. Though the towers are still upright, their aura is attenuated, and they are losing bone and muscle by the minute. These are habitats for living, but there is nothing personal about them. They lack color, actually a muddy taupe, if you pin me down, but that is the absence of color. They lack style, opting for the international style of bare bones titivated with doodads, pilasters stuffed with rubble, fake cornices holding up air.

Around them when no one was paying attention, some vaguely industrial enterprise has sprung into being, a workplace for the damned, ramshackle shanties, rusty warehouses, railroad tracks that go nowhere, a slimy body of water like Eliot's dull canal behind the gasworks. This city of dreadful night is a place to die in. What future can there be here for the young? It baffles me that Sanjar can see this place in his future, but so he does, and he has put his money down for an apartment. He says the girl of his dreams helped choose it.

"She must love you to pieces!" I say gloomily.

"Till death do us part," he says.

The rows of baleful towers, battlements of merde, mock his words. They have a model in the neo-Gothic Moscow of the 1930s. Clearly something was wrong with the Soviet idea from the start. The wrongness must be rationalism's, embracing bloodless abstractions while pretending to a materialist philosophy. More than wrong, perverse, championing life but installing death in its tabernacle, eviscerating the language to make it say the thing that is not, condemning us, its worst sin, to live in a nonphysical world. Many of these counts might be urged against Islam. It insisted from the beginning on merging church and state. That meant you couldn't challenge the state without repudiating the church. But no Muslim dared look with inquiring eyes at the church, embodied in the Koran. He couldn't see this sacred book for what it is, a collating of the Prophet's words with the words of the Hebrew Bible, the New Testament, and the preaching of Zoroaster.

But the Islamic faith, though lifting from others, had a benighted first commandment peculiar to itself. Unlike the creeds it built on, it bade its followers turn away from the world. It anathematized the art that dwells lovingly on our human face. Like communism it closed our eyes, "seeling" them the way a falconer sews up the eyes of the falcon. This hoodwinked creature makes an obedient servant and will never be led astray by the beautiful world it can't see. I shake my head with an almost physical revulsion, having had enough of false prophets. "Take me to your art museum!" I tell Sanjar. To my astonishment, there is one.

A two-story rectangle lined with shelves and free-standing cabinets at right angles to its walls, the museum is a time capsule going back more than three thousand years. Its earliest ceramics, some that make my eyes blink, are almost as old as King Tut. I note, on a bas-relief surface, a man and woman embracing. "Forget about the dreadful city!" I say to my young tour guide, confident that he won't understand me. "'This will go onward the same/Though Dynasties pass.'" I think of the Emperor Wudi and his favorite concubine, Lady Li. Their tombs stand side by side in China's old capital, Chang'an, and when the moon rises a thin wraith of smoke ascends from her tomb, circles his, and disappears. That is a version of the bittersweet love, sweet while it lasts, on the bas-relief in the museum.

Any day soon, Ashkabad is going to recede in memory, but I'll not forget its rhytons, drinking vessels made from horn. Mostly goat and bull hides furnish the horn, though some are of ivory, terra-cotta, even glass. What sets them apart from run-of-the-mill tableware is the carving. Where the horn bends toward its point, the artist has carved the head of a lioness, a bull, a griffin. On one, a human face like the mummified faces of Egypt, looks back at me across a great gap in time.

The heart of the collection comes from two ancient capitals, now gone under earth, Nisa, the capital of the Parthian empire, and Merv, after Baghdad the greatest city of Islam. It makes the reading of history less melancholy to know that these monuments of the far-distant past, each a metropolis, enjoy a modest afterlife in art. Thanks go to the archaeologists. Excavating in the ruins of Nisa, they discovered a reliquary room, fifteen meters long, six and a half meters wide. Gladdening the eye, it was stuffed with treasure, the poet's "infinite riches in a little room." Four pillars, standing on a base of greenish sandstone from the Kopet Dagh Mountains, supported the ceiling. Shelves lined the walls. This, I realize, was where the museum in Ashkabad got its ground plan.

Some rhytons from Merv and Nisa are adorned with a frieze in relief. Under the rim of the vessel, where once a fur-clad dignitary or his consort set their lips, the frieze functioned as a cornice. The carver let his fancy run riot, decorating the cornice with fabulous beasts, a Minotaur, a centaur supporting a bacchante, a scene of Dionysian revels. Elegant they are but not fastidious, on the contrary intensely sensual, flesh of our flesh. The human figures wear a Parthian costume, long shirt and trousers with a mantle over the shoulder. Greek and Oriental features merge, assigning a new identity to the men and women who lived in this vanished place. But they themselves haven't vanished. They still live, like the figures on Keats's Grecian urn, not in life but art.

Like the medieval *Biblia pauperum,* moralized pictures whose moral is implicit, the rhytons of Ashkabad constitute a book of the people. The written word was lost on this preliterate society, so the rhytons preferred showing to telling. They came up from their hiding place in Nisa at the end of September 1948, docketed and laid away by the provident scientists who retrieved them. A week later in the small hours of October 6, an earthquake of great magnitude struck the area, annihilating the city of Ashkabad. More than 110,000 people died. Stalin's statisticians (he was still going strong then) put the number at a tenth of this. Catastrophes beyond imagining weren't admissible in the old USSR. One way or another, though, the earthquake missed the treasures of the reliquary room, and for once something was saved from time's tooth.

OUTSIDE THE MUSEUM an impromptu carnival is in full swing. I smell shish kebab cooking, and suddenly a skewer is thrust in my face. Instant happiness!

Here in Ashkabad I have everything I could want. "Such nice people!" I mutter, as much to myself as to Sanjar.

"You know why?" he asks me. "Ashkabad means to love."

The market seems to bear this out. Tolkuchka, as the bazaar is called, is from the Russian "to push!" Sanjar says. But it isn't a mob scene, more like a festival. We have cycled past the ruined fortress built by the Russians, the czarist ones, also the airport and the Kara-Kum canal. Without warning, the market is all around us, as if lowered from the flies above the stage. All the world's a stage. Women are cast in the lead parts, driving hard bargains. "Take it or leave it!" They say this with a smile, though, not a fishwife among them.

The knot of women around me specializes in shucked corn, prayer socks (for when you must take your shoes off before entering a mosque), tins of tea from Iran over the border. It is hot, and they are sweating through their cotton blouses. Many, dressed in bright red, are selling finely tooled silver jewelry. Others offer skullcaps threaded with gold, bright green scarves in honor of the Prophet, striped wraparound cloaks, "chapans," secured at the waist with a sash in all colors of the rainbow. This is their art and makes them believable.

Made-by-hand carpets, colored deep red or burgundy, are the glory of the market. These favorite colors, Sanjar says, symbolize light and life. Almost all the patterns are quasi-abstract—some look to me like Leger paintings—and passed on from one generation to the next. The persistence over time means that the way they see things doesn't change. If they hint at nature, a camel, for example, it is stylized, the idea of a camel, never the thing itself. This seems odd. Turkmen live immersed in nature but hold it at the length of a convention. Why should they do this, and what does it say about them?

I think it says they are people of the desert, with a view of the world and its creator that reflects their distinctive place. Christians, freed of the desert, worship a personal God who smells of mortality. "Thou shalt be recognized in the midst of two animals," reads the book of Habakkuk, taken as predicting the birth of the Christian Messiah. The Septuagint (Seventy), early translators who rendered this text, got it wrong in particulars but knew what they meant. Near Bethlehem in Judaea, pious pilgrims are shown a cave, the Milk Grotto, where Mary, God's mother, nursed her son. No earthly mother nursed the God of the Koran.

Christianity has a God who resembles the God of the Koran, but off the Christian religion's main line. Once I spent a holiday exploring the Tuscan hill towns in the emptied-out country south of Florence. Little oases, some are still as remote today as they were in the Middle Ages, Gubbio, for instance, where St. Francis converted the wolf. An equivocal saint, enamored of spirit but not much cherishing the body, he strewed ashes on his food. His temper has something in common with the ascetic temper of Islam. "Do to my body whatsoever is permitted you," he said to the devils who beset him.

Petrified ruins, the medieval towers of San Gimignano climb the empty sky like Arab *kellas* in the desert. Medieval mystics had their revelations in these lonely hills. The god revealed to them was a nullity like silence or the void. When they described him, they fell back on analogy, being hard put for details. For most men, however, God lives in the details. Some do without them, cutting straight to the big picture. The gain is in clarity, anyway they think so, but coarseness is its concomitant, like the statues at Bamiyan, impossibly larger than life.

I have an analogy suggesting how clarity and coarseness make a pair. Seen from the sky, Turkmenistan is like the flat country around Holland, Michigan, between the Great Lakes. The geography rubs off on the people who live there, not much ambiguity in how they see things. Farmers in the countryside, descended from Dutch Calvinists, grow tulips, a cash crop, but otherwise the local color is monochrome. I went to Holland once, to give a speech at Hope College. Eyebrows rose when I lit my pipe, and they had much trouble finding an ashtray. (I used to be a smoker, before we all learned to know better.) Later, over dinner at the Warm Friend, I asked for a drink, but this restaurant was dry. I wasn't the perfect guest, and I fear they found me confusing.

Muslims don't drink either, alcohol being taboo in Islam. No quarreling with their code of behavior, except that it's partial. Deploring self-indulgence, it comes down even harder on mercy. In some parts of the Islamic world, if you fall off the wagon, they punish you with eighty lashes of the whip. Umar, the second caliph after Muhammad, finding his son drunk, scourged him to death. No tulips grow in the country outside Ashkabad, but the spring rain, a merest dusting, turns the desert purple for a while. Then the wind blows the flowers away.

The bazaar is going full tilt, and the ground between the makeshift stalls is littered with garbage, shreds of paper, and plastic bottles and containers, some of this rubbishy deposit ankle deep. Flies buzz the garbage, a glistening carpet of them, black as tarpaper. The dirt road at my feet is caked with salt along its margins. The salt, from eroded water, tells of the encroaching desert. It breeds kidney problems and physical deformity. What am I doing here? My elation snatched from me, I feel an irrational urge to be clean. I cry for water, more like a croak than a cry.

A skinny man who could be any age from forty to sixty, the kind they call nondescript, is standing beside me. He has stubble on his chin and a large plastic bottle hooked over one finger. His shirt and trousers are Salvation Army, and his toothless smile is Walter Brennan's in an old Western, but it is clear that he has good intentions. "Water?" he seems to be saying. His plastic milk bottle is full of it, and he wants me to have some. Gratefully I accept, tilt up my elbow, drink, and let the warmish water splash on my face and run down my neck. "Thank you thank you!" I bow and hand back the bottle.

"Wait!" he says, and turns away. I see him talking with the flower woman at the next stall. When he returns he has a flower in his hand, a daisy from Turkmenistan. "From the city of love," he says and, giving me a toothless grin, tucks the daisy in the top buttonhole of my shirt.

My elation, gone only minutes ago, comes sweeping back like the tide. "Yes!" I say, aware that my voice has a tremor in it. In my sojourning through Central Asia, I find myself close to being unmanned like this half the time. But the head of the daisy in my buttonhole has already fallen, and when no one is looking I pinch off the wilted flower and drop it underfoot.

The face Ashkabad wears is like this, happy one moment, dejected the next. Conjured out of nothing like a rabbit from a hat, the city resembles its improbable dictator, Turkman Bashi. But the Muslim religion its people practice reveres many Judeo-Christian prophets, Jesus included. However, it denies the Incarnation. This leaves its tabernacle empty, a problem Muslims have never resolved. Their god means to do good, and the daily prayers they recite faithfully assert this. But being thin-blooded (my possibly deficient sense of him), he finds it hard to suit the deed to the word.

Alexander was present to my mind as I began to write about this maze of contradictions, and I return to him here as I finish. How is he a great man rather than a black-and-white cartoon? I answer is that he yoked together dissimilar sides, like the sorb apple before it was sundered. I'm not thinking of his bisexuality, to my mind an aberration (saying so, I'm aware that I've set the fox in the hen coop)—but the uncommonly large spectrum of possibility he shows us, emotional and psychological, sad, happy, civil, wild. In his complexity he calls to mind the rhytons in the local museum.

I wish I could bring one home! Mostly, however, as I near the end of the bazaar, pickings are slim. Ho hum to the trays of baubles simulating the real thing. But wait! At the end of the road, I come on a double lane of carpets. Heaped up in cylinders of different length, they glow softly in the bright sun. I thought I had bought my fill in Bukhara, but the urge to acquire still more of the beautiful artifacts wells up strongly, and I poke and prod with the tip of my shoe, uncovering one after another. Inevitably I find one I have to have, a smallish Beluch from Persia, an old piece, woven on woolen warps rather than the usual cotton. I know the gods are with me when I realize that this specimen includes a tree motif and a broad kilim skirt, glorifying both ends of the composition.

"You don't often see that in modern prayer rugs," says the vendor, a young man, uncharacteristically hatless and beardless. "I am Hasani," he says, offering me his hand. We haggle only a little to satisfy the convention: I think we have too much respect for the thing we are holding at opposite ends to worry overmuch about price. Having met the price he's quoted, I turn to go. But he isn't finished with me or his carpet. He wants to be sure there won't be a hassle with customs. Sadly, he says, they aren't above asking a "tip" to let something like this leave the country. He proposes to cycle out to the airport, even though it will be dark and the road does without lights. "I shall see to it," he tells me, "that all goes, as you Americans say, 'according to Hoyle!'"

"No need!" I tell him. But this is one insistent young man. At 10:30 that night there he is, standing beside my luggage and leaning on his bike. He is calm, but he is arguing and not to be talked over. The customs officer has a thin, vulpine face and nothing on his mind but dollars and cents—or manats. His talk is largely sputtering. "I'm asking less than a tenth of what it costs!"

"I'll report you," says my carpet seller. He is implacable, and the customs man sees this. Sighing bitterly, he tosses his chin, stamps my form, and with exaggerated politeness ushers me through the gate with my bags. When I look back, my friend has yet to leave. He is staring fixedly at the door I have just walked through to be sure they won't send me back. "Such a nice man!" I say to myself. But he is more than nice. He is thick-skinned; he has to be in a country that will eat you alive if you let them. What other qualities must he possess? I add shrewdness, the knowledge of what ropes he has to pull. He's beginning to emerge as a man to reckon with.

Once again I think of the rhytons and the lesson they have for the people of Ashkabad. My feeling for the city has been ambiguous, shading to negative. This is a modern city, meaning here today, gone tomorrow. But its considerable art, embodying the past, is still quick, and it may be that the past will rise again to save it. That young Hasani is already learning what the past has to teach him makes me believe in the future.

10

The Return of the Mongols

My next venue is Mary, a small industrial city to the east in Turkmenistan. The limo driver who takes me out to the airport is a talker like cabbies everywhere. "Famous men of Islam," he says, as we pass a pair of worthies aloft on their pedestals. "Famous men" gets me thinking. What did they do to boost our fortunes? In fact, did they make any real difference?

When I was growing up, my teachers wanted me to think that the great man defines his context. Today's conventional wisdom supposes, on the contrary, that the common man in the aggregate counts more than the man whose like "we shall not see again." Dante counts less than the weightier Guelphs and Ghibellines who made his gorge rise, and Shakespeare less than his audience. Fashionable critics and historians put their money on the audience. Some, promoting the "death of the author," deny that he or she exists at all.

The flight for Mary doesn't leave until well after midnight, giving me plenty of time to sort this out. On my mind are the great Russians of the twentieth century—Osip Mandelstam and Nadezhda, his wife; Anna Akhmatova; Boris Pasternak—men and women who raised our stature a cubit. But others, notably Lenin and Stalin, their contemporaries, dreamed a perverted dream that wreaked havoc, and whose legacy remains with us. Their footprints are still visible on the sands of time. I am about to find them.

A glance at the map shows you the Aral Sea in relation to Ashkabad, a straight line to the northwest. I am aware of this since a branch of the Silk Road went in that direction, crossing the Kyzyl-Kum Desert. Soviet planners, looking at the desert, saw in their mind's eye fields of blooming cotton. The Aral Sea, actually a lake, the world's fourth largest, was there for the taking, and they tapped its waters to irrigate the dry land. It was understood that the waters might drain away and disappear into the desert, and they have. This destroyed the ecology of a huge region, bringing misery to thousands of people. Perhaps their masters knew this would happen and didn't care.

Central Asia's two great rivers fed the Aral Sea, flowing west from the Pamirs and the Heavenly Mountains that separate China and the Stans. Their deltas, fecund with life, made a complex skein of smaller rivers and lakes, marshes, reed beds, and forests. The sea itself extended two hundred miles from north to south, more than a hundred from east to west. Passenger ferries plied its waters, clear enough to see through a long way down. Its swimming beaches drew crowds in summer, and the fishing never failed, yielding twenty thousand tons per annum. But as cotton production rose, the waters fell.

By the 1990s they had fallen better than five feet. The eastern and southern shores receded like a rolled-up carpet, and rusting hulks of fishing boats lay keeled over on sand dunes, sixty miles from the water. The fish died from pesticides and fertilizers and the disappearance of their spawning grounds. The two seaports that depended on the fishing industry died with them. Sixteen thousand fishermen lost their jobs, and almost four times that number of canners, fish mongers, distributors, and the like.

The weather, everyone's standard topic for small talk, became a burning issue. Winters got colder and longer, summers got hotter. Dust and sandstorms, their teeth sharpened by salt and the residue of chemicals from the cultivated fields, blew across the blighted land. Toxic defoliants, finding their way into the Amu-Darya and Syr-Darya, begot cancer, respiratory disease, a long list of ailments. In the region called Karakalpakstan (far west Uzbekistan), fewer than one baby in ten lived beyond infancy. The Soviets, until their empire crumbled, aggravated this horror, using an island in the Aral Sea for testing biological weapons.

Uzbeki Air, taking off on time, banks to right itself, and the ground below comes up at us, sparkling with light. In minutes, however, absolute blackness replaces it. We are over the desert. The lights are off above the passenger seats, and my seatmates, like most on this late flight, are dozing. I sit with eyes open, thinking about the evil done by Stalin and the USSR. I needn't be told that murderous tyrants and the violence they unleashed aren't peculiar to the twentieth century. Uzbekistan and Kyrgyzstan, two of the nation-states carved from Stalin's former domain, were proficient in killing before men put a name to them, and for prowess in that line, no one beats the Mongols. But Stalin was one of a kind.

The provincial from Georgia, underbred and ill schooled, lived in a state of war against his fellow men. He grew up deformed in one arm, like Tamburlaine, and the scars of early smallpox left him unlovely to look at. Trotsky, among Communism's founding fathers the intellectual par excellence, inspired his particular aversion. When the Bolsheviks sought to expand their newly won power to Central Europe, Trotsky focused on Warsaw, Stalin on the Polish-held city of Lvov. Trotsky needed his help if Warsaw was to go Communist, but Stalin hung fire, incurring the Party's censure. Later he had his revenge. He engineered Trotsky's murder—with an ice pick, appeasing his implacable soul. The Polish veterans of Central Europe's civil war, thousands of them, were massacred on his orders in the Katyn Forest. He saw to it that the uprising against the Germans in the Warsaw Ghetto was crushed. And at Yalta he got Lvov, a personal trophy, for the Soviet Union.

His climb to the top began when Lenin chose him as general secretary of the Communist Party's Central Committee. Defining the aparatnik, he handed out assignments, not plums necessarily, mostly drudgework, like sitting on committees. But the man who was willing to spend his days in dreary meetings cast the all-important vote when the meetings finally ground to a halt, and Stalin made sure that many of these seat warmers were his cronies. (Molotov was one, the mediocrity to end all.) Having gained control of the apparatus, he set out, after Lenin's death, to destroy its old leaders. None should stand near the throne, nor bear witness to his ignoble beginnings. The show trials of the 1930s were reenacted in the meanest cell in the party, where men of education or intellectual leanings were methodically destroyed. Pol Pot was his scholar.

But the anti-intellectual was complicated, himself an intellectual manqué. This accounts for his high ranking among history's evil men. Brutes with low foreheads who kill for money or power are easy to explain. Stalin was driven by the need to rationalize experience, starting with the peasant life that produced him. The family farm, aggravating obscure resentments, made his blood boil—or run cold—and he collectivized agriculture, an ugly word suiting the deed. The serfs had been freed before he was born, but he took back their freedom. The straitjacket he imposed on the land bred terrible famine, the worst in the Ukraine. In 1932–33 five to ten million starved to death. He wanted to be rid of the kulaks, well-to-do peasants, and this was a fortunate chance or possibly deliberate, an act of genocide.

Fitting the nation to an industrial yoke, he got his labor unpaid from the tens of thousands he shipped to the gulags. If they didn't pick up their feet, he killed them. This took sangfroid but did wonders for efficiency. If he killed enough of them, they began to pay attention. A xenophobe, he uprooted his non-Russian subjects—Tatars, Chechens, Turks, Finns, Volga Germans, Jews—relocating them to Siberia and the far north. All by himself he redrew the ethnic map of Russia. Cynically he joined hands with Hitler, and when Hitler, as might have been expected, betrayed him, he was unready, almost costing his country the war. He wouldn't make the same mistake again, and after the war was over, he rang down an Iron Curtain across Europe. Colonizing the Eastern Bloc and the Baltic states, he prepared a new reign of terror. Only his death forestalled another Great Purge.

No one will ever know how many died at his hands, estimates ranging upward from three million, a figure documented by the official records and negligible seeming. Historians such as Robert Conquest put the number at sixty million. But the wickedness on Stalin's head, though colossal, doesn't strike the core of what he was and did. His was the mysterious sin against the Holy Ghost for which there is no forgiveness. He treated people as things.

IT'S NOT A DESERT below me but a necropolis where Central Asia's lost civilizations lie at rest. Three of them, Khorezm, Parthia, and Merv, are more vivid to my mind as I sit down to write than my birthplace in New Jersey. The latter is only a statistic, but the charnel house of history passing underneath the plane must engage all who are conscious of last things. When I was living in London after the War, I spent much time in graveyards searching out the famous dead. I found Milton in St. Giles Cripplegate, Isaac Watts and Daniel Defoe in Bunhill Fields, Marx, George Eliot, and Michael Faraday in Highgate. Under a stone in St. Botolph, Bishopsgate, lay the infant son of Ben Jonson, "his best piece of poetry." Exploring graveyards goes with my conservative temper, like sifting through the ruins of long-vanished cities. I hang tight to the past as a sailor at sea might fix his eyes on a landmark, his best hope of surviving into the future.

The dead are everywhere in Asia's heartland and engender speculation. "Did these bones cost no more the breeding but to play at loggats?" (a game like bowling). Hamlet, posing the skull of Yorick, asks the question, and I repeat it to myself as I travel east against the sun. Beneath the wing tips to port and starboard is the once-mighty empire of Khorezm, or rather its ghost. Taking in the Amu-Darya delta where Turkmenistan and Uzbekistan come together, Khorezm extended east into modern Afghanistan. Seljuk Turks, a warrior people, were its overlords, ruling from their capital, Kunya Urgench. When the Arabs overran the Khorezmian empire at the end of the seventh century, they destroyed all its literature and banished all its educated men, "so that," writes the polymath Al-Beruni, a native Khorezmian, "everything became covered in darkness and even we do not know for certain any . . . of their (earlier) history."

Though I live much in the mind, doing my best to make sense of experience, I find it hard to come to terms with Kunya Urgench. The Arabs, killing the last Sasanid emperor, begot the city's byword, "inimical to kings." Subsequent history confirmed it. Few today recognize the name, but once it was "worth the whistle." The Arab traveler Ibn Battuta described Kunya Urgench as "the largest, greatest, most beautiful, and most important city" of the Seljuks, a synonym for irresistible power. Early in the thirteenth century, Genghis Khan and his Mongols destroyed it.

The vanished city was located east of modern Urgench and Khiva. On the ruins scale it ranks near the top, home, my books say, to two million people in the days of its glory but reduced to a population of zero as the wheel turned. In the tenth century, its Academy of Learning counted among its members Al-Beruni and Avicenna. The former, adept in geography, history, and astronomy, was also a poet of price. Everyone knows the latter. The academy stood on Forty Mullahs Hill, where a terrible tale unfolded. Genghis Khan wrote the script. Having subjugated Northern China in the first part of the thirteenth century, he turned west against Khorezm. Its shah, Muhammad II, had put to death the occupants of a Mongol caravan, and when the Great Khan sent a trio of envoys to demand satisfaction, they were murdered as well.

Retribution came swiftly. A Mongol army of ninety thousand attacked from the north, thirty thousand more from the east. The shah's army was larger still, but the Mongols had the victory. Following their practice, the Scourge of God, as he called himself, winnowed the inhabitants like a threshing machine. He culled out the city's artisans and craftsmen, one hundred thousand of these, meaning them to beautify his Mongolian capital, Karakorum. The women and children he sold into concubinage and slavery. The men and boys, all who stood taller than the butt of a whip, he massacred. Then his soldiers tore down the dam that held the river in check, flooding the city and turning it into "the abode of the jackal and the haunt of the owl and kite."

Incredibly Kunya Urgench rose again. Maybe Faulkner in his Nobel Prize address, too sanguine on my reading, had it right after all. "Man will not only endure but prevail." Maybe the human race, though not open to correction, isn't open to destruction either. Growing back like grass in spring, it almost denies the chance for tragedy. A century and a half after the Mongols leveled the city, Kunya Urgench decided that life must go on. But inching itself back up, it attracted attention, and late in the fourteenth century Tamburlaine led his armies against it. It took him five separate campaigns, but at last, in 1388, he finished off the city for good. To verify that it had once existed, he left standing the tallest minaret in Central Asia and a pair of mausoleums. One honors a daughter of the khan of the Golden Horde, the other Sherif Sheikh, a ruler of Kunya Urgench's golden age. It seems a meager memorial.

TODAY CENTRAL ASIA is a land of sleep and dreams, and in the delta they go to bed early. If you want action you must hop a plane for Ashkabad. But my focus is elsewhere, and I want to pay my respects to Parthian Nisa, another lost civilization. Before leaving Ashkabad, I drive out to see what is left of it. Imagine three cities more or less in a line, below them the Iranian border. The middle one is Ashkabad, to the east and south Merv, a few kilometers west of it Nisa.

It will have looked grand atop its citadel, a natural belvedere in the foothills of the KopetDagh Mountains. Arthur Upham Pope offers a detailed version of the palace at Nisa in his *Persian Architecture* (1969), and Josef Wiesehöfer in his history *Ancient Persia* (1996) tells what Soviet excavations at the site suggest of the city as it was. Among the treasures retrieved by the archaeologists are more than fifty ivory rhytons. Wiesehöfer's reconstruction of Old Nisa gives his sense of the treasury building in which they were housed. To the naked eye, unassisted by scholarship, it shows as little more than mounds of dirt.

The belvedere is still there. Stopping the car, I lever myself up the hill, only to find someone before me. A sign in English and Russian advertises an archaeological dig, a modest one by the look of the gnarled old peasant with his wheelbarrow, shovel, and pitchfork. Evidently digging is both his pleasure and business, and though he spends his days hip deep in history's wreckage, he whistles tunelessly, merry as a cricket. Were I to take over the tools in the wheelbarrow, I believe I could unearth traces of Alexander, the Seleucids, the Persians, the Arabs, last of all the Mongols. Were I to ask about them, he'd shake his head and counter with a question. Would they be from Berzangi, the next village over?

The city he is excavating, at the rate he's going the labor of a lifetime, was first of all Parthian, founded by an Iranian king in the third century B.C. Trading with China, and Rome when they weren't at swords' points, Parthians flourished until another dynasty, the Sasanids, defeated and replaced them in 224 A.D. Four hundred years later, the last Sasanid king was captured and put to death by the advancing Muslim armies, and the Sasanian empire became a part of the caliphate. One up, one down, and so on. Everyone knows how the Parthians turned in their saddles to deliver a parting shot, a "Parthian shot," laying their enemies low. A horseman myself, also a skeptic, I'd like to find out how they did this.

Twenty-three hundred years ago, Parthia challenged Rome for domination in the East. Its empire lasted three centuries before the birth of Christ, less than three after. Encompassing much of Central Asia, it stretched one way to Iraq and Syria, the other to the Indus, flowing down through Tibet to the Arabian Sea. Susa, one of the oldest inhabited sites on earth—at least seven thousand years old—was a capital of the Parthian state, sharing this role with Ctesiphon and Ecbatana. These are storied names, fabled in history. Shakespeare, intensely skeptical in his reading of history, remembers Parthia. Mark Antony is praised for taking its measure, but we learn that it was his lieutenant who did this. That makes the lieutenant fear for the head on his shoulders. "Who does more in the wars than his captain can/Becomes his captain's captain." The moral is to keep a low profile if you don't want it permanently marred. Central Asia's ruins approve this.

But "ruins" doesn't meet the case altogether. For centuries after Parthia disappeared as a living entity, it led a posthumous existence, and that, I have come to realize, is the heart of my narrative, an account of death and transfiguration. Cultivated at first in the eastern provinces of the empire a hundred years before Christ, its art of Gandhara reached its apogee under the Buddhist Kushans in the first five centuries of the modern era. This Central Asian people deserves resurrecting. One of its sculptures shows the Greek god Atlas, like a caryatid, holding up a Buddhist temple, two immiscibles, you would think, yet their juxtaposing lets us see how one culture, fusing with another, makes a third at least as vital as either.

Alexander the Great took Gandhara in his stride, bequeathing it to one of his generals, Seleucus. In the early fourth century, the Seleucids, his descendants, lost it to an Indian dynasty, whose greatest ruler, Asoka, spread Buddhism throughout this part of the world. Buddhism succumbed to Islam; then came the Mongols.

The Parthian dynasty Asoka gave way to ushered in the golden age of Greco-Buddhist art. It is hard to believe that the sequence is serendipitous, like the propagating of flowers by pollen carried on the wind, for the religion and art that come with it are an index of man's difference from the lower orders. An older culture called them nature's "germens," seeds of life. Arriving in the thirteenth century, they laid siege to Nisa, and having bullied its inhabitants into surrendering—terrorized, they must have been, like a rabbit in the claws of a stoat—razed it to the ground. I study the pieces that lie at the foot of the mountains, willing them to come together again. Slowly they rise before me: palaces; towers, more than forty of them; temples, one dedicated to the Zoroastrian cult; and tombs of distinguished persons, surrounded by a thriving commercial city. Nothing making an integer survives, and even the mountains that frame the scene look worn down by time, half the size of Iran's over the border.

THE WALL THAT ENCLOSED the citadel zigzags up like a scotched serpent. Mixed with its broken segments are bits of the underground water system, carried by clay pipes. A large mud-brick building has reduced to its skeleton, all rectangles like a cubist painting, except that the color is gone, leached out by the elements. Some sections are cut with slits to shoot through, others with small square holes into which beams, likely supporting a firing platform, would have been fitted. Something colossal rose on this high ground, but whatever is animal, mineral, or vegetable has long since turned to dust, and to retrieve it you must do as Shakespeare instructs us, summon "your imaginary forces."

The king of Parthia, habituated to command, saw no need to do that and could hardly have imagined that one day all he commanded would vanish. In one sense, however, it hasn't. Oppressed by history and the carnage it tells of, I look about for some point of purchase to stand on. And I find one! Ashkabad's museum is a still point in our turning world, preserving the past for the future. Among its treasures is an ivory head of Aphrodite from the second century B.C., stylized hair and a glowing face, its wide-open eyes looking straight up at the viewer. Memorizing the hair, I think of Wallace Stevens: "Alas, have all the barbers lived in vain,/That not one curl in nature has survived." This rhetorical question expects an affirmative answer, something like "All is vanity," but the poem itself and the lovely head testify against it.

From the same period is a Parthian face "gone under earth's lid" more than two thousand years ago. The face, incised on a drinking horn, has character: a fleshy nose; full, sensuous mouth; curling mustache and beard. On the head is a Trojan-like helmet. Aeneas, Anchises, and the boy Ascanius are here, and I find a fifth-century Buddha from a temple tile at Merv. These details testify to coherence, an attribute of beauty, and after more than two or three millennia are still there to gladden the heart.

IN AN OLDER TIME, a traveler could go from Uzbekistan to Turkmenistan as easily as stepping up the curb to the sidewalk. But little men with touchy egos man the border posts today. They take themselves seriously, thanks to the witches' brew stirred by Russia and Great Britain when they vied for control of Asia. Kipling called the contest between them the Great Game, its mischief still potent. The clans used to be seamless on either side of the border, but the imperial powers insisted on difference, and having divided, they conquered.

Where Uzbekistan and Kyrgyzstan share a common border, violence has boiled over like a kettle on the hob. Kyrgis are killing Uzbekis, though both are Muslim and speak the same Turkic language. But the people of little Kyrgyzstan are mostly nomadic, while those of its larger and more prosperous neighbor are sedentary, living in towns and cities. A lot of them have crossed the border and settled in Kyrgyzstan, especially in the south, where, like

Chinese in India, they have got their hands on all the levers of power, not least economic power. This has fostered resentment: Kyrgis hunt down Uzbekis as French Catholics did French Protestant Huguenots in the bloody massacre of St. Bartholomew's Day. Five hundred years later, things seem not to have changed much.

French Catholic mobs, rampaging through Paris in 1572, paused in their killing when they saw a man with a white cross on his hat and a white scarf on his arm. He had to be one of them. Step by step the mobs in southern Uzbekistan came to a halt before a house marked "Kyrgyz" or simply "KG." Stalin foresaw this Pavlovian behavior in dividing the Ferghana Valley among Kyrgis, Uzbekis, and Tajiks. Soil is rich in the valley and water abundant, a combustible combination sure to breed endless quarreling among its three claimants. This was a tub for Leviathan to play with. Willing to be distracted, they let him go on undeterred.

It was to avoid a hassle at the border crossing that I dropped the rental car in favor of a flight to Mary. This has meant a day to waste, but I discover that an interlude is just what the doctor ordered. Sitting still in an outdoor café, I watch the crowds on the sidewalk, homely affecting faces, a few with a bigger-domed forehead that make me feel more cheerful about life's revolving wheel. Mary is a newish Soviet city, deplored by the guidebooks but not as bad as they say. No one here goes without, thanks to the natural gas discovered under the desert in the last century. The beer is quite good, and the people are friendly. I give the city two cheers. But Mary has only one reason for being. It serves as the gateway to Merv.

By the time the plane touches down, the sun is picking out the mud walls that ring the huge Seljuk city called Sultan Kala. It's no distance at all across the desert by taxi but a universe away in emotional time. Emotional time is historical time multiplied by the full range of human feelings, outrage, despair, trepidation, and horror. My authorities say that different walled cities were built here at different periods, not one atop another as is usually the case but side by side. The Seljuk city was the big one. It rose beside the earlier Gyaur Kala (Castle of the Infidels), dominated by its citadel, Erk Kala. Aerial views, available through the Merv Project at the University of London, show what looks to be a pancake inside a griddle.

The griddle is a good metaphor for Merv, laid out on the Hellenistic plan like our nation's capital. Its walls were square and bisected with gates and towers, but this outer garment was always loosening its belt. Merv in other words was an irredentist city, casting greedy eyes on its neighbors. It had long absorbed Gyaur Kala when it reached its zenith in the twelfth century. By then it ranked just after Baghdad as the second city of Islam. It had some impressive rulers, and the name of one of them, Alp Arslan, still resonates for me. He defeated the Byzantines in a once-famous battle, Manzikert (1071). How melancholy history is! I remember the poet's lines from my schooldays: "'But what good came of it at last?' quoth little Peterkin. 'Why, that I cannot tell,' said he. 'But 'twas a famous victory.'"

Sultan Sanjur's mausoleum outlived his famous victories and still stands, a gaunt giant, as you approach across the desert. The classic form of the Persian mosque with its four *iwans* is owing to him and his fellow rulers in Khorezm. He built his own monument, and its deeply delved foundations have outlasted time, even earthquakes. The walls were thirty-eight meters high and three meters thick, crowned by a blue-tiled dome. From a day's march off, you could see it. Like St. Peter's in Rome, it excites a feeling of awe that seems to me less religious than aesthetic. As in many churches of its time and earlier, for instance Sancta Sophia in Constantinople, the dome sits on a thick column, grotesquely like the head and neck of an overdeveloped athlete. This confronts the architect with a problem: how to fit a round solid on the square solid beneath it without seeming to squash it in place. He solved his problem at Merv by the use of squinches, concentrically wider arches that projected, each time a little farther, around the internal angles they concealed. Outside a curved arcade fulfilled the same function. The clever architect was Muhammad Bini Ateiz Seracsin, who signed his name to the base of the dome. Looking closely, I can just make it out nine centuries later.

OVER TIME legends immortalized the city. Some had it founded by the Persian prophet Zarathustra three thousand years ago. Here, they said, Scheherazade wove her tales of the *One Thousand and One Nights*. Then there were its entertainments. Sultan Sanjur liked a party, and in a windowless castle nicknamed "the house of maidens' tears," he threw parties to remember. All the guests were men, and all the women were slaves. This story rings true.

Home to more than a million people, Merv was master of much of Asia between the Aral Sea and the Mediterranean. It was a cultivated city, and one of its world-renowned libraries numbered 150,000 books. It was tolerant in an intolerant age, accommodating Jews, a Christian monastery, a community of Buddhists. Men of intellect found it to their taste, and among its inhabitants was the astronomer and poet Omar Khayyám. Getting out of the taxi, I walk today's sullen waste, recalling that once it luxuriated in flowers. A network of irrigation ditches crisscrossed the land, creating civic parks and private gardens whose beauty ravished the eye and lifted the spirit.

Omar Khayyám found, however, that the beauty inclined him to sadness.

> I sometimes think that never blows so red
> The Rose as when some buried Caesar bled;
> That every Hyacinth the Garden wears
> Dropt in her Lap from some once lovely Head.

But even sadness summons to delight, why we still read Omar Khayyám.

> Ah, make the most of what we yet may sound,
> Before we too into the Dust descend.

Marv-i-shah-jahan, men called their city, Queen of the World. Into this hugely attractive culture came the Mongols.

They struck with catastrophic force, and Central Asia needed many generations to climb out of the wreckage. Entire peoples were decimated, their economies and lifestyles destroyed. Peasants abandoned their land, no longer fed by the *qanats,* underground water systems on which life depended. Huge geographic areas, like that enveloping Merv, have never recovered. Balkh, Herat, and Nishapur were annihilated, with them the province of Khorezm. A government official wrote of the Mongol period at its end: "Even though there be generation and increase until the Resurrection, the population will not attain to a 10th percent of what it was before."

History records a startling paradox, however. Though its conquerors left Persia a ruin, Persia survived them. More than that, it engulfed them, and the conquerors became the conquered. The Mongol Khanids, under their great chief Hulagu Khan, the grandson of Genghis, were effectively "persianized," turning from violence to cultivate the arts of peace. Especially in architecture, their towers rose higher and their domes swelled in girth. With the Timurids in power, not only architecture but calligraphy, poetry, and historiography underwent a qualitative change, a sea change, and you could say that, tutored by their Persian subjects, they inaugurated a new golden age. But first they had to get through the horrors.

THE MONGOLS came with blandishments a child might have seen through. Genghis Khan, proffering greetings, called the sultan "my son." He wanted tribute, however, a tithe of the city's grain and his choice of its most beautiful women. The Seljuks responded by killing his emissaries. They were foolish, also brave beyond thought.

The Mongols ruled the greatest land empire the world has known, extending at its height from Korea to Hungary. That didn't happen by chance. They waged a new kind of warfare, based on light cavalry whose mounted archers and swordsmen struck with sudden fury, then galloped away. Each soldier traveled with five or more horses. If the army numbered more than one hundred thousand men, as when it attacked the Khorezmian Shah in 1220, there must have been half a million horses on the hoof. Their very appearance filled enemies with something like paralysis. Still more fearsome were the riders, their blackened faces burned by the sun, or fire-red and yellow, whelked with "botches and blains." (They rarely washed.) Their bodies were steely, their eyes narrow and piercing, heads shorn, mouths like a slash from cheekbone to cheekbone. The Chinese called them Mongols, the people of Mongolia called them Tatars. Europeans confused this with Tartarus, the Underworld, and *Tartars* became a byword for devils out of Hell. In medieval art the devil is invariably black.

Cold, hunger, and thirst they endured uncomplainingly, but when strong drink was before them, both men and women threw it down like drunkards. Gluttonous at the table, they roasted and consumed an entire horse at a sitting. They were polygamous, the son taking the wives of his dead father, only the mother excepted. Nomadic and illiterate, they despised the rest of the world, locating themselves at its center. Oddly they disliked shedding blood. That didn't mean taking pity. A fastidious son of Genghis had the Persian caliph wrapped in a carpet and beaten to death. "Regret is the fruit of pity," said the Great Khan. Acting out this saying, he killed to the last man.

In the part of the world that includes Merv, the earth is mostly loess, a clayey substance like putty. Covering the toppled castles or *koshts* that stood up here like medieval towers, it doesn't hide their bulk, only their sharpness of outline. The two great mounds my taxi stops in front of look like spooks hiding under a bedsheet. "Merv!" says the driver, shrugging his shoulders. Relics of the earlier city, Gyaur Kala, the mounds stand on end like big pipes—in fact the bigger one is called the Organ Pipe, though it will never make music. Their sides are cut with vertical clefts like the corrugated doors of a boxcar, their tops are indented with crenels, through which defenders fired their weapons. Or might have, had they not taken the Mongols at their word.

Behind the *koshts* are fragments of the old walls, broken by what look to be gates, and at intervals the sketchy outline of a tower. This countryside is a crucible, however, distinction collapsing into a few primitive forms. An opening is a window, a partial opening a hearth, an obstruction a door or wall. Through the open space between the two castles runs an incline of hard-packed mud like frozen lava. Bizarrely it calls to mind the lava that coats the big rocks half buried in the harbor at Santorini, another vanished civilization absurdly covered in curds and cream. The twin castles themselves, lacking the beauty of form, are anonymous seeming and evoke neither time nor place. They call to mind a modern sculpture in front of a public building.

A buttress holds up the one on the right, a donjon-like tower the other. Surmounting the incline is a platform, and I imagine Hamlet and Horatio walking below the battlements that go with a castle. But no clock strikes midnight, and the sun, no longer waterish, has sent malignant spirits packing. I hear the whirr of pigeon wings, a constant in the empty space between walls. Raising my eyes, slowly, for who can say what I'll see, I look out on fields that run flat to the horizon. There is nothing in them but osiers and pale green tamarisk trees, only a few feet high. A car goes by on the one-lane road, the same road I took to get here, and I see telephone poles in the distance. Though I try hard to conceive of the carnage eight hundred years ago, I find I can't make myself do it.

I have another reason for visiting Merv. West of Sanjur's tomb, a final item on my itinerary is the mausoleum of Muhammad ibn Zayd, founder of the Shi'ites. Near falling apart, it is being put back together. Broken rungs from corrugated castles litter the desert around it. Standing in a grove of saxaul trees, said to be holy, the mausoleum has an impressive central dome and some nice little ones setting it off, and the yellow bricks in the north wall go back a long way. I carry with me a memory of the seashell design in the mihrab—*scallops;* wouldn't you know it, the same scallops Christian pilgrims wore in their hats on the way to St. Thomas's shrine in Compostela.

Some see this surprising sameness as pointing to the basic sameness of Christian and Muslim under the skin. Others propose cultural influence, still others a gallimaufry of archetypes, like symbols on a slot machine ready to fire when the right combination comes up. The truth, more prosaic, is that the seashells must tell of real scallops fished from the sea, the Mediterranean or the Aral Sea or some wandering lake such as China's Lop Nor. This doesn't mean that things are always what they seem. Hanging on the trees around the mausoleum are strips of white and garish-colored cloth that look like ratty laundry but are hope offerings left by last year's pilgrims. If they return in festival time, the feast of Khudajuli, their previous year's wish will be granted. So many readings of matter-of-fact cluster about this remote place in Asia, all deriving order from chaos.

It is pleasantly cool inside the mausoleum, and I exchange friendly nods with the toothless old man who guards the black marble cenotaph in the center of the floor. But I hear chickens clucking and children giggling, and taking my Dictaphone in hand, I go out to record them. A little boy, less abashed than the others, speaks a phrase into the machine, and when I play it back at him he's convulsed, they all are. Their happiness, while it pleases, subdues me. One of those gloomy poems of Robert Frost's comes to mind. "Weep for what little things could make them glad."

THE ARMY GENGHIS KHAN sent against Merv arrived in the dead of winter. He was determined to plow the city up utterly, like Carthage when the Romans were through with it, and he chose as best suited for the job his third and fiercest son, Tolui. But Tolui, making a circuit of the city walls, could find no way in. So he resorted to trickery, preparing catapults and battering rams for the siege he never intended. At the same time, he offered terms. He would spare the inhabitants provided they surrendered. The credulous burghers opened their gates, and he killed them as they emerged.

Not all died supinely. Some fought to the last on Forty Mullahs Hill (Kyrk Molla). The bones of these defenders are still visible at the base of the hill, among them decapitated skulls. Each soldier was instructed to bring in between three and four hundred heads. Reports put the initial slaughter at half a million, rising to a million. I read that from the sun's reflection "the plain seemed to be a tray filled with blood." Nothing about the aversion to bloodshed. After much of this, the smell of blood gets in the nostrils, but there is more and worse to come. Having destroyed the city, the Mongols withdrew, disappearing over the horizon. Survivors, thinking themselves safe, crept back to pick through the ruins. When they had all come back, Tolui returned and butchered every one left. Finally Merv was at peace.

The Mongols, both in their duplicity and their absolute lack of ruth, look forward to Stalin. Like him they stopped at nothing to achieve their ghastly objectives. But compared to him, they were pikers in killing, monstrous, no doubt, but not in a class by themselves. What sets Stalin apart is less brute force than his intelligence, and in exerting it he transcended his subservient time. All the Mongols ever wanted was power, but he was an ideologue and wanted to build the kingdom of God, or some evil simulacrum, on earth. His perverting of the intellect gives him his special character, like Lucifer, a prince of darkness.

Half-hearted attempts at rebuilding the city of Merv came to nothing. Most of the ruined structures are still buried, with the people who lived in them, under the impartial earth. I study the earth with eyes asquint, holding back tears. The taxi driver, waiting behind the wheel, wonders what ails me. He thinks it's time to be going and looks pointedly at his watch. I am bending to get back in the cab when I see in the distance a sight that chills my blood.

A hand seems half-rising from the floor of the desert, its fingers sticking up at the sky. My University of London catalog says this isn't an apparition but another ruined *kosht,* "Five Finger Castle." It seems too small for a *kosht.* Perhaps the fingers were meant as a turf balk or windbreak, or could they have had an iconic function, lost with the time that understood it? Or just possibly, were they raised in supplication? My catalog informs me that their shape was conventional, but that is all it says, and no other version survives.

Tower of Silence, outside Yazd, Iran. Photograph by the author.

Qanats and wind tunnels, Yazd, Iran. Photograph by the author.

Tomb of Cyrus the Great, Pasargadae, Iran.

Delegations bearing gifts, from Eastern Stairway, Persepolis, Iran.

Warrior, from Eastern Stairway, Persepolis, Iran.

Pishtaq Arch and Ablution Pool, Isfahan, Iran. Photograph by the author.

Chehel Sotum Palace, Isfahan, Iran.

Imam Mosque and Square, Isfahan, Iran.

AZERBAIJAN
Baku
TURKMENISTAN
Amu Darya
TURKEY
Caspian Sea
Tabriz
Ashgabad
Merv
Atrak
Harirud
Mary
Mashad
Mt. Demavend
Tehran
Dasht-e Kavir
Baghdad
IRAN
AFGHANISTAN
Tigris
Karkheh
Isfahan
Euphrates
Yazd
IRAQ
Pasargadae
Helmand
KUWAIT
Persepolis
Shiraz
PAKISTAN
Persian Gulf
SAUDI ARABIA
Gulf of Oman
UNITED ARAB EMIRATES
OMAN
Cartography by Manoa Mapworks, Inc.

11

Persia of the Ages

Ashkabad lies just above the Iranian border. I need to cross the border and head west for Tehran, where I have arranged to meet with Mary. My wife is a "multi-tasker," too busy at a multitude of chores to come with me. Now, however, she has got her life in order, and we can do the last leg of the trip together.

A young Iranian male, handsome but sullen and wearing the orange garb of an airport employee, is waiting as she gets off the plane in Tehran. Inside the hall I blow her a kiss and get an impersonal smile in return. Mary doesn't like public displays of affection. She has buttonholed the same flight attendant, who seems not to be listening. "Why are we standing here?" and the like. (I can read her lips.) When her chin tilts up like that, she's the image of Myrna Loy. He doesn't answer but holds up his hand, a cop directing traffic. She tries again. "Excuse me?" This time with an edge to it. Her first taste of Iran, and you'd think she might play the docile woman's role, doing what they want her to, but not Mary.

Going on a half century ago, youngsters like this one stormed the U.S. embassy and took its staff of fifty-two persons prisoner in the name of the Iranian Republic of Islam. They waited 444 days to be free. But the taciturn young man is the only one of his kind. A well-groomed Iranian woman, first off the plane, sees Mary tapping her sensible shoe in annoyance and turns back to ask what's wrong. "Never mind him!" she says, speaking English. "He's an Arab!"

"How can you tell when he won't open his mouth?" Mary asks her.

"That's how they behave!" the lady says. "When they invaded my country, they brought nothing but destruction. Even the Mongols were builders, not them. Persia got through that time, though. It kept its culture and its precious language, never fear."

But Mary's new friend is only getting started. "Do you know what happened when *they* took over? The dress code happened. They made divorce impossible without the husband's permission. They saw to it that the women sat behind the men at Friday mosque."

"That seems much," Mary says.

"Actually it's funny," the lady says. "We have to touch our heads to the floor at prayer, you know, and women, when they do this, elevate their bottoms! It gave scandal to the men in back of them!"

When Mary, having passed through customs, tells me this story a few moments later, I realize with a shock that the outpouring of emotion was directed at the Arab conquest of Iran, thirteen hundred years ago. Memories in this part of the world go back a long way.

The nice lady is a forerunner of many. We encounter them everywhere, in the countryside as well as the city. In front of the mosque in Abarkul on the road out of Yazd, another woman and her daughter ask our guide in Farsi about Mary and me. Switching to perfect English, the woman welcomes the two of us to "my country." Her daughter puts her mite in, and I nod my effusive thank you's, getting the gist. Pushing back the mandatory scarf that conceals her hair, the woman lifts an etched amber disk from her neck, on it a winged figure. "Ahura Mazda. You've heard of it?"

"Zoroastrian?" Mary says.

"They were here in the beginning. Long before Islam. This pendant is for you. I hope it will bring you good luck." Lifting the chain in both hands, the woman puts it over Mary's head, touches her daughter's arm, and is gone.

In the bazaar in Tehran, an old man with a stump for a leg gets up from his stool when I pause in front of his hat shop. "You know where I got this leg?" he asks, and proceeds to tell us. Attached to a unit of American engineers at Fort Benning, Georgia—those were the days when we were training the Shah's army—he'd thought the explosive he kicked away from him was a dud. Mary looks sympathetic. "But never mind the leg," he says, smiling at her. "America is best."

Ducking into a stall hung with clothes for gents and ladies, I watch while my wife buys an outfit, de rigueur for the well-dressed Iranian woman. A new scarf comes first, more serviceable than the skimpy bit of silk she brought with her. She has to hide her hair completely, as if Delilah had the long, sexually empowering tresses, not Samson, also every trace of woman's flesh except the face and hands. To hide her flesh, she has an old raincoat, long enough but lacking style. We replace it with a manteau—they use the French word, grotesquely out of place—extending from the head to just above the knee. Slacks cover the rest of her.

Iranian women wear what the mullahs tell them to, though it assigns a doubtful character to all the daughters of Eve. Up to now it hasn't crossed their minds, or they haven't been able to say no. A minority dress in flowing black from head to toe, like the nuns of my childhood without the white wimple. But most of them, while they follow the letter of the law, mock its spirit unmercifully. Stiletto heels are the mode in this straitlaced city, shocking pinks and luscious purples storm the eye in their head scarves, and the required long cloak and pants, cleaving to their form, reveal it. Their masters want them to deny the body, but like a bell crier in the streets, they proclaim its sexuality, asking the world to notice.

Mary is trying on her new manteau, turning this way and that in the shop's full-length mirror. Despite her no-nonsense manner, she has her share of female vanity, and it endears her. While she is making up her mind, I try to engage the salesman in small talk. An agreeable young man, a lot like scruffy Americans his age, he has a beard coming, and with luck it will cover his acne. He wants to be friends, but he has no English. I have no Farsi. Though each of us is willing, neither is able. At last, the sale consummated, he sighs, puts a hand on each of my shoulders, and kisses me on both cheeks.

For two and a half millennia, Iran has been kicked from pillar to post, thrall to the Achaemenids, then Greek Alexander, subsequently Genghis Khan and a host of others only less ferocious. Bringing the list up to date is the Ayatollah Khamenei, spelled a little differently than the revolutionary Khomeini but cut from the same cloth. His cold eyes, looking out of photographs, say what he is. But Iran is resilient. Possessing its soul in patience, it has endured all its oppressors, taking none to its bosom. Alexander, "going Persian," married a Persian wife, Roxane, and at his wedding, thousands of his soldiers took their vows with him. Who was the conqueror here, who the conquered? Sex is the people's current weapon of choice against their oppressors, difficult for the mullahs, their cramped nature limiting what they can know. I think their rule will be short-lived. *Farr* is the word Iranians use to describe the right to rule. It depends on their behavior, and if they behave badly, they are open to removal. My guess is that their intolerance will cost them their *farr*. The uncivilized regimen foisted on young men by these old men forgets that we're flesh and blood, and not called Homo sapiens for nothing.

From my vantage point in America thousands of miles away, Iranians seem to be backed in a corner, but closer up not many look cowed. On the grounds of Tehran's White Palace, formerly the summer residence of the Pahlavi shahs, city dwellers out for a lark are strolling or sunbathing on the grassy lawns. Upstairs in the ceremony hall, they are scuffing their shoes on the biggest carpet ever woven in Iran. It is their carpet. Peterhof outside Russia's capital is like this, once reserved to the czars, now a people's playground. In front of the White Palace where the stairs go up to the entrance is a gargantuan pair of black boots, outsize copies of the leather boots worn by Reza Shah, the father of Iran's last ruler.

Renaming Persia Iran, he returned it to the old name it bore in the time of Cyrus the Great. Reza Shah wanted his country to resume the glory the Achaemenids had bequeathed it. At the same time, he wanted to be Ataturk and move his country into the modern world. The mullahs bore him a grudge for that and made sure he paid for their animosity. The one thing that got their hackles up was change. The boots without legs in them are an emblem of change. Little kids think them funny. When the revolution came, the people took an ax to the shah's statue, everything but the boots. He had lost his *farr*. This truncated statue, all that is left of his former high-and-mightiness, is a symbol of the world turned upside down.

But the new world in Iran isn't a chaos. Its revolutionary idea is to live and let live. I speak of the people, not their masters. The writing is on the wall, though, and the masters might want to consult it before the fate of Reza Shah overtakes them. Being arrogant as well as myopic, however, it's likely they'll stick to their guns. This means that change, when it comes, will be wrenching.

The Iranian male has a surprise in store too. Like St. Paul he thinks the man is the head of the woman.

"How can he believe that!" asks Mary, a rhetorical question, playing along with me.

"He doesn't," I admit. "In his heart he knows it's a half truth. But he has an ingenious expedient. The entry door from the street has a bifold panel. The right-hand panel, the thicker one, is for him, the left-hand panel for her. When he knocks, she recognizes his big bow-wow sound and claps on her head scarf before she opens up."

"Her knock is different?" says Mary.

"So faint you can hardly hear it," I say. "That isn't true of them all, of course." Some are like Mary's, though I don't say so. "When Eros is part of the scenario," I tell her, "they take a good look at Delilah, estimating her power to make mischief. Before it can scorch them, they put out her fire."

But things are changing in Iran. We go down for dinner in the old hotel where we're staying, the Laleh, which used to be the Intercon. Once it was stylish, but it's been allowed to run to seed, no water in the pool, the landscaping untended. But it is keeping the Islamic side up, and Mary, entering the dining room with her hair exposed for all to see, is guilty of a no-no. Her head scarf is still on the dresser in the hotel room, and suddenly aware, she puts her hands to her head, eyes widening.

But the men in the room, taking it all in, laugh and give her the thumbs up sign. For them the edict of the mullahs and the convention it appeals to seem threadbare. Our guide, Karim, an educated man who has traveled in the greater world, laughs with them. He jokes at the crudities of President Ahmadinejad, "Dinner Jacket," he calls him. His bantering makes us feel hopeful.

Point counterpoint, however. An afternoon in Isfahan's Armenian Quarter puts a damper on too-easy assumptions. In the Quarter, a Christian enclave in the sea of Islam, the women, Christian or not, must wear the head scarf. "As they should," says our sophisticated guide laconically, not giving the matter much thought. His prepossessions, unexamined in the nature of such, run deep. Not wanting to embarrass him, I forbear asking why Armenian Christians should cover up like their Muslim sisters. But I make a mental reservation. East is East and West is West, and before they come together, this twain will have to travel some way.

Their clothing, the kind they wear voluntarily, not by fiat, says that many of them don't want to go the distance. Some women, even young ones, choose to wear the chador. This black cloak shrouds their bodies like a tent. When they pull the "visor" across their face, only their eyes are visible, peering out furtively. Ill-omened blackbirds, they lean forward when they walk, feeling for earth, eager, it seems, to have it shoveled over their heads.

I have to thank my father for giving me a prophylactic against them. I might not have understood how out of this world they are unless I had passed through his hands. He was the kind of man who checked to see that all the windows and doors were shut tight and bolted before he went to bed. He looked forward to the day when he might write finis to sending out Christmas cards, his monthly visits to the barber, his twice yearly visits to the dentist. I still see him cleaning out the icebox, as if he were about to close it for good.

THE CITY STREETS around Tehran's Archaeological Museum, close to the main post office and Khomeini Square, are pestiferous with little cars Mary would like to swat at. "Almost as bad as Seoul or Bangkok," she says.

"The modern world is more in our face in this city," I say. "One big reason is the way they keep down the price of gas. It's a version of Rome's bread and circuses. Everybody's on the road, as if my lungs didn't know it! Emissions control is a brand new idea they think might be worth looking into."

Partly, I realize, geography is the culprit. Much of this country is high plateau, four to five thousand feet above sea level. The air is polluted, as bad as it gets, and the mountains standing over the city seal it in. I find myself short of breath, sometimes doubling over with spasms.

"A lot of it is the way Iranians drive," she says. "They're like berserker Italians."

"Under the skin Iranians are a breed apart," I say. I remember some historian describing their Persian consciousness—*iraniyyat* was his word—making them unlike any other. "Their culture was a thousand years old when the Arabs arrived. And it shows."

We are returning to the city from a visit to Mount Davidand, their tallest peak. A spectacular sight, it goes 18,600 feet, guaranteeing that tourists and locals alike will clog the highway out and back on a sunny afternoon. We move at petty pace, two lanes of traffic flowing one way, two another. After an hour of this, it gets on the nerves.

"We're caught in a neap tide," Mary says. "Unless something is done, we'll be spending the night here."

The carpet dealer Maggi comes to my mind, a charming scoundrel who snookered me into buying a tribal carpet I dearly wanted but couldn't afford in my wildest. How did he do this? He clinched the deal by telling me that I had more taste than the generality of men. "Most of them think a tribal rug is the work of peasants," he says. "If they can't afford a city rug, they'll buy the machine-made stuff dyed with chemical dyes before they'll buy a tribal."

"How sad," I say.

"But you're different," he says. "It's obvious you have discrimination."

"Well," I say sheepishly, "I'm not so sure of that!" It's a Hamadan he's pushing at me, nomad work, the wool from mountain sheep, the design geometric, my preference. It doesn't need to argue its merits.

"Over ten years, the money will amortize anyway," he says. "Don't deny yourself the pleasure."

He wasn't being dishonest, only plying his trade. All at once I realize that this is what the traffic jam we're locked in requires. *Audace! Audace!* Where are you, Maggi, when we need you?

Suddenly, without signaling, the driver in front of us makes a U-turn. Before you can say "Down with Ahmadinejad," he has darted into the lane beside us, paralleling our car but going in the opposite direction. Just down the road is a turnoff on his right and a straight shot back to town. The only way to reach it, though, is via the direction he's taken. Executing this maneuver, he isn't playing chicken, only doing what he can with the sliver of wiggle room at his disposal. Nobody hoots an angry horn. But he has put a bee in their bonnet, and acting on his better idea, they convert the four lanes of traffic to three. We are out of there in a jiffy!

That wouldn't satisfy an Italian. He wants to reduce you to a puddle of helpless agitation. Doing this, he employs a colorful vocabulary. Something like "I have just come from sleeping with your mother." Iranians aren't that imaginative. The different principle they live by is that nobody's feathers be ruffled.

A great surge of energy came in with the Revolution, and the new highways and apartment houses in and around the city show how it galvanized the country. Now, however, under the dead hand of Ahmadinejad, the energy has leaked away. In the election that brought him to power, he was the populist candidate, promising to give the downtrodden a hand up. But he does what the mullahs want him to, and their interests aren't served by shaking things up. So change from the top is nonexistent, and change from the bottom is verboten.

Failing intervention from the outside, protest doesn't stand a chance against the bayonets of the Revolutionary Guard. The Guard runs the country, its missile and nuclear programs, its economy, the secret police. But though Ahmadinejad and his patron the Ayatollah are stronger today than a year ago, their power seems increasingly naked, more a matter of force than conviction. It depends on censorship, prison terms, even execution. Mostly a tactful visitor (like me) skirts political discussion, but it breaks through, a mole under the surface. Some hardy souls have demanded the prosecution of those who stole the last election. That takes chutzpah. I have talked with a few who oppose the Islamic Revolution itself. (I do this gingerly, looking at a point above their heads.)

There is a kind of protest that is more difficult to defend against than the sticks and stones that break your bones. How are the men at the top to react when the people they are lying to, hosing down, or beating on with billy clubs respond less with rage than with something akin to humor? This seems in the nature of Iranian people, not morose like some Russians, costive like some English, gabby like some French, volatile like some Italians, but inclining to be happy. This doesn't say they are hypergelastic, like some Americans. Nor will they roll over if push comes to shove. Hungarians are good-natured but died for freedom when the Russians invaded.

The geniality of Iranians is worth commenting on a little. Masters of a first-rate cuisine, they regard sitting down to a thoughtfully prepared meal as a decidedly sensual pleasure. Here are some quotes from an Iranian cookbook, Mary's and mine. "Drops of butter on the face of Qa'meh (a finely minced meat) tell us of the dew on tulip petals." Or: "Delighted is the Pomegranate which has a secret with Sugar!" That sounds like Hāfez—or Blake!

Their minced kebab, prepared by thrusting a long, flat-bladed knife through the molded hamburger and grilling it slowly, can be forked into the mouth like custard. Their rice, light and dry, almost a condiment, tastes of pomegranate and walnut. Their finger food, pistachios, *paladeh*, sorbet made of rice flour (this needs a spoon), flaky baklava, nougats, sinewy delights that hint of cardamom, *pashmak*, a cotton candy, all tell of a people content in their body. It shows in the way they behave. A well-dressed older man whose round belly seems lined with good capon can't keep his eyes off my portable oxygen. Ruefully, he says, "No more smoking, eh?" I agree, and he shakes my hand, calling back "Good luck!" over his shoulder.

Customers in the fabulous sweet shop in Shiraz, bustling in and out with a smile on their face, might be saying to the world, "All is well." What they do say, to whoever makes eye contact, is *Salom*. Welcome. Exploring the Atigh Mosque, this city's oldest, we come on a trio of roustabouts slumped against a wall, shoeless, unshaven, possibly drinking. Are these bums going to make trouble? Surprising me, they say in unison, "Salom," and we answer in kind.

My eye lights on lovely young women everywhere I look, "a frieze of girls," the title a friend of mine hit on for his autobiography. On Friday, an Iranian holiday, our Sunday, they throng the mosques and madrassas, troops of them in their school uniforms, learning their culture. Flirty but not self-conscious, too young yet to be aware of women's wiles, they mill around us wanting to talk, take our picture, be friends. Why can't we be friends? Like an adolescent girl, I put the question, feeling its pathos, also its naïveté. I know about their crimes and misdemeanors, a good deal more about ours, how we deposed Mossadegh, their prime minister, installed the young Shah and licensed his out-of-control spending, even propped up Saddam. Perhaps the crude lefties are right, and it all comes down to oil. We want it, they have it. So Iranians, voicing their grievances, have reason.

The first constitutional government in the Near East was Iran's, ratified by the Shah in 1906. With it came at least the rudiments of a free press and an accelerating impulse to a real democratic society. But the CIA, acting on instructions from our President Eisenhower, ousted Iran's Mohammad Mossadegh in 1953. The idea was to contain Communism. The result was to turn the embryonic democracy into a cauldron of anti-American resentment. The Iranian revolution of 1979 was its sequel.

All this embittered history says to me that we must be the first to hold out the olive branch. The gesture must be genuine, not fraught with disingenuous motives. Yet it must be leavened with intelligent self-interest. We are impoverished as we persist in our enmity, Iran being too rich a culture for us to deprive ourselves of it. As I quit the hotel in Shiraz, I see that all the flags of the nations are banked in a corner of the lobby, all but the Stars and Stripes. This omission seems too bad. We must hasten the day when we repair it, while understanding that more than being nice is involved.

IRAN'S ARCHAEOLOGICAL MUSEUM goes back ten thousand years. Much of what's in it is lifted from the clayey soil of Persepolis. There, in the lee of the Zagros Mountains, Cyrus the Great and the Achaemenids who came after him reared a colossal shrine to the world's first empire meriting the name. At its greatest extent, it stretched from India to the Mediterranean, but not everything about it was on the grand scale. I carry with me in memory the carved image of a sitting dog, dead who knows how many centuries but so alert it might come running if I whistled. Alexander the Great, certifying his barbarian side, made a bonfire of Persepolis, and he and his soldiers capered drunkenly as they torched its incalculable treasures. But the columns and sculptures, toppled by the flames, fell into the earth, where the soft, enfolding soil preserved them. Archaeologists have a multitude of clues to work with, and with their aid they are piecing the shattered egg back together. Twenty-three centuries have gone since Alexander burned Persepolis, but "now at last," says A. T. Olmstead, concluding his *History of the Persian Empire* (1948), "Achaemenid Persia has risen from the dead."

Its culture was a potpourri, and the museum reflects this. Among its contents is a mosaic tile that seems to be Pompeian, not Persian. The toga-clad figures breathe the pathos of doomed men and women who know that death is coming their way. But the identification on the wall says this relic is from Parthia. Its king defeated the Roman emperor Valerian in A.D. 260 and made him captive with much of his army. The artist at work on the mosaic was one of these captives, reason for the sadness his work communicates, but he had his life spared because he was skillful at tiling. He always knew that art had its uses.

His art of mosaic seeks to render people in situations that engage emotion, theirs and the viewer's, sad on this occasion, joyful, it might be, on some other. Beside him in the museum is Picasso, recognizable at once, his primitive African sculpture almost a contemporary icon. The caption on the wall says that the donor wanted "to enliven moribund convention," presumably the staple stuff on exhibit. He—or the work he donated—does something rather different. It sets in a clearer light the superior quality of much of the work that surrounds it. The sculpture, characteristically iconoclastic, diminishes what it renders. Its range is limited, and the masklike visage withholds emotion rather than expressing it. This generic art hews close to the convention it takes off from, fitting comfortably in its narrow niche. The Parthian tile maker ranges more widely, and runs the danger of losing his way. But that is how he finds his way.

A city of consequence, if more than bricks and mortar, must include at least one first-class museum, and the Jewel Museum in Tehran has no equal this side of the Tower of London. It has its downside, a shortness of air. To reach the vault, I walk down a long, narrow staircase, breathing harder as I descend, but the tightness in my chest is compensated by what opens to my eyes. The shahs, when they sat to their toilet, must have liked what they saw in the mirror. The Globe of Jewels betters the great globe itself, if your taste, like mine, runs to the man-made artifact over the thing it mimics. Its sea is made of emeralds and the land of rubies, except that Iran, without peer, is all diamonds. Fifty-one thousand precious stones do for the leftover bits.

Much of the bric-a-brac that tourists like me gape at once balanced on the head or limbs of Iran's rulers. The Pahlavi Crown or Sea of Light, a pink diamond weighing in at 182 carats (that's times 200 milligrams), must have taken getting used to. But the royal person who wore it first, Fatteh Ali Shah, a scion of the Qajar dynasty, was clearly to the manner born. Early in the nineteenth century, a British diplomat stood entranced in the blaze of light that enveloped His Royal Highness. "On his head the lofty tiara of three elevations . . . [was] entirely composed of thickly-set diamonds, pearls, rubies, and emeralds," its points "finished with pear-shaped pearls of an immense size. . . . The jeweled band on his right arm, called the Mountain of Light," had for a complement the Sea of Light on his left. Both these superb diamonds found their way into the Persian regalia thanks to the rapacious Nader Shah, the eighteenth-century ruler who plundered India to glorify his kingdom. Splendor as the yield of violence is a familiar topos for Iran.

Where royalty was, I am now, and staring at these enormous baubles, I feel a charge of sexual energy coursing through them. In my superheated fantasy, I feel a frisson of something like it myself. I see the Queen of Iran, an expensive beauty, on her wedding night. She is wearing a white gold tiara and two loopy earrings, solid gold. That is all she is wearing. I compute the cost of bedding this modern Semiramis, my fingers ticking off vast sums of money. Rials beyond thinking! But I can offer as earnest the Kiani Crown, studded with twenty-seven thousand gems.

The Carpet Museum, a short walk from our hotel, gets only a line in the guidebook. I take it seriously, however, and Mary isn't surprised.

"You are the Grand Acquisitor," she says. "A good thing these carpets aren't for sale."

"All I ask is half an hour's walk through the collection," I say. It turns out that half a day is more like it. But though poring over the museum's treasures is time well spent, I have to accept that they are out of my sphere. I take away more than baffled cupidity, however. Many of them are representational, gorgeously so, forcing me to modify the preference for pure form I'd thought the Islamic standard of value. But the deeper I delve in Iran's multilayered fabric, the more unnatural seems my categorizing instinct. At any rate it doesn't work for Iran. Islamic faith testifies against the multilayered thing in the Hadith, sayings attributed to the Prophet. But how strictly his followers observe the prohibition of representing humans or other figures from the natural world depends on whether your tilt is to Sunni or Shi'a. The latter, gaining the upper hand in Persia from about 1500, seems more accommodating to flesh and blood. Much reason it should be. Most of Iran is desert, endless wastes of gray-brown dirt, rock, and stone. Against this dreary landscape are the formal gardens that enliven Persian carpets. One of my authors says finely that all Persian carpets are woven gardens, "the artistic precipitate of the nomad's dream" (P. R. J. Ford, *Oriental Carpet Design*, 1992). "After all," I say. "Iran is an amalgam, one state of mind mixing with another. Just the kind of thing decorum says no to."

"What does the Bard say?" Mary asks me. "No, not Hāfez, Shakespeare! 'Hot ice and wondrous strange snow'—that's the kind of pairing we should be looking for. There, for example," and she points to a carpet depicting Nader Shah and his court. The brute of a ruler is kneeling on his divan, contemplating who knows what enormity, but lovely ladies and sagacious counselors stand around him, converting his gall to milk. He is nice old Nader Shah, a sense enforced by the warm hues that depict him. They shouldn't be warm; decorum says they should be frigid!

But nature at a remove puts decorum to flight. Yellow flowers such as larkspur, or vegetable dyes, red madder or indigo blue, impart the warmth the carpet radiates. Some of it comes from crushed insects, some from shellfish or dyer's weed, growing wild in the Middle East. The coloring is artificial, but its source is nature, and the transforming of Nader Shah isn't arbitrary, like that of old Scrooge from skinflint to hail-fellow-well-met. It is a natural transformation, but nature mediated by art.

Later, via the Internet, I supplement the museum's collection with color photos from reference books. Two good ones are David Black's *Macmillan Atlas of Rugs and Carpets* (1985) and Eiland and Eiland's *Oriental Rugs* (1973). They reinforce the idea building in me that Persia in its art is at a distance of some degrees from the rest of Islam. As early as the earliest surviving Persian carpet (beginning of the sixteenth century), the "figure in the carpet" seems indebted to the natural world. Often it evokes the classical Persian garden. Or a geometric scheme blends with flowers, animals, even humans, in a single frame. Examples so abound across the spectrum of time and place as to beget the feeling—anyway, in me—that Iranians love nature more than art.

The primacy of nature is suggested by an antique carpet from Tabriz. Sliced into segments, twenty-five in all, it resembles a series of miniature paintings, each in a separate envelope. The scenes are discrete, some violent, some composed, almost all devoted to some aspect of the physical world, but they make a unity like the poem they are rendering, Iran's national epic, the *Shahnama* or *Book of Kings*. The carpet I am looking at is dated 1220 AH, that is, After the Hegira, the flight of Muhammad from Mecca to Medina in 622 A.D. With that date the Muslim calendar begins. Simple addition tells me that the carpet was woven in the first half of the nineteenth century. But the poem it takes off from is much older.

Ferdosi, its maker, labored on it for twenty-five years, finishing his magnum opus early in the eleventh century. He meant it for Persia's ruler, Muhammad of Ghazni, but the sultan, a Turk, declined to accept it because there weren't any Turks in the story. It makes a good yarn to go with the pathos of Ferdosi's death, penniless, old, and sore at heart. But he saved the Farsi language, under siege from Arabic, and he saved Persia's history and culture. It is said that every Iranian, whatever his education or lack of it, has passages from the *Shahnama* by heart.

The tale of Sohrab and Rustum, familiar to English speakers from the long poem by Matthew Arnold, is almost its centerpiece. It tells how young Sohrab, leader of the Tatars, and his father, Rustum, Persia's great champion, meet in single combat beside the Oxus. Epic similes are of a piece with the helter-skelter of Persian carpets (apparent, not real), replete with extraneous-seeming matter but composing a unified whole. Death-and-transfiguration is the ground note, for the heroes as for the great river, leaving its beginnings far behind in the high cradle of the Pamirs. But the Oxus keeps going, till at last the dash of waves is heard, "and wide His luminous home of waters opens."

The poem, a narrative in couplets, offers an account of Persia's history, incidentally its psychology, even its soul. Read aloud, my translation, by Dick Davis, sounds like Pope's *Odyssey.* It has brio and marches to an affirmative beat. Drawing the sting from the Arab takeover, it gives Persia's people a version of themselves to be proud of. The carpet from Tabriz is like the poem in microcosm, another reading of the representational art Iran's psyche is prone to.

Outside the museum the street is swept clean, little bundles of rubbish piled by the curb, waiting for the pickup truck. Cleanliness is next to godliness, Iranians think, and Americans aren't so different. The mullahs are clean, too, anyway fastidious. The Zoroastrians, there before them, were cleanest of all. Not wanting to pollute the earth, they laid their dead in towers of silence (*darhmeh*), brick or stone structures open to the air and built on a mountain. The vultures came down to pick the bodies clean, and when naught was left but bones, the priests dropped them in a pit at the center of the tower, dousing them with acid until they decomposed.

The population of vultures has declined, and bodies don't disintegrate as promptly as they used to. Today the Zoroastrians, still a presence in Iran, bury their dead in a proper cemetery. But they remain faithful to the imperatives they honored three thousand years ago, and they line the grave with concrete so the body won't come in contact with earth.

THE SILK ROAD, linking Persia to China and India and the other way to Europe, ran through Shiraz in the east and in the west through Yazd on the edge of the southern desert. That part of the road is still substantially intact. Travelers can stay the night in a rebuilt caravansary deep in the Old City. Centuries ago they came from Venice and Chang'an, meeting in the courtyard to swap stories of their faraway lands. If they wanted to pray, Yazd had a mosque to serve the need, going back to pre-Seljuk times, that is, before the eleventh century. Both mosque and caravansary are dun colored and purged of adornment. Austere St. Bernard, whose abbey at Fontenoy reflects the same impulse to negation, would have understood and sympathized. This is the other face of Islam. Shunning a pantheon of gods, no Father, Son, and Holy Ghost, no Blessed Virgin Mary, its rubric is *ars celare artem,* the art that hides art or, better, abjures it.

Yazd is one of the oldest inhabited places on earth, not worn-out, however, but lived in. Its "Old City," an oxymoron since all of it is older than time, is lined with handsome plane trees called *chinar* in the East. I am reminded of some leafy streets in Rome, the Via Nomentana, for instance, going north outside the walls. On Yazd's twisting, narrow streets, the houses are of sun-dried brick, and the women who live in them wear black chadors. They jar on the nerves when I meet them in a populous modern setting such as Tehran, but here the vibes are good. Yazd, unlike Tehran, is a product of "the dark backward of time" and reflects this in its social intercourse. The truths by which we recognize its religion aren't handed down, as by God to Moses, but grow out of the environment and are imposed on man by nature. But *conservative* and *natural* are synonymous in Yazd.

The enduring vitality of this city, remarked by Marco Polo eight hundred years ago, is a function of water, rare in the Dasht-e lut Desert. Heat can blister the skin when May turns to June, but wind-catchers called *badgirs* overlook the city like towers in San Gimignano, and however slight the breeze, they catch it and pass it on to the houses below. The currents of wind, crossing a pool of cooling water before they enter the house, lower its temperature. At the same time, warm air, blocked from entry, travels a circular path up and out, moved along by a shaft in the body of the wind-catcher. The process, complex and efficient, has been going on for thousands of years.

The water doesn't fall like grace from heaven but is a product of the toil and craft of men. Some of it comes from wells dug deep in earth, but however deep, they must be higher in elevation than the site they mean to irrigate. Gravity flow propels the water, and naturally men's eyes, canvassing for it, look up to the mountains that cover half the country. In Yazd they look to the Cshir Mountains, ridged by frost and thaw and walling in this part of Iran's central plateau. The mountains poke up through an arid waste, like Titans reaching for heaven. Some go fourteen thousand feet, and snow covers their peaks. Surface erosion suggests to me that they are limestone, but their reddish coloring argues for sandstone, like the Flaming Mountains of China.

Two stand out above the others, the Cshir-kuh, or Lion Mountain, and Oghab-kuh, or Eagle Mountain, exactly like an eagle revving its motors for takeoff, the wings furled, the arrogant head lifted up and surveying the scene. This is Zoroastrian country, and stone platforms where the cult members lay their dead loom over the traveler on the southern outskirts of Yazd.

Emptiness, the rule when the Swedish explorer Sven Hedin roamed this barren country a hundred years ago, is still pervasive. No condos are building, no highways take the desert in hand. How scary must it have been when, in the heat of summer, Hedin, slightly off his head, climbed up to the boneyard on top of the mountain. His mission accomplished, he brought back skulls for his mad professor in Tehran.

In the little town of Abarquh, between Yazd and Shiraz, I run my hand across the bole of a bent and blackened cypress, stiffened with iron clamps and said to be four thousand years old. Pieces of white cloth are tied to its branches, the work of yearning believers I've encountered before, not only in Asia. "They are like children," Mary says musingly. But she wouldn't think of sneering at them. "They imagine that a woodland deity dwells in this tree, and on feast days they pray to it, making a wish. All of us do something not so different, isn't it so?" The rags have been there a long time and are rotted by rain. She looks at them wistfully. "It makes me sad that the deity isn't paying attention!"

We might be in the Outer Hebrides or far Western China, any remote place on the map still in touch with older and nonrational ways of thinking. Like Mary I'm not "uncanny," so don't see the same world as the people of Abarquh. But they have my respect. People who call themselves atheist make me look around nervously, waiting for the thunderbolt to strike them. I'd think twice before denying arcane power to a four-thousand-year-old tree.

Sheep in the fields are scattering fearfully, herded by border collies. Carrots are putting out their parasols of white flowers, wheat is greening, mixed in with yellow poppies. All this luxuriant growth comes from underground water pipes, the *qanats.* Bringing the water to the desert floor, they feed it into a network of smaller canals. Collected and stored in underground vats, sometimes for ages, the water is covered by brick domes on the surface, protecting it from dust and soil. Wind towers, a pair of them, stand up like sooty fingers pointing to the presence of two of these subterranean reservoirs. Draft between the towers keeps the water cool, "cooled a long age in the deep-delvèd earth."

All this activity is "by hand," part of the nexus of feeling the ancient cypress tree plugs into. What sort of spirit, woodland or other, accounts for the tree's vast age? What is the right response to the low-tech engineering that supplies the water? Men, when they couldn't turn on the tap, got along well enough without benefit of machines. Stone or mud-brick maintenance stations, opening on the underground via a stone staircase, saw to it that the water flowed freely. From earliest times it has sustained the people of Iran, not only physically. More subtly it touches a chord in their psyche.

The sound of running water echoes down to the present from the Achaemenid age, in the park at Susa, for example. The sound is muted, not violent. Nature controlled, not nature unleashed as in "sounding cataracts," is how they like it. Formal gardens are part of Persia's identity. Called *chahar bagh,* they channel the water in a cruciform pattern, harking back to the four rivers of paradise. The Koran specifies the rivers, but the pattern they describe tells of paradise regained.

The garden we visit in Yazd glorifies a pavilion-like park, the Bagh-e Dolat Abad. Iran's tallest "badgir," topping one hundred feet, is the park's chief attraction but has a bonus we have come to expect, the rippling sound of water. Outlined by greenery and flowers, it filters the clamor of the boisterous city outside. All we hear is the fountain in the center of the crossed arms, cooling the water as it throws it into the air. A form of air conditioning, the best kind, it calls to mind my place of origin, halfway across the world. The climate in Hawaii, year round, is like Iran's in spring, except that spring is eternal there, coming to us "at the farthest, in the very end of harvest." But high-rises along the ocean front block the natural flow of the winds, and spring dies in its cradle. The cry goes up for A/C, costly, frigid, and staring us down like the blind eye of Polyphemus. The trade winds can't play, throttled by the masses of concrete. Nature has no choice but to abdicate, and the machines take over.

They say the machines are acquiring intelligence, and maybe in time they will learn manners. When the Mongols descended on Iran, they brought along unspeakable horrors, razing town after town, pillaging everything of value, massacring every inhabitant who put up his head. Worst of all, they destroyed the elaborate system of *qanats,* built up over centuries and crucial for survival. Bukhara is said to have lived at death's door for more than six hundred years, after the Mongols silted up its water. They did this deliberately, liking to be cruel, but time has mitigated their fury. The Il-Khanid dynasty, successors of the terrible Genghis, when they stopped killing, cultivated a new mode of architecture that makes me question the priority that always goes to Greece and Rome.

Il-Khanid architecture is often a hodgepodge. On my reading, however, this attests a willingness to reinvent what worked well enough but might work better yet. Lord Curzon put the name and fame of Samarkand and its Registan about the world, but who will tell of the splendors of Yazd? For example its Friday mosque, begun in the fourteenth century but not *de novo.* On the same site stood a twelfth-century building, before that a Zoroastrian fire temple, dating from the Sasanian time (224–642 A.D.), a leaven in the yeast before Islam ever came on the scene.

An anonymous genius of the eleventh or twelfth century looked at the *iwan,* the barrel-vaulted hall that opens on the courtyard, and saw an opportunity in its plain inner surface. He centered arches or squinches at an angle over the corners of the surface, creating an octagon. Set at angles to this octagon, a row of smaller arches formed a sixteen-sided polygon. This "*muqarnas* system," appearing at Yazd in the Davazdah Emam or Friday Mosque (1037), appears again in the Great Friday Mosque at Isfahan. Brightening the polygon, as if small electric bulbs were screwed into its surface, the *muqarnas* are so many glazed concavities hoarding the light. Between them the tiled surface portal might open on the interior of heaven. Undulating forever, the Persian arches are like eternity in stone.

This is a mosque, but not strictly conventional, and a new mind is working on its ancient aspect, for example, the urge to climb the heavens, illustrated by the huge *pishtaq* or entrance and the pair of unusually tall minarets that surmount it. To either side, on a front view, stood what look in outline like oratorios, small chapels for prayer, reminding us of what we came for. The new mind is concerned with what I'd call the gratuitously beautiful, however, a phrase for the *muqarnas.* They are squinches and so function to carry the weight. Mostly, though, we don't need them, except to admire.

The Zoroastrians, whose original fire temple preceded the Friday mosque, still worship their supreme being, Ahura Mazda. This impalpable deity resembles Allah in having no visible icon. Light is its symbol; hence the fire that must burn forever. The fire in Yazd is housed in a modern temple, the Ateshkadeh, and Mary, taking my arm, wants me to gaze at its sacred eternal flame, burning continuously for fifteen hundred years. I feel the same affect as when I placed my hand on the four-thousand-year-old cypress.

On the facade of the temple, a winged bas-relief figure in blue and yellow tile looks down on the omnipresent pool of water that fronts it. The figure symbolizes the spirit that finds its way to Ahura Mazda after death, an emblem that appears on the Achaemenid buildings of Persepolis. What it means is a constant in Persia's history and psychology. The old man stands for wisdom, the possession of age, the feathered wings for purity in thought, word, and deed. In the long tail, divided in two parts, we recognize our ambiguous legacy. The first part is good, the second is evil, and this ancient fire cult, like Islam and Christianity, joins the two parts together.

12

The Pattern of the World

Modern Iran is huge, bigger than France and Spain, seven times larger than the United Kingdom. But greater Iran, an intermediate area between the limits it reached in history and the present-day state, its territory fixed in 1907, is much larger. All of what is now Iraq used to be part of it. Spreading north through the Timurid empire to Bukhara and Shakhrisabz, it included what was once known as Khorezm, that is, Turkmenistan and Uzbekistan, in its sphere of influence. Before it was done expanding, Iran boxed the compass. It absorbed Egypt to the southwest, north of it Arabia, on the east Transoxiana ("the other side of the Oxus"), even Afghanistan. Ferghana, high in the northern Pamirs and home to the Heavenly Horses, was Persian. So was Northern India before the coming of the Mughals.

The heralds of its empire were the architects and master builders who created Samarkand, most of them Persian and more than one hundred surviving by name. Among these heroes of art is Oavam ad-Din bin Zaynad-Din Shirazi, whose name says he came from Shiraz in Iran. In the first half of the fifteenth century, he played the different roles of designer, decorator, astronomer, and master mathematician, helping diffuse the Persian style far beyond his country's borders. Between the years 1300 and 1500, this polymath and others like him labored in the service of beauty and truth. It doesn't seem to me extravagant to liken their achievement to that of the Renaissance in Florence.

Six hundred years later, Shiraz still lifts the heart. City of Love, men call it, of gardens, especially roses. Such poets as Hāfez sang the praises of its Shiraz grape. Unhappily it no longer produces the wine that bears its name. The mullahs have seen to that. Our first night out in town, we dine on traditional Shirazi food, rice and tomatoes followed by stewed eggplant. "It tastes much better than it sounds!" Mary says. In lieu of wine, however, we are offered Coca-Cola. This gratifies the mullahs, who get their jollies from denying us the pleasure of an innocent glass. But of the celebrated trio of wine, women, and song, two are holding their own, the women nice to be with, and song, expressed as poetry, diverting both the senses and soul.

People in Shiraz carry on a love affair with living. Their calendar, descending from Zoroastrian times, tells you as much. Skipping over the dark days of winter, it begins on the first day of spring. This is when Iranians celebrate their feast of No Ruz, a holiday that seems not to end. It is as if they turn back the clock at midnight on New Year's Eve, letting the revelry continue. Bonfires blaze in the streets, and people jump over them, asserting their health in the new year. Poetry is part of the pervasive joie de vivre, not the inchoate kind, a conventional misunderstanding, but thought-provoking, speaking to the brain as well as the heart. Joy, unless merely factitious, needs a collected head to go with its green tail.

Both are the possession of two famous local poets, Sa'di and Hāfez. The first, a real sojourner in Islam, "went out on the roads," as the saying goes, spending much of his life far from his native city. Coming home near the end of life, he wrote his two books, died, and is buried in his garden. Sa'di is a humble poet, of the earth earthy, sometimes almost a writer of almanac verse shifting from poetry to didactic prose à la Poor Richard. An anecdote of his tells of a prodigious eater and a more sparing eater who are locked up for no good reason without any food. Their innocence is established two weeks later—too late for the well-fed man, but his skinny companion survives. Sa'di isn't surprised. "When a person is habitually temperate, and a hardship shall cross him, he will get over it; but if he has pampered his body . . . and shall get into straits, he must perish."

Hāfez is less inclined to point the moral. A contemporary of Petrarch, he tossed off his short lyrics, ghazals, without apparent effort. But make no mistake: his is considered poetry, as the French say, "written." Petrarch is remembered by scholars, Hāfez by the people. They throng to his tomb in the city, a venerated shrine that charges admission. It doesn't make you think of Graceland in the United States. The tomb sits under a tiled dome held up by stone columns. Cypress trees and pools of cooling water surround it. At sunset the floodlights go up, and poetry set to music is piped over the public address system. People bring the poems with them—every home must have a copy: Hāfez and the Koran, there is no third. In England a hundred years ago, Tennyson and the Bible had that kind of status.

Opening Hāfez at random, Iranians find their future disclosed. Much emotion goes with this popular ritual, the *faal-e Hāfez*. Obviously it depends on the reader's or diviner's interpretation of the passage he hits on. If love poetry, is it carnal, and do I glimpse my beloved in it? Or, lowering the temperature, does it make God the object of arousal? That Hāfez's poems are open to different readings limits their scope. Readers who aren't into poetry think the scope is widened. But cerebration isn't this poet's game, and without it we don't have a finite range of meanings—the fruitful ambiguity poetry at its highest pitch depends on—we have a smorgasbord of meanings. When this poet speaks truth, it is an unsupported ipse dixit, declared, not deduced. If he raises questions, they are generally rhetorical, like this, to the breeze in the tulips: "Who were the martyrs these bloody winding-sheets wrap?" He can't take the question further since, as he tells us, the universe is a riddle his reason is helpless to solve.

His range is circumscribed like a Fauvist painter's, or, among poets, like Crashaw's or Hopkins's. The world he apprehends is a maze of swirling shapes and colors, assaulting his sensibility, sometimes bowling him over. Trouble, he says, is forever catching at the skirts of the time, and there is little we can do to fend against it. Adam walked warily, the Koran tells us, but lost paradise even so, all for eating a kernel of corn. How is Hāfez to help himself, dazzled as he is by "these hundred stooks [shocks] of fantasy"? To be that susceptible to the world leaves him open to trouble, and inevitably sadness follows. There is no chance that the heart, his or ours, will find its way on the roads of old age. Life's foundations are rooted in wind, the house we live in is jerry-built. Hence the injunction to seize the day—less a jolly toper's than that of a man at wits' end.

The mingling in Hāfez and his city of exhilaration and encroaching darkness is another instance of Islam's two faces. Shiraz's major theme (to make a stab at it) is grace-in-living, but its obbligato tugs toward abstention, fatalism, and prayer like a chant of woe. You can say of the daily prayer call that it orders men's lives, surely a good. But chaos is in the voice of the muezzin.

The city's best bazaar, the Vakil, evokes that kind of mixed response in the things it sells and the building that displays them. *Vakil* is "regent," the modest title chosen by Karim Khan, the first and best ruler of the short-lived

Zand dynasty (1750–95). His building is a thing of beauty, its wide, vaulted passages keeping us cool in the heat of the day. Shoppers crowd the main avenue and the alleys opening off it, but the elegant brick walls solace the eye and seem to true up the people. Architecture as moral suasion.

If you are selective, you can do good for yourself in the Vakil. I carry away a kilim, nomad work. Flat to the eye and fingertips, its stylized design shows an image of the Tree of Life and a Grandma Moses–like *badgir* (wind tower) in the background. Mary's jewelry box, lacquered wood overpainted with transparent varnish, has for its motif the nightingale and the rose, much loved by Iranians. The tablecloth we get for the two of us has been washed in the river to fasten its palette of colors. "It doesn't quite glow, too subtle for that," says Mary, holding it out by two corners. However, we've had enough, at least she has. "Better quit when you're ahead!" she tells me, reining in the Grand Acquisitor.

The tide has turned when no one was looking, and the architectural masterpiece is awash with creepy knickknacks slickened over with synthetic dyes. The paintings for sale hope to hang on our wall, but we hurry past them, embarrassed for the painter. The glass bottles and bric-a-brac cluttering the shelves advertise their chief function, dust collecting. Dead white statuettes, approximating a masculine female body, are the kind they give you when you hit the bull's-eye. In a recurring nightmare, I see a vast swell of this rubbishy stuff flooding west from China, its ancestral home. What has happened to the infallible taste that went into weaving their carpets and building their classical temples?

Mary is more tolerant. "It's only half the story," she says, snuffing up the smell of the East. Cumin, barberry, coriander, Malabar pepper, it pours from barrels and open sacks, leaning against storefronts. We point to what we want, inhaling the pungency, and the vendor weighs and bags it up for us. Further on the ice cream man is scooping gobs of creamy chocolate from a vat between his knees. Other vats lined up beside him ask us to try them. We buy vanilla suffused with rose water, the consistency of taffy. Orange trees are growing and bearing in front of his shop. They go back to pre-Seljuk times, he informs us. How can we not be happy?

Just outside the bazaar are bits and pieces of a seventeenth-century theological college, tumbled by earthquake. But the entrance portal and the stalactites (*muqarnas*) within the arch still remain to delight, and I stand taller when I take in the redness, almost pulsing, of the mosaic tiling. Suddenly the Atigh Mosque is before us, Shiraz's oldest. This building is a living thing. Begun in the ninth century, it kept adding to itself like old clapboard houses in New England. Hāfez used it as a workplace, and its turreted House of God (*khodakhaneh*) bears an inscription in raised stone, as if attesting his presence. The calligraphy is *thulth*, uninflected by any meaning I can put in words, so close to pure form. "The noblest script in Islam," our guide calls it.

If the mullahs would go away, I could stay on here. That is what I think, voicing my opinion aloud. But they remain, a physical presence you can't ignore, tyrannizing the people through their vigilante groups called *komitehs*, smashing recordings of Western music, vetoing any law passed by the Majlis that doesn't accord with sharia, expropriating the land of those who supported the old regime (and as often as not, hanging on to it themselves), punishing apostasy and adultery with death, thieving with the amputation of a hand, lashes, as many as a hundred, for illicit sex or drinking alcohol. "Hateful!"

"Maybe the people share your opinion," Mary says. "But all the same, they remain devoted to the mullahs for helping make them free of the Shah."

"That was then," I say. But the way she puts it pulls me up short. Could it be that their way of thinking stands for something in the psyche of Islam? Does that explain why they feel other than contemptuous for those bullies in turbans?

"You've been doing a lot of pontificating lately," Mary says. "What was that part about Islam's two faces?"

EVERY HOTEL in Shiraz has a tour of Persepolis, a little to the north and west. Its neighbors, on familiar terms, clip it short when they pronounce it, saying "Perse-plis." Built by Iran's first rulers, the Achaemenids, this fabulous city comes down to us today as bare bones. But even the devastation wrought by men, far worse than time's, hasn't obscured its grandeur. It breathes the spirit of high civilization, among the cultures of the ancient world ranking with Egypt, India, and China. People often call it the soul of Iran.

Soul is a comprehensive term, and the mullahs' reading is circumscribed by the Islamic faith, a moat defensive. When they venture to speak their mind, they put Persepolis much lower. Mostly they keep mum on their slighting opinion, aware that the people are loyal to their history. To the mullahs whatever precedes Islam is irrelevant, even immoral as it depicts the natural world. It does this lovingly, another count against it. We remember that Muhammad put all that under ban.

The Achaemenids saw another world than he did. It wasn't "fallen," and they didn't idealize it either. But being closer to the earth in that earlier time, they were closer to heaven, a paradox I needn't labor. When Xerxes was king, the skin of the satyr Marsyas was still displayed in Asia Minor. Apollo had flayed him alive for challenging the god to a musical competition. Earth and its creatures are never far distant in the world of the Achaemenids. Their drinking vessels (rhytons) often take the shape of a beast, half mammal, half bird. Their sculpture favors the bull, almost Cretan in its hugeness, huge but not gross. Stone images of mythic creatures, winged and crowned with a man's head, stand before the entrances of the royal Throne Hall. You must pass these gigantic guardians (*lamassu*) to enter Xerxes's Gate of All Nations. Despite their fearsome appearance, they are warding off evil, something like the hair of the dog.

As the visitor ascended the grand entrance stairway to bow before the king, he saw the heraldic symbol of Persepolis, the lion tearing the hindquarters of a rearing bull. This image comes close to being erotic, the lion embracing the bull's flanks as it sinks its teeth into the skin. The bull's head, turned back to look, isn't agitated: on the contrary, its beautiful face is composed. Yet what is happening is violent. This, said Professor Olmstead, "contrasts strangely with Zoroaster's admonition of loving care for the sacred kine." Mary thinks that beside the point. The bull isn't being devoured but propelled forward to a better season, she says, and the savage scene intimates the coming of spring. "Of course there is violence in springtime," she tells me, catechizing a backward pupil. "Read your Hāfez!"

Though Persia's sculpture, in sheer size and weight, evokes comparison to Egypt's, it doesn't strike us as monumental, a pejorative. My word for it is humane. We aren't oppressed by titanic figures bearing down on us, who are only ciphers. Achaemenid sculpture looks accommodating, as if Iran, before Muhammad, lived easily with the physical world. That didn't guarantee the empire a long life, and perhaps its relative equability cut the life short. Though the greatest in history up to its time, it lasted only 170 years (500–330 B.C.). But at its zenith it stretched from the Nile to the Oxus, and from the Aegean Sea to the Ganges. A succession of impressive rulers bore a part in creating it, none of the stature of its founding father, Cyrus, surnamed the Great.

The Old Testament records his conquest of Babylon, the preeminent power before him. But the way he wielded power was different. Babylon's previous ruler, the Assyrian king Assurbanipal, whose likeness is on my study wall at home, makes this clear. Having aggression in myself, I find it useful to keep his ferocious visage before me. When a car on the highway cuts in front of me, I cock my thumb and forefinger, lean out the window, and blow him away. The trusty six-shooter I cradle in my hand is of course pure fantasy. Assurbanipal was, however, for real.

He wrote: "I decapitated six hundred enemy soldiers and burned alive three thousand. . . . I carved up the (city's) governor with my own hands. . . . I grilled others on fire; I cut off their hands, fingers, eyes, and noses, ripped thousands of eyes from their sockets and tongues from their mouths. . . . I razed their temples and suppressed their gods. . . . I sowed salt and thorns." Assurbanipal makes a good antiseptic. Cyrus, though a sufficient soldier, promised (on the word of Herodotus) to "respect the traditions, customs, and religions of the nations of my empire," vowing to impose monarchy on none. "Each is free to accept it, and if any one of them rejects it, I resolve never to reign through war."

Even after the lapse of two and a half millennia, he casts a huge shadow, moral even more than physical. He freed the Jews from their Babylonian Captivity (539 B.C.), sent them back to Jerusalem to rebuild the Temple, gave them the money to do it. In his empire almost two dozen different peoples lived peaceably under the central government at Pasargadae. The Cyrus Cylinder, now in the British Museum, inscribes in cuneiform writing on its clay surface the world's oldest charter of human rights. (Magna Carta was still nearly two thousand years in the future.) This document and the men who produced it reflect back the light of a cosmopolitan society in a largely barbarous age.

The reign of Cyrus the Great brought order and stability to Persia, both alive, not sclerotic, also magnificence, worth having. The king, ethically sophisticated and politically sagacious, made life viable for his subjects. He created a network of imperial roads, paved with stone or brick, sometimes bitumen. Relay horses carried the mail, delivered to the farthest corner of the empire within fifteen days. Nothing traveled faster than the king's royal couriers, said Herodotus, and nothing stopped them from traversing their allotted stage, "neither snow, rain, heat, nor darkness." (We see where the modern postman comes from.) One road led from Mesopotamia all the way to Bactria (modern Afghanistan), thence to India, and on to Central Asia and the Far East. Later this became known as the Silk Road.

Cyrus was a Zoroastrian, worshiping Ahura Mazda, a god of light. He saw life as a struggle between the worst and the righteous, or you could say between the *civitas Diaboli* and the *civitas Dei*. He, or his prophet, whose sayings are set forth in writings called the Avesta, sometimes sound to my ear like St. Augustine or certain passages in the New Testament. He lived in an age when men mutilated other men and tortured them to death, and on one side he is a child of the age. But thinking about him, and about other dynastic rulers who are like him in ability, some moral, some not, I am tempted to recite the proverb: "Best government, good czar; worst government, bad czar"—except that even worse is when we are rudderless, and like Scotland in the time of Macbeth, "float upon a wild and violent sea."

Cyrus made his first capital at Pasargadae, northeast of Persepolis, on the same ground, says tradition, where he had defeated the army of the Medes, led by his grandfather Astyages. With this battle the Achaemenid empire got its start. Historians call the place the Camp of the Persians, still a nomad people when they appear in history. A park encloses the palaces they built, murmurous with running water and an early example of the *chahar bagh* (cruciform design). At Pasargadae Cyrus is buried, his white limestone tomb a ziggurat ascending in six stages. The tomb is still there, though the inscription, reported by the geographer Strabo, is gone. "Passerby," it read, "I am Cyrus, who gave the Persians an empire." The Arabs, when they conquered Persia, were about to destroy his tomb, but were told by disingenuous locals that it held the remains of King Solomon's mother. Dissuaded, they spared it but got a new inscription from the Koran.

Darius, third of the Achaemenids and also known as the Great, wanted a new capital, not trailing other men's baggage. Persepolis, covering an area of 1.3 million square feet, is largely his work, though he didn't live to complete it. (I take my details from Arthur Upham Pope's *Persian Architecture*, 1969.) A huge platform, cut from solid rock and measuring nine hundred by fifteen hundred feet, accommodates this sacred national shrine. The visitor approaches by way of a majestic double staircase, twenty-two feet wide and returning on itself. On the north and east sides, the staircases are adorned with bas-reliefs commemorating the annual festivities when subjects came to pay tribute. The platform and monumental pavilion they ascended to is guarded by colossal human-headed bulls, and through the Gate of All Nations, so proclaimed by Xerxes, they entered a splendid world dominated by his Apadana palace, with its central room almost two hundred feet square.

Columns were everywhere. The palace rested on thirty-six of them, each sixty feet high and topped by ten-foot capitals in the shape of a bull, lion, or griffin. The interior, a forest of columns, presented "an unearthly vision of the sacred groves of heaven." In this reception hall, the supreme king received his vassals. The immensity of it all is suggested by Herodotus in his account of the royal birthday banquets, when fifteen thousand guests at a sitting honored their royal lord. The festive time reached its peak during No Ruz, when friends trooped off to their friends' houses, ate their food, gave them presents. On the thirteenth day, they picnicked with their extended families and threw on the ground the germinating seeds kept in the house since New Year's Day. This guaranteed early marriage and fertility for their daughters.

A look at the sculptures on the Apadana staircase is worth the pains, for ancient Persia has nothing better to show. Detail is lavished everywhere, on the way the men talk together or hold hands in friendship, the different hats and clothes they wear, the Persians in long robes, the dress of the Medes cut shorter. Indians lead a donkey, Cappadocians a horse, Bactrians a camel, the double-humped variety Marco Polo rode. We see the elite of the imperial soldiery, including the One Thousand, distinguished from the Immortals by the golden pomegranates they carry. Ancient Persians didn't stint on adornment. The *tachara* (palace) of Darius was notable for the polished stone of its walls, earning it the title Hall of Mirrors. But the gold plating on the walls has been stripped long ago, the tiles and paintings have vanished, like the color from the marble capitals, the sumptuous wall hangings have rotted, and of the elegant wood carving, only a scattering of charred beams remains. And yet enough has escaped time's tooth to leave the traveler in awe.

Before Darius died he chose his tomb site on the same plain as Persepolis, the nearby rock face of Naqsh-i-Rustam, named for Persia's greatest soldier of *Sohrab and Rustum* fame. Three of his successors, one of them Xerxes, had their graves dug from this rock. Its outer surface is shaped like a cross with an opening in the center, giving on the funerary chamber. On the upper part of the surface, a king is represented, beside a fire altar held up by vassal nations. An inscription on the central tomb identifies the king as Darius

(521–485 B.C.). Nothing remembered the man he was except his bones, picked clean by vultures.

Like his predecessor, Cyrus, he had imperial yearnings, pushing one way to India, another to the Danube. He decided to conquer Greece, a mistake, paid home at Marathon, 490 B.C. We, who always sympathize with the Greeks—sentimentally, as if they reflect our image in a looking glass—are no longer like them. The day of the town-hall meeting and participatory democracy, when perhaps we were like them, is over, except in small-town New England. What we have become has little in common with Athens before its Syracusan adventure. Paradoxically our powerful and ever-expansive state is closer in spirit to the Persia of Darius and Xerxes.

Xerxes, wishing no doubt to make good his father's failure, had another try at Greece, but the gradual decline of the Persian Empire dates from his defeat at Salamis (480 B.C.). Still he was a great builder, completing the magnificent structures Darius had left unfinished on the terrace at Persepolis. I thank Herodotus for a poignant glimpse of the king, unfaded after much of my lifetime. Preparing to crush the Greeks once and for all, he assembled his invading force at the Isthmus of Corinth. The entire navy was with him, and three of his six army corps, each sixty thousand strong. Seated on a white stone throne near Abydos on the Hellespont, he reviewed his troops. The amorous Leander swam the Hellespont nightly, from Abydos to Sestus, keeping his tryst with Hero. Cursed by heaven, the two of them died, as all must who are human, but Xerxes, though he knew of their fate from the poet Musaeus, thought he knew better how to propitiate the gods. He burned incense and prayed with his face to the rising sun. At dawn he poured libations from a golden cup, honoring the spirits of those who died for Troy. He was the champion of the East against the West, and the outcome of the war about to begin represents one of history's great hinges.

For seven days and nights, the army, 180,000 men, struggled across the bridge, urged on by the lash. They were an Oriental army, and that was how they were made to give battle. In short time all were dead. The famous lovers had perished not because of what they did but what they were, and the Persian soldiers, laboring under our primal curse, were fated too. Perhaps Xerxes hoped that his praying would lift the curse. But though he had all the accoutrements of godhead, none of it availed him, and he felt the breath of mortality as he awaited the clash of arms. He was the descendant of Cyrus the Great, whose tomb bears the words: "All that is left of me is dust." The tragic sensibility was the possession of men in his age. Oddly *hubris*, the Greek word, is more appropriate to our time than theirs.

The Achaemenid dynasty lived on, though impaired, after the Greek debacle, but its hour had struck. Arrogance grew on its rulers, in proportion as their authority lessoned. A prince of what might be called the Decadence executed two members of the royal house because they came before him with their hands not hidden in their sleeves. This was a breach of protocol. The bureaucracy hurried on the process of decline. It imposed increasingly heavy taxes and involved business in an evermore tangled web of regulation. The small farmer went to the wall, swallowed up by huge combines, the government verged on bankruptcy, a lawless proletariat crowded the cities. My fellow traveler and spouse, a keen student of today's political scene, is intensely skeptical in her reading of it. Looking over the plain at Persepolis, she says, "What's past is prologue."

Art participated in the general falling off. Darius III, last of the Achaemenids, continued work at Persepolis; but his reliefs are recycled from elsewhere, and the sculptured tomb he began but didn't finish is rough and coarse compared to earlier carving. The age of Darius III shows how much has been lost. A suitable comparison is that of the age of Constantine to the age of Augustus. It remained for Alexander the Great to deliver the coup de grace.

His attack on Persia was of the nature of a holy war, or given its brutality more like a Sicilian vendetta. Persepolis he described as the most hateful of all the cities of Asia. Xerxes had burned the Acropolis in Athens, and in requital Alexander gave the Persian capital over to his soldiers. One detail will suffice for what they did. A marble statue of a seated woman, carved just before the Parthenon sculptures, its only peer, stood in the museum hall of the Persepolis treasury. Breaking in on the treasury, Alexander's soldiers knocked off and smashed the head of the statue, threw the decapitated torso into a corridor, and where it had stood, left a mutilated hand. "Alexander could not have shown more plainly how thin was his veneer of Greek culture," said Olmstead.

Coming out of Macedonia in northern Greece, before him and his father, Philip, a semibarbarous backwater, he led a tightly disciplined and brilliantly generaled army against numerically superior Persian forces in a trio of great battles, culminating at Gaugamela (331 B.C.). Festal games celebrated his victories, and the story is that as the drinking grew far advanced, an Attic courtesan, Thais, told the king it would be his most memorable triumph to burn the topless towers of the city and extinguish its glory forever. So it was done. To the sound of flutes and pipes, the king, torch in hand, headed up a drunken procession, and in moments all was aflame. But much of Persepolis escaped the holocaust, the fire baking and preserving its magnificent reliefs. For many centuries the reliefs and other survivals were lost to the world but saved for posterity, covered over by dust and sand. But in the 1930s the vanished city emerged from its long "occultation," like the Mahdi of time. Those who come to pay homage will hardly credit their eyes, for at sunset the palaces of Darius and Xerxes appear to knit themselves together as they tower above the plain, and in the half-light they regain their first grandeur.

ON A SUNNY DAY in Isfahan, we are drinking black tea and nibbling nougats in the garden of the Hotel Abbasi. A renovated caravansary, the hotel is hushed in the heat of mid-afternoon, the hour of siesta, and most of our fellow guests are snug in their beds. Other than the splashing of water, falling back on itself in the fountains scattered about the lawn, the only sound is the twittering of birds in the big trees that stand, sentinel-like, above them. Roses are blooming fore and aft of us, and closing my eyes, I inhale blissfully, a sybarite with nothing better to do. In the seventeenth century, an English traveler to Isfahan said no city in Asia could outvie its gardens for grandeur and fragrance. He called them another paradise.

Sanitation was nil in the medieval city, and they say its smell hung in the air a mile off. But the silence was palpable, and inside its cocoon a man could hear himself think. On my post-Luddite side, I crave the return of silence. The great concavity of the hotel, two stories of arcades, rises about us like a Zoroastrian tower of silence. I don't crave to be dead!—only not invaded by sound. Letting my mind idle, I imagine the identity of the traveler who stayed in our room four hundred years ago. Ezra Pound has a poem spoken by a river merchant's wife, left alone in China while her lord journeys far afield. We don't get to meet him, but I guess at what he was like, a businessman avid for money and keen in its pursuit but with a soft spot for a good-looking woman. Staring at himself in the glass above the dresser as he makes ready to go back on the road, he sees the crow's-feet at the corners of his eyes and wonders if age has begun to claw him.

Cities like this one used to be recognized by a sign of the Zodiac. Isfahan's was Sagittarius the archer, and a version of him appears on the main portal of the Royal Bazaar. Half man, half tiger, he is shooting his bow and arrow backward, aiming for the dragon's head growing out of his tail. The dragon, in the nature of such, is emitting hideous noises, and the archer has had as much as he can stand. Right on, archer! Silencing his raucous side is necessary, if his better side is to survive.

Shah Abbas I, who knew what he was doing, selected the sign of Sagittarius as his city's emblem. By far the most able ruler of the Safavid dynasty, he straddled the sixteenth and seventeenth centuries (1587–1629), a late contemporary of Shakespeare's. The coincidence is fitting. Abbas the Great, as he is remembered, understood that man cut an ambiguous figure and that repressing his discontents was the condition of a civilized life. This holdover of the ancient Zoroastrian duality, good and evil in one lump, makes a persuasive psychology, reflected in the creating of Iran's most beautiful city.

But Isfahan is not only a feast for the eye. Its center, the enormous square now called Imam Square, had a more implicative name when it was first conceived. Naghsh-e-Jahan, as it was, gives us a phrase for the city in its essence. By intention it is the pattern or design of the world. Obviously the world wasn't like it, not yet. But Shah Abbas meant his new city for a pattern—the word chosen deliberately—and hoped that others would follow its lead.

The main street of the city, Chahar Bagh or Four Gardens, runs south in a straight cut along the west side of the square and down to the river. Zayandeh Rood is the river, literally life-giving, and of its eleven bridges at least three are worth an afternoon's excursion. They serve for transit, of course, also to dam the water and irrigate the palace gardens flowering along the banks. One of them, Chehel Sotun or "Forty Pillars," is still mirrored in its long pool. In fact there are only twenty pillars, but their reflected image doubles the number. Built in the columnar porch style—*talar* is the word—the palace remembers the Achaemenids: think Persepolis and its Palace of a Thousand Columns.

Murals on the walls depict battle scenes and entertainments. Nader Shah defeats Mahmoud of Ghazni, he on a white elephant. When the Mughal prince Humayun, deposed from his throne, shows up seeking sanctuary, Shah Abbas II lays on a lavish banquet, complete with musicians and dancing girls. The frescoes of Vank cathedral, the big Armenian church, dating from the early seventeenth century, are similar in feeling but even more physical. I get the sense that Christian and Muslim in these years are concluding a concordat, not inevitably a good thing.

We cross over the river on the Si-o-Seh or Allahverdi Bridge, the work of a favorite general of Shah Abbas I. Later we nod to his portrait in the Chehel Sotun Palace. Women are doing the wash in the shallows. Lording it over them, a phalanx of Persian arches, thirty-three in all, marches across the bridge, each feeling for its perfect point as if it were platonically there. When the light turns golden at close of day, they show us their special character, color plus form. Zoroastrians believed that the saved entered heaven via thirty-three gates. But the number glances also at the life of Jesus, ending with his crucifixion at age thirty-three. Allahverdi Khan, the builder, was a Christian.

Teahouses at either end of his bridge offered refreshment, until the mullahs, alarmed at the propinquity of young men and women drinking tea and assessing each other, shut them down. The bridge gives access to the Armenian Quarter on the south bank, where life is less straitened. Reserving it for another day, we walk west toward the Khajou Bridge, notable for its two levels of terraced arcades, the upper for walking quickstep, the lower for recreating the soul. An unearned gratuity, it is like the grace of heaven. Picking our way with care over the slippery surface, we sit on what is left of the stone seats reserved for Shah Abbas II and friends while they enjoyed the view. Wherries, a flotilla's worth, are plying the river. I might be looking at London's Thames in the first years of the seventeenth century. Civilization needs running water.

Shahrestan, the oldest of Isfahan's bridges, dates from the twelfth century, though the pillars reach back to Sassanian times (A.D. 224–692). None of these is your generic bridge; they satisfy aesthetically, and in their particularity deserve the name of architecture. This is true of the caravansary where we spend the night, true of the lowly pigeon towers still standing beside the river near the tumbled ruin of an ancient fire temple. Once each of them accommodated fourteen thousand guano-producing birds. Alas for the pigeons, chemical fertilizers have made them de trop.

But Isfahan the pattern of the world is waiting, and I mustn't tarry too long on incidentals, however delightful. Imam Square is its beating heart, a huge rectangle more than fifteen hundred yards long and almost five hundred wide, bigger than St. Mark's, Venice, and Moscow's Red Square, second only to Tianenmen Square in Beijing. We want it big but not infinite, and it is good that Beijing gets the palm. Tianenmen Square is an enormity, proclaiming the insignificance of man. Imam Square is all about the realizing of the individual man, and though establishing this is a task of magnitude, the size involved has limits.

Shah Abbas began to construct Imam Square in 1602, approximately the year of *Hamlet.* He meant it as a venue for public theater and meetings of the citizenry, parades and fireworks, all the needs of a modern capital of nearly half a million souls. Polo matches were held in the square, and the stone goalposts are still in place. Executions were held there too: he wasn't a soft-hearted ruler. On the periphery the Shah planted trees and dug an open canal lined with stones to hold the running water.

Like Tamburlaine before him, he culled the best in each kind for this labor of his life, assembling a team of architects, calligraphers, and painters, headed by the engineer Ostad ("Master") Ali Akbar Isfahani. The square was to be bounded on its four sides by two stories of arcades, as it is today, though the upper level, there largely for symmetry's sake, is empty. Building went on nonstop for the next fifty years. European travelers, awed by Isfahan's repleteness, called it "half the world." In 1666 Chardin, a French visitor, counted 162 mosques, 48 madrassas, 182 caravansaries, 173 *hamams.* Some are work for the ages.

Its handling of light and color is unlike that of any other civilized venue I know. Emphasis falls on cream and vermilion, light blue and median blue, as in the blue-tiled designs of the Masjid-i Iman Mosque. The walls of smaller porches in the mosque's inner courtyard favor deep blue and yellow for their painted tiles (*hafti rangi*), in which the design is painted directly onto the tile. Each *iwan* leads to a vaulted sanctuary, two of which, the east and west, have floral motifs on a blue ground. Sometimes the Isfahan style goes in heavily on white, too heavily, Westerners think, an effect of busyness. The white calligraphy above the entrance portal is perhaps a case in point, and it must be agreed that Persians love showiness, for example, the dome of half the mosques you point to—until, as the light changes, the white softens to cream and the red to rosy brown.

Four major monuments interrupt the double arcades, on the south the Royal Mosque, Isfahan's religious center; on the west the Mosque of Shaykh Lotfollah, honoring the Shah's father-in-law, a distinguished theologian; on the east the Ali Qapu Palace, conflating Arabic "Ali" (high) and Turkish "Qapu" (gate), that is, the Sublime Portal, the city's administrative center; and finally, on the north, the Qeisarieh Portal, opening on the Great Bazaar (Bazare-e-Borzorg). This arched passageway links Imam Square to the Friday

Mosque or Masjed-i-Jami, a survival of the Seljuk era and a popular choice, including mine, for Isfahan's noblest building.

The Friday Mosque is outsize, Iran's largest. It is old, replacing a mosque of the eighth century on the same site, and it is unusually complex in design. Professor Pope, a great panjandrum of scholars, says it is made up of twenty distinct structures. I single out the big dome in front of the main *mihrab,* built by the famous vizier and patron of architecture Nizam-al Molk (late eleventh century), and at the northern end a second dome, the Gonbed-e Khaki. This jewel of great price, dating from the same period, is the work of Taj-al Molk, Nizam's principal rival. Both had an eye to uncluttered form, recalling in their enmity and complementarity those masters of Roman Baroque, Bernini and Borromini. I think the smaller dome is near perfect, not least in its plainness—no tile work, brick alone.

The mosque in its entirety represents, says my professor, a thousand years of mosque building in Persia. It is modest, despite its preeminence, not opening itself all at once. As I prepare to leave, my eye falls on a *mihrab,* wrought all over with floral decoration and delicate calligraphy, not a fraction of its stuccoed surface left untended. The guidebook says this *mihrab* is the work of the last Ilkhanid king, Ojeitu, a fourteenth-century Mongol who converted to Islam. I liken it instinctively to medieval Christian carvings in ivory, possibly a Jesse Tree thick with the ancestors of Jesus. It belongs, in its perfection, in a special place in the south of France, and I see it in my mind's eye, Moissac, among the great treasuries of art. The coincidence of this church with the Jameh Mosque attests the kinship of Christianity and Islam.

Kinship, not sameness. Simply, as they are great, Islam and Christianity are like each other. But likeness-in-the-grain needs more than magnitude. It needs a similar reading of the ways of the world, and such a reading is wanting. The deeper we delve in either religion, the more profound do their differences show.

At the other end of the square, the entrance to the Royal Mosque (Jameh-Abbasi or Masjid-e Imam) is meant to counterpoint the huge *pistaq* arch of the Bazaar, flanked by turquoise minarets. I note the inscription on its portal, signed by a peerless calligrapher, Ali Reza Abbasi. Next to his name is the date of his work, 1616. This year Shakespeare died, and it seems harmless to imagine the calligrapher saluting a kindred spirit from afar. The gateway to the mosque, a vast honeycomb, is alive with stalactites (*muqarnas*). Turquoise tile spills over the surface of the portal, and peacocks, three pairs of them, strut on the panels. Our guide says this intrusion of the natural world doesn't violate Muhammad's interdict against mingling art and nature "because peacocks symbolize the cosmos." I have no idea if this is true, but the exception to the rule suggests to me a wholesale rejecting of the rule. The seventeenth century in Isfahan merges art and nature cheerfully, letting the interdict go its own way.

In from the entrance an ablutions fountain cools the main courtyard, surrounded by the familiar four-*iwan* pattern. A double-decker porch varies the pattern and bids us notice its *hafti-rangi* (prefabricated) blue and yellow tiles. Flowers like none in nature grow on the doors, walls, domes, and minarets, and after four centuries their verdure hasn't staled. When the Qeisarieh Portal was finished, the Shah topped it with a clock and belfry, symbols of his triumph over the Portuguese in Hormuz. He had one eye trained on earth, the other on heaven.

Peacocks or their trailing tails surface again in the Sheikh Lotfollah Mosque, framing a vase on the portal. Shah Abbas meant the mosque to serve as a private chapel for the women of the harem, but though smaller than the Imam mosque, it needn't "vail its crest." Mosaics on the portal and on the walls and ceiling of the sanctuary or prayer room leave the competition well to the rear. But color is its chief distinction. Blue and yellow flow together on the stalactites above the portal, cream brightens the tiles of the dome, changing to pink around sunset. Intertwined flowers and complex geometric designs flourish on the exterior portal. But then a startling change: in the passage the brightness of day yields to semidarkness. There is propriety in this. "To see God clearly, we go out of sight," wrote John Donne as the century was beginning.

Color is qualified by shadow, the sunlight, filtering through the high lattice windows, being mitigated or strained. So we have a third state, neither light nor shadow but partaking of both. Robert Byron (in *The Road to Oxiana*) describes the Lotfollah Mosque as blending color and abstract form. The inside of the mosque he calls "Augustan," referring, I assume, to the eighteenth century in England, the Augustan Age or age of reason. Whatever he meant, that is the term we want. It connotes urbanity; light that is clear but not dazzling; a mundane state of mind, even though the eye is fixed on the hereafter; elegance, reason's unlikely carapace; and last, a preoccupation with form.

The Great Bazaar, a warren of arched passageways topped with small domes like skylights, first surfaces in the annals a thousand years ago. Its shops cluster together by trades: tinkers, artists, carpet makers, the various groups known as *timeheh,* each under its own arcade. A high dome, Chahar Sough or "Four Bazaars," rises where passageways cross, spilling daylight from the roof. The bazaar has a pool in its midst, caravansaries, madrassas, even bathhouses. A sound body must support a sound mind, with an "upright heart and pure" (the desideratum is Milton's) to go with it. But this version of Augustanism accommodates the world of Hogarth's paintings as well as the architecture of Bath, and in frescoes on both sides of the Qeisarieh Portal men sitting around a table are carousing and getting drunk. Maybe this melding of contraries comments on the psyche of Iran.

Today, our last in Iran, I bid farewell to the city. I am sitting on the elevated terrace of the Ali Qapu Palace, named for Shah Abbas's hero, the son-in-law of Muhammad. The terrace, hoisted up high on its eighteen slender columns over the domes and spires of Imam Square, is my theater box, no better view in town. The ceiling above it is crinkly with an intricate design, nonrepresentational, like that on an older carpet. Braziers stand about in the palace's smaller rooms, taking the chill off the air. Many rooms have fireplaces that open at the back of the hearth to the outside, another illustration of the Persian fondness for bringing the out-of-doors within doors.

From this privileged point of vantage where the Shah watched polo and his parading soldiers, we look down at twilight. Stick figures below us are buttonholing friends, like actors in a silent movie. Local families, spreading a cloth on the grass, are opening picnic baskets and getting ready for supper. Horse-drawn buggies, their drivers' eyes peeled for tourists, are going lickety-split around the periphery. The square, a vast living room, is the model of a public place. My heart fills up with love.

Without warning, a fight breaks out in the near foreground. Young men, as many as a dozen, have been chaffing one another mindlessly, throwing water from the fountains in their cupped hands. As I watch they up the ante from teenage imbecility to violence. A punch is thrown; I see the arm flash out and a youth crumple on the grass. Those standing over him begin to kick him in the head. I scream at them to stop it, though at this distance they can't possibly hear me. Then, as suddenly as it began, it is over.

What has happened to the idyllic scene that was Imam Square only a moment before? Why have these unfledged adolescents turned savage, as if to give paradise the lie? Evidently there is trouble in the Garden of Eden, but where does it come from? Donne has an answer: "And that this may truly Paradise be thought, I have the serpent brought." But he, a peccant man, didn't need a serpent, bringing the evil with him. Am I to locate it in these young good-for-nothings? Are they victims of their "sociology"? Is there a crack in the bowl? Too many questions.

However you derive the evil, it has tarnished the perfect place. More accurately, says Mary, it has cleared my imperfect seeing, the perfection being a myth I concocted myself. Against the idyllic scene, I must set the bigoted rule of the mullahs and their cat's-paw Ahmedinajad, the confining of women, symbolized by the chador, the insistence that we give up our glass, the innocent pleasure of polite men and women. All this does a number on my estimate of Iranian people, those good friends.

I ask myself how the rigorous faith they profess works into their behavior. Perhaps they honor it more in the breach than the observance. In the time of Abbas the Great, everyone in the city, smaller than today's but still substantial, went to Friday mosque. Now, in a population of three million, only ten thousand attend. So I am told, and if true, the decline is spectacular, paralleling the decline of organized religion in the West. Europe is no longer churchgoing—I generalize in the interest of brevity—and in the United States my sophisticated colleagues have turned Laodicean, equating things major with minor and unwilling to make a fuss about either. Though evangelicalism is surging, its emotional brand of faith isn't one I'd have recognized in my youth. "The best lack all conviction, while the worst are full of a passionate intensity."

That makes a good, resonant conclusion. But like the epigram as a kind, its clinching tone is in excess of the facts. True, Iranian people are damaged by their ideology, and I mustn't discount original sin. But their country, though skirting disaster, hasn't foundered, and clear-sighted men and women are doing what they can to keep the ship off the rocks. The job is hard, even painful; nonetheless they haven't lost their joie de vivre. Its strong sense is what I take with me as I shuffle offstage, tipping my straw hat with my walking stick to salute them.

13

The Pilgrim of the Heart

When Marco Polo returned to Europe after years in the East, he made the journey by camelback, horseback, and sail. It pleases us to follow him. We leave the Fertile Crescent behind and go north before going west, getting on the old branch of the Silk Road that went through Anatolia to the Black Sea. The Persian Royal Road, there before it, ran from Susa on the lower Tigris, today little more than a memory. It carried on to the port of Smyrna on the Aegean, known to the Turks as Izmir. According to Herodotus it ran the other way as well, to India and the Far East. Going on two millennia later, Marco Polo used it. So do we.

Royal messengers did the entire journey in nine days. Ordinary travelers took three months. Now that I have the bit in my teeth, I don't want to dawdle, and we cut out the whistle stops. Our destination is Trebizond, poignant in memory. Once a Byzantine trading port, it held out longer than any other Greco-Roman city against the Ottoman Turks. Before we glimpse its towers, we smell the sea.

Cargo ships go out with every tide, and ours brings us by easy stages through the Bosporus into the Sea of Marmara. Taking on fresh cargo, we drop anchor for half a day in Istanbul. Marco Polo knew it as Constantinople and would have been horrified that this greatest city in Christendom could have succumbed to Islam. But "gain and loss have always been partners," Mary observes, and Istanbul, re-created by the Ottomans, is magnificent in its different way. Looming out of the grainy air, its minarets and shining domes lift this weary traveler's heart.

A short boat ride more and we are into the Aegean, closing in on Euboea, the big island that hugs the west coast of Greece. In Marco Polo's time, it was known as Negroponte, the objective of our trading vessel, also a junction for travelers from the east. The man we are following was going home to Venice, so took another boat round the southern tip of Greece and north into the Adriatic. Venice is the terminus ad quem of the Silk Road, but Rome is the lodestar whose power to draw a sojourner in distant lands never weakens. In Rome I mean to end my long journey.

The eternal city tugs at the heart, the seat of emotion. But the heart is also the condition of health, and its waxing and waning rhythm keeps us in fettle. When the two are in sync—when, to invoke the medieval physiology, the elements are "nicely" or precisely mixed in us—we are at the top of our powers. But in age the heart's vitality wanes, and the downward slide begins. Conscious of that, I cope as I can.

Passing the Italian boot to starboard and the island of Sicily to port, we sail up the Tyrrhenian Sea to Civitavecchia. In the Middle Ages, Ostia was the port of Rome, for centuries the gateway for all westward-bound traffic. I have an eighteenth-century print by Piranesi on my living-room wall that shows the island in the Tiber emerging from the water, raised on the timbers of a shipwreck in pre-Republican times. Livy tells about it, how a grain ship coming from Egypt sank in the river opposite the city and, with the passing of years and the help of thrifty Italians, turned into the island it is now. Gain and loss once again, though: as the Isola burgeoned, Ostia waned. Raiding Saracens, Arab pirates, were the culprit, with a strong assist from drifting sand that silted up the harbor. We disembark at Civitavecchia, a little to the north, and find a taxi. "Al centro," I tell the driver.

The trouble with the center is that staying in it is *troppo caro:* it costs a bundle. But across the Corso in the old Campo Marzio is a *pensione* on the first floor above the street, that is, the second floor, clean, cheap, and super convenient. This is where we put up, meaning to renew acquaintance with a few of our holy places before writing finis to our travels. As I am unpacking, I have a try at assessing them. My trek through Central Asia can be plotted along a great arc from Kazakhstan in the far north to the Caspian Sea, but mostly it means the people, some of them long dead, whose lives intersected with mine.

Much of their story is as homely as mine, though occasionally glamour touches it, "like the lightning in the collied night," and its equivocal character matches that of my narrative. By and large I am partial to "my" people, adopting toward them a proprietary point of view. But being real, they often fall in the flaws of their nature. I am paraphrasing Shakespeare, whose view of character is both skeptical and generous. He withholds high marks, having learned abundantly that "reason panders will." This makes trouble, not least as his characters impinge on history. "The evil men do lives after them, the good is oft interred with their bones."

But character, as he conceives it, and as I do, following his lead, is more fallible than wicked. This inclines him to temper the wind to the shorn lamb. Not that we are acquitted of culpability. Our behavior, whether good or evil, testifies to choice, though chance has first of all to put us in the position to choose. Central Asia disputes this. Mocking volition, it says that factors beyond our controlling determine what we do. America, by contrast, is the land of opportunity, offering such as Ulug, my self-appointed protégé, the chance to live life to the fullest. Except that nothing is tendered us gratis. If chance puts opportunity in our way, we must grasp it by the forelock. That is what I shall say to Ulug if he is given the chance to live among us.

As if I have conjured him up, the jinni I can't get rid of, I find that he's sent me an e-mail. "When you reach home," he writes, "please send my application forms to the State Department and your recommendation to Harvard. See enclosures. I list you as my primary sponsor. This should be done ASAP."

The nerve of him! Impatiently I type a sentence, hoping it will take him down a peg. "You'll hear from me when I get to America, not before." I shut off the computer and, suddenly hungry, turn to my wife. "Let's have a bite before we call it a day."

Ducking out of the *pensione,* we head for Falcone's, just in from the Corso above Piazza Venezia. They remember us, though it's been a long time. "The *carciofi* is good," says Mario, the only waiter. We go for the artichokes, trusting his laconic judgment, after that a bowl of minestrone the texture of porridge, and a thin-as-a-postage stamp carpaccio of octopus. "Due dopii"—two cups of espresso—plus a tot of grappa for me, and it's time to say *buona sera.*

I lie down in my skivvies on the *letto matrimoniale,* my eyes closing before my head hits the pillow. Music, faint but unmistakable, jerks me awake. It's Mozart, an early caprice, playing on someone's radio in the room adjoining ours. I could pound on the wall, but I listen. Mozart was hardly more than a boy, no older than Ulug, when he tossed off this "essay" for piano. The notes run smoothly, like water in a Persian *chahar bagh,* and though he hadn't yet come into his force, you can hear where he was headed. How did he progress from this little vignette to an unguessed-at greatness? How did he put on the new man?

I ponder this question, lying there in the dark. Abruptly, without conscious thought, I have the answer. We must take counsel of the past, incarnate in those who came before us. Mozart did that, standing on the shoulders of his Baroque and classical forebears, estimable, all of them, but not a patch on the master. Maybe I can play their part in giving a lead to Ulug. With luck he can learn something from my hoard of shiny pebbles, bits of string, and colored glass. He might even help revive the old man, in need of a bit of reclamation.

IN THE MORNING, much refreshed, we attend to our devoir. First on the docket is paying our respects to the Capitoline Hill, Rome's nerve center before Christ was born and still the living thread connecting the ancient world to our own. The Campidoglio is a short walk down the Corso and across the piazza. Purple wisteria are blooming beside the monumental staircase Michelangelo built. The museum at the top is stuffed with treasures, most notably the statue of the Dying Gaul, the embodiment of all lost causes. Life is oozing out of him, his body semirecumbent, his heavy limbs feeling for earth. *Ave atque vale.*

Around the dying soldier are busts of the Roman victors, "grave and reverend signiors" like the Doge's council in *Othello,* hard when they had to be, men who knew how to govern. I feel a certain kinship with them, having cut a figure in the world in my time. They might as easily be Muslims of the great age, Saladin or Harun-al Rashid. All are beyond their youth, with lines at the mouth and branching from the nose, wrinkles at the corners of the eyes. They wear the look of gravitas. I hear them saying, like Shakespeare's old King Henry, "Are these things then necessities? Then let us meet them like necessities."

But imperial Rome went down fifteen hundred years ago, and Islam, though a far more recent arrival, is long past its zenith. Already in the thirteenth century, its energy had begun to dissipate. It no longer entertained fresh ideas, and most of the manuscripts that survive from that time are copies or commentaries on work done before. After 1100 Muslim orthodoxy steadily hardened, squeezing the intellectual life from the faith. This hardening, or turning downward toward entropy, seems a constant in the history of nations.

The next hill over, going west, is the Palatine, where in the beginning the wolf gave suck to Romulus and Remus. You see her doing this in bronze beside the stairs leading up to the Capitol. The image of the mother offering her breast is everywhere in Italian art, a reason we believe it. Sometimes it verges on sentimentality. In at least a few of the old paintings in the Villa Borghese up beyond the Veneto, the Madonna's face is too sweet as she looks down at the little fat boy. Almost always, however, he makes a credible infant, and is staring with avidity at her nipple, which she squeezes with two fingers, pushing it at him. There's nothing in any other religion, certainly not in Islam, that's like this.

The Palatine is inextricably part of my youth. I can't say how often I climbed its southern face, enthralled by the strewn-about relics of antiquity. But no less moving were the bright globes of the orange trees, the purple oleander, the gnarled trunks of the olives and the dusty sheen of their leaves. This time, even with Mary pulling me along—"Keep going! You can do it!"—the climbing is a chore, no longer *vale le pene.* Somebody's sarcophagus, planted with hydrangea, looks like a concrete bathtub. The clipped boxwood bordering the path smells of urine. So the Palatine, that so buoyed me up when young, fails me in age. I remember the excitement, a generation and more ago, when I discovered this magical place. No fatigue then: I lived in a different body. This time I never reached the Belvedere that overlooks the pines of Rome.

We keep on trucking, though, past the Colosseum and into Via Labicana, a long, gritty street of *carrozerie,* auto repair shops, on our left what remains of the Golden House of Nero, tucked into the side of a hill. "Let's have a peek," says Mary, and stooping our heads, we enter a large room with a vaulted ceiling. The fresco on the vault stops us in our tracks, though we've seen it before. Hector, about to begin his death duel with Achilles, is saying goodbye to Andromaque. Shortly he will die his ignominious death, dragged at the horse's tail, but the colors of the fresco are still fast after two thousand years.

In the upper world again, we pass the Basilica of San Clemente but don't stop. Though it is one of Rome's noblest, we have something else in view, not better, only one of a kind. Crossing the street, we toil up Via di Querceti to a heap of old stones that might have had its first avatar in the desert outside Yazd. The ninth-century abbey of the Quattro Coronati, Four Martyrs, is set back from its free-standing baptistery, also worth seeing, and we get the key from one of the "enclosed" order of nuns. Just as we remember him, the Emperor Constantine is sitting in his bath, his naked body covered with spots—leprosy, the story goes, though they look like impetigo. Help is on the way in the person of Papa San Silvestro Primo, Pope Sylvester I, who extends a healing hand and the leprosy is gone. I love this cartoonish fresco, but it isn't why we single out the Church of the Four Martyrs.

Inside we are admitted to the cloister, its special glory, helped by the large coin I fish from my pocket. The enclosed garden isn't manicured but clearly tended by loving hands. An arcade surrounds it, over which runs a balcony where the nuns have hung out their wash on a clothesline. Flowers are blooming, not showy, but they have their particular scent, and I see wavy papyrus, reminiscent of the East. A fountain in the center throws up water, the only sound. We think of the *chahar bagh* in Yazd's eighteenth-century garden, rippling endlessly, never tumultuous.

The old Shahrestan bridge in Isfahan, built in the twelfth century, is of the same age and generically the same kind as the fountain in this obscure corner of Rome. For both modesty is key, with a crucial overplus not easy to put in words. Calmness settles on me as I watch the water rising and falling, a repetitive action like the beating of the heart. I lay a hand on my heart, gingerly, aware that this pilgrim grows old.

Backtracking brings us to the closest *fermata,* and the 223 bus whisks us past "the gasworks," my phrase for Rome's overall awfulness beyond Porta San Paolo. Our goal is the grave of St. Paul the Apostle in the huge basilica "outside the walls." Almost in front of us as we get down from the bus is an unpretentious *ostaria,* and we make a light lunch of spaghetti *vongele* with a glass of the house wine. The waiter addresses me as "Dottore." *Perche?* Why does he do that? "You have the persona," Mary says slyly. "Intelletuale."

The fire of 1823 consumed much of the basilica, one of Christendom's grandest, but the Papacy strained every sinew to restore it. The result, however, on the word of a grumpy Victorian, is "a very ugly railway station." It's a drafty barn of a place, no question, but has its splendors. The cloister, not enclosed by the church and untouched by the fire, is an oasis in the desert for those sore in body and spirit. The giant paschal candlestick in a corner near the high altar is a nonpareil among beautiful things, and not to have seen it will diminish your travels. Mary traces the spot, her finger hovering above it, where the makers signed their names: "I, Nicholas de Angelo, with Pietro Bassalecto, completed this work." Around the base are oxymoronic figures, including animals with human heads. This special kind of grotesquerie is absent in Islam.

St. Bernard, almost Islamic in his psychology, looked through the flesh to the spirit within. Naturally he detested all preoccupation with the surface. Not far away, in the Tre Fontane, he had his vision of souls in purgatory ascending to heaven, and there St. Paul awaited his death. When they cut off his head, it bounced three times, and three fountains sprang up on the site.

The apostle is buried in the basilica beneath the altar canopy, the work of two medieval cynosures, one of them Arnolfo di Cambio. We meet Arnolfo again, or would if we had time, in Sta. Maria Maggiore, the ancient basilica on the Esquiline Hill. Pull up the metal ring inset in a paving block, and you can descend the stairs beneath the floor to see his marvelous sculpture of the Nativity. The Virgin and Bambino have yielded to sixteenth-century replacements, too bad, but standing around them are the three wise men, genuine *magi* come all the way from Persia. The heads of the ox and ass, poking out from their stalls, overgo nature.

The well-worn story of the birth in a manger comes with a point, not the same as a moral. Implicit in what we see with our eyes, it needn't be flogged to death. The setting makes a difference, locating mother, father, and child in a stable with animals who warm them with their breath. Looking at this tableau, I think of the text from the Apocrypha: "And he shall be recognized in the midst of two animals." There are animals in the Koran, like the one that carries Muhammad on his night journey through the heavens, but none so coarsely palpable as these.

The scene is dynamic, befitting a great story. It begins in utter humbleness, abasing its protagonists, but ends in glory, presented by the kings of earth. Gorgeously caparisoned, they enter to bear witness. Angels are singing, and a blazing star lights up the sky. Although a god is the central figure, he is born of woman, making him blood of our blood. How far St. Paul, an intellectual (like me), believed all this on his pulses is a question. Had he lived some centuries later, he might have embraced the vision of the Prophet.

Perhaps the suffrage he gave to the word made flesh was, as mine is, more willed than intelligent. Above the grave in his basilica is the first in a series of mosaic roundels with portraits of all the popes. They girdle the entire circumference of the church, beginning with St. Peter, the rock Christianity is built on. St. Paul never saw them, but I, gazing up, feel, or it may be only want to feel, the sustaining presence of a company that surrounds me and has gone on before. Perhaps it is waiting for me when time comes round.

Both Islam and the Pauline version of Christianity seem more enamored of the Logos than the incarnate god. But classical Islam, though it knows nothing of the Incarnation, shared the Christian sense of man as connected to a greater than himself. This sense is the burden of Islamic art and architecture, accounting for its stunning success. Shah Abbas I, as the old song was nearing an end, wrote its finale in the triumphant orders of Imam Square.

OUR FLIGHT to Chicago isn't leaving till mid-afternoon, time in the A.M. for one more excursion. We can't risk a long walk, and turning our backs on Piazza Venezia, we take a bus in the opposite direction. It lets us down in Via di San Vincenzo leading into the little piazza filled almost to the brim with the famous Trevi Fountain. Begun in the fifteenth century, restored in the seventeenth, and finished in the eighteenth, the fountain overlaps the re-creating of Esfahan, Shah Abbas's capital, and like it assimilates life to art. The spectacle that opens to our eyes as we enter the piazza shows us life at its most violent, and we aren't yet jaded enough not to blink. Gods and goddesses, emerging from stone, mingle with tritons, old Ocean with his chariot, galloping horses, jagged rocks, wind-blown trees, over all a leaping cascade of water. "White water," I think.

But the wildness is ordered, putting us in mind of Isfahan's baroque fantasies. Like them it yokes together modes of feeling and perceiving from opposite ends of the spectrum, and its range gives the sense that we inhabit half the world. The Chehel Sotun Palace is a primer, illustrating what this means. Intended as an entrance to the parklands between the great square and Chahar Bagh Abbasi on the west, it was completed by the middle of the seventeenth century and rebuilt after a fire early in the eighteenth. This makes it virtually contemporary with the Trevi Fountain. The palace is imposing but doesn't seek to cow us. Its slender, ribbed pillars, twenty of them, direct the eye upward, away from mere grandiosity to the exquisite inlay work of the ceiling. Note that it isn't true to life but to art. The Trevi Fountain is like that, assertive but stylized, not naturalistic, of the psychology of Handel.

Going back in mind, I walk Shah Abbas's city, approaching it from the banks of the river where the cloth makers are drying their wares. I revisit

Imam Square and its fabulous Jameh Mosque, doing my best to sort out its different strata, from the Seljuks (the Kufic inscriptions give them away), through the Mongols and the Timurids, ending with the baroque overlay of the Safavid style. I wander the bazaar, not buying but looking, and at day's end I take tea in the Qeisarieh Tea Shop above its main portal. Unasked, they bring a dish of *gaz*, nougats mixed with chopped pistachios, to the table. The grizzled old serving man will be gathered to his ancestors soon enough, and I with him, in company with my nearest and dearest. Some of the Shah's work is already gone. But something endures, and much of the great song still resonates. While there is time, I have tried to pass its character on.

CPSIA information can be obtained at www.ICGtesting.com
Printed in the USA
LVOW12*0530230114

370582LV00004B/9/P

9 781611 173161